AMAZING RECIPE MAKEOVERS

½ THE
- FAT
- CALORIES
- SALT
- SUGAR

*But with all the flavor!

AMAZING RECIPE MAKEOVERS

½ THE
- FAT
- CALORIES
- SALT
- SUGAR

*But with all the flavor!

OVER 200 RECIPES BY THE EDITORS OF Cooking Light

Oxmoor House

©2016 Time Inc. Books

Published by Oxmoor House, an imprint of Time Inc. Books
225 Liberty Street, New York, NY 10281

SENIOR EDITOR: Rachel Quinlivan West, R.D.
EDITOR: Meredith L. Butcher
EDITORIAL ASSISTANT: Nicole Fisher
ASSISTANT MANAGING EDITOR: Jeanne de Lathouder
ART DIRECTOR: Christopher Rhoads
PROJECT EDITORS: Melissa Brown, Lacie Pinyan
PHOTOGRAPHERS: Iain Bagwell, Victor Protasio
PROP STYLISTS: Kay E. Clarke, Mindi Shapiro Levine
FOOD STYLISTS: Victoria E. Cox, Margaret Monroe Dickey,
    Catherine Crowell Steele
RECIPE DEVELOPERS AND TESTERS: Nathan Carrabba,
    Rishon Hanners, Julia Levy, Callie Nash, Karen Rankin
SENIOR PRODUCTION MANAGER: Greg A. Amason
ASSISTANT PRODUCTION DIRECTOR: Sue Chodakiewicz
COPY EDITORS: Dolores Hydock, Kate Johnson
INDEXER: Mary Ann Laurens
NUTRITION ANALYSIS: Carolyn Williams, Ph.D., R.D.
FELLOWS: Olivia Pierce, Natalie Schumann,
    Mallory Short

ISBN-13: 978-0-8487-4704-6
ISBN-10: 0-8487-4704-6
Library of Congress Control Number: 2016933120

First Edition 2016

Printed in the United States of America

10 9 8 7 6 5 4 3 2 1

Time Inc. Books products may be purchased for business or promotional
use. For information on bulk purchases, please contact Christi Crowley in
the Special Sales Department at (845) 895-9858.

We welcome your comments and suggestions about
Time Inc. Books. Please write to us at:

Time Inc. Books
Attention: Book Editors
P.O. Box 62310
Tampa, Florida 33662-2310

CONTENTS

WELCOME!

Here at *Cooking Light*, our goal is to empower you to cook and eat healthfully and mindfully. But we know that always making the right choice can be hard. Especially when your favorite recipes might be categorized as the less-than favorable choice.

What if you didn't have to give up any of your favorite foods? We've figured out how to make the most decadent recipes more healthful, without sacrificing flavor, so you can indulge at any time. And we've done this in an amazing way! Throughout, you'll see unlikely ingredients pop up that have nutritional benefits. Think ground mushrooms to bulk up a lasagna meat sauce, mashed avocado to replace some of the mayonnaise found in egg salad, or even pureed butternut squash to make the base of a rich macaroni and cheese sauce. We've also come up with some new and radical cooking techniques to boost flavor but lower the fat.

Through a little creativity, we were able to make over 200 of the most luxurious recipes and reduce the calories, sodium, fat, or sugar by half. In many cases, we were able to achieve this goal and then some. Enjoy!

The Editors of *Cooking Light*

SECRETS TO SUCCESS

Learn all the tricks to making food delicious and light! Here are some tried-and-true techniques for making dishes more nutritious without sacrificing an ounce of flavor.

STUDY THE RECIPE. Closely examine the original to identify where changes can be made. Look at each ingredient to see where you can take away, add, or substitute.

LIMIT SODIUM.

Try the recipe with half the recommended salt.

REDUCE PORTION SIZES.

When plating, start with a smaller amount and see if that satisfies you.

CHOOSE A FLAVORFUL CHEESE.

Aged cheeses like Parmigiano-Reggiano pack a punch, so less is required to build flavor.

SPRINKLE CHEESE, CHOCOLATE, OR NUTS ON TOP RATHER THAN MIXING INTO BATTERS.

As toppings, they deliver concentrated flavor.

REDUCE SUGAR-CRUMB TOPPINGS. Half the amount is often enough.

SUBSTITUTE PANKO, EXTRA-CRISP JAPANESE BREADCRUMBS, FOR ORDINARY BREAD OR CRACKER CRUMBS. Doing so can reduce the crust's fat, calories, and sodium by half.

THINK BEYOND FAT-FREE.

Sometimes no-fat foods don't satisfy. Try blending fat-free and full-fat varieties, which can reduce the fat and calories without sacrificing flavor.

INCREASE LOW-CALORIE INGREDIENTS, SUCH AS ADDING EXTRA VEGETABLES TO CASSEROLES, AND FRUITS TO BREADS, MUFFINS, OR SNACK CAKES.

FINELY CHOP NUTS, BACON, OLIVES, AND OTHER HIGH-FAT OR HIGH-SODIUM INGREDIENTS. They will distribute more evenly, allowing you to use less without sacrificing taste.

Opt for leaner meats, such as center-cut or loin meats and skinless, white-meat poultry.

ADD ZING WITH CITRUS. A squeeze of fresh lemon or orange juice can help brighten the flavors of veggies and meats without added sodium or fat.

When you need oil, use canola, which has nearly half the saturated fat and more healthful, unsaturated fat than other oils.

PUREE VEGETABLES TO ADD BODY.

Mash some of the beans in a chili or the potatoes in a chowder.

Opt for lower-sodium broths and no-salt-added tomatoes; always rinse canned beans in a strainer under cold water, which cuts sodium by up to 40%.

KITCHEN ESSENTIALS

Use this handy list to keep your kitchen stocked with the basic ingredients you need for healthful cooking.

CHECK THE PANTRY FOR THESE STAPLES.

- Baking powder
- Baking soda
- Unsalted chicken, beef, and vegetable stock
- Cornstarch
- Flour: all-purpose and whole-wheat
- Milk: nonfat dry milk powder, and fat-free evaporated milk
- Oats: quick-cooking and rolled
- Oils: olive, sesame, and canola
- Unflavored gelatin and gelatin mixes

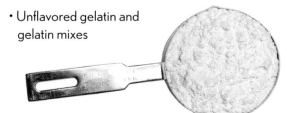

KEEP THESE CANNED FRUITS AND VEGETABLES ON HAND.

- Unsalted canned beans and chickpeas
- Unsalted canned tomato products: paste, sauce, whole, diced, and seasoned

YOU CAN ALWAYS MAKE A MEAL WHEN YOU HAVE THESE WHOLE GRAINS AND PASTAS.

- Bulgur and quinoa
- Corn tortillas
- Dry cereals without added sugar
- Dry pastas, especially whole grain
- Rice and rice blends

ADD FLAVOR
WITH THESE CONDIMENTS AND SEASONINGS.

- Dried herbs and spices
- Fresh citrus: lemons and limes
- Mayonnaise: canola or olive oil–based
- Mustards
- Seasoning sauces: hot sauce, ketchup, lower-sodium soy sauce, and Worcestershire sauce
- Vinegars

STOCK UP AND STORE THESE FOODS IN THE FREEZER.

- Cooked chicken: diced or strips
- Frozen fruits
- Frozen vegetables
- Ground sirloin, pork chops, and other lean meats
- Seafood

FILL THE FRIDGE WITH THESE ITEMS.

- Cheeses: reduced-fat
- Milk: fat-free milk and low-fat buttermilk
- Rolls and pizza dough, preferably whole wheat
- Sour cream: low-fat
- Yogurt: low-fat or fat-free Greek

BULK UP ON FIBER-RICH FOODS.

- Beans and legumes
- Dried fruit
- Skin-on fruit and vegetables
- Whole-grain bread and crackers

USE MORE PLANT-BASED OILS.

- Avocado oil
- Canola oil
- Extra-virgin olive oil
- Olive oil
- Walnut oil

Lemon-Ginger Fried
Chicken, page 18

RADICALLY REVAMPED COMFORT FOODS

BETTER THAN
FRIED CHICKEN

HANDS-ON: 20 MIN. TOTAL: 8 HR. 50 MIN.

Try this spicier version of an old favorite. Marinating overnight makes the meat super flavorful and tender, so plan ahead, and enjoy without the guilt.

2 cups nonfat buttermilk
2 tablespoons Sriracha (hot chile sauce, such as Huy Fong)
2 garlic cloves, minced
3 bone-in chicken breast halves, skinned and cut in half crosswise
2 bone-in chicken drumsticks, skinned
1 cup panko (Japanese breadcrumbs)

4.5 ounces all-purpose flour (about 1 cup)
1 teaspoon freshly ground black pepper
1 teaspoon paprika
½ teaspoon kosher salt
¼ cup peanut oil
Cooking spray

1. Combine first 3 ingredients in a large zip-top plastic bag. Pat chicken dry with paper towels; add to bag, seal, and shake to coat chicken. Chill 8 hours or overnight.

2. Preheat oven to 425°.

3. Place panko in a food processor; process until finely ground. Combine flour, panko, pepper, paprika, and salt in a large zip-top plastic bag. Remove chicken from marinade; discard marinade. Working with 1 piece at a time, add chicken to flour mixture in bag; seal bag, and shake to coat. Remove chicken from bag; repeat with remaining chicken. Discard remaining flour mixture.

4. Heat 2 tablespoons oil in a large cast-iron skillet over medium-high heat. Add half of chicken to pan; cook 6 minutes or until golden brown, turning to brown on all sides. Remove chicken from pan; place on a wire rack coated with cooking spray set over a baking sheet. Lightly coat chicken with cooking spray. Repeat with remaining oil and chicken.

5. Bake at 425° for 30 minutes or until a thermometer registers 165°.

Serves 4 (serving size: 2 pieces): Calories 433; Fat 15.9g (sat 2.9g, mono 6.3g, poly 4.3g); Protein 37g; Carb 33g; Fiber 1g; Sugars 1g (est. added sugars: 0g); Chol 116mg; Iron 2mg; Sodium 622mg; Calc 55mg

BISCUIT-TOPPED
CHICKEN POTPIE

CLASSIC: Calories per serving: 561, Sat Fat: 19g, Sodium: 895mg, Sugars: 5g
MAKEOVER: Calories per serving: 334, Sat Fat: 5.9g, Sodium: 543mg, Sugars: 5g

HANDS-ON: 35 MIN. TOTAL: 1 HR. 15 MIN.

Enjoy the fluffy deliciousness of the biscuit topping while still delivering a healthy meal the whole family will love.

FILLING:

1 tablespoon canola oil
1 1/2 cups chopped onion
1 cup chopped carrot
1/2 cup chopped celery
1 garlic clove, minced
1.1 ounces all-purpose flour
1/4 teaspoon kosher salt
1/4 teaspoon black pepper

4 cups unsalted chicken stock
2 cups shredded cooked chicken
  breast
1 cup frozen green peas, thawed
1 (3/4-ounce) package fresh poultry-
  blend herbs
Cooking spray

BISCUITS:

4.5 ounces all-purpose flour
1 teaspoon baking soda

1/4 cup cold butter, cubed
1/3 cup buttermilk

1. Preheat oven to 425°.

2. To prepare filling, heat oil in a large saucepan over medium-high heat. Add onion, carrot, and celery; sauté 4 minutes. Add garlic; sauté 30 seconds. Weigh or lightly spoon 1.1 ounces (1/4 cup) flour into a dry measuring cup; level with a knife. Stir 1.1 ounces flour, salt, and pepper into vegetables; cook 1 minute, stirring constantly. Stir in stock; bring to a boil. Reduce heat to medium; simmer 8 minutes, stirring occasionally. Stir in chicken and peas; simmer 5 minutes. Remove from heat. Remove rosemary from herb package; reserve for another use. Strip leaves from stems of remaining herbs; chop leaves to measure 2 tablespoons. Stir chopped herbs into filling. Pour filling into a 2-quart baking dish or cast-iron skillet coated with cooking spray.

3. To prepare biscuits, weigh or lightly spoon 4.5 ounces (1 cup) flour into a dry measuring cup; level with a knife. Combine 4.5 ounces flour and baking soda. Cut in butter with a pastry blender or 2 knives until mixture resembles coarse meal. Stir in buttermilk. Turn dough out onto a lightly floured surface; knead gently 5 to 6 times. Roll to a 9-inch circle. Cut with a 2-inch round biscuit cutter, rerolling scraps. Arrange biscuits over filling; coat with cooking spray. Bake at 425° for 35 minutes or until browned.

Serves 6 (serving size: about 1 1/2 cups): Calories 334; Fat 12.8g (sat 5.9g, mono 4.1g, poly 1.5g); Protein 23g; Carb 31g; Fiber 3g; Sugars 5g (est. added sugars: 0g); Chol 62mg; Iron 3mg; Sodium 543mg; Calc 55mg

CHICKEN AND DUMPLINGS

HANDS-ON: 66 MIN. TOTAL: 66 MIN.

Classic chicken and dumplings makes everybody feel warm and happy. This version features light, herby dumplings cloaked in rich sauce with plenty of vegetables and light and dark chicken. The dumplings are packed with herbs and brightly flavored lemon zest, so you'll never suspect that the chicken stew portion is light and healthy.

CHICKEN STEW:

1 (3- to 4-pound) whole chicken
3 quarts water
10 black peppercorns
4 garlic cloves, crushed
4 thyme sprigs
2 celery stalks
1 large onion, peeled and halved
1 large carrot, peeled and halved
1 bay leaf
1 rosemary sprig

Cooking spray
1 cup chopped onion
1 cup chopped carrot
1 cup chopped celery
2 tablespoons chopped shallots
1.1 ounces all-purpose flour (about ¼ cup)
2 tablespoons cornstarch
3 tablespoons heavy cream

DUMPLINGS:

¾ cup 1% low-fat milk
1 large egg, lightly beaten
6.75 ounces all-purpose flour (about 1½ cups)
3 tablespoons chopped fresh parsley
1 tablespoon chopped fresh thyme

1 tablespoon cornmeal
2 teaspoons baking powder
½ teaspoon salt
½ teaspoon grated lemon rind
Freshly ground black pepper (optional)
Chopped fresh parsley (optional)

1. To prepare chicken stew, remove and discard giblets and neck from chicken. Place chicken in an 8-quart stockpot. Add 3 quarts water and next 8 ingredients (through rosemary sprig). Bring to a simmer; cook 45 minutes. Skim fat from surface of cooking liquid occasionally; discard fat. Remove chicken from pan; cool slightly. Strain stock through a sieve over a large bowl; discard solids. When chicken is cool enough to handle, remove skin from chicken; remove chicken from bones, discarding skin and bones. Tear chicken into 2-inch pieces; set aside.

2. Return pan to medium-high heat. Coat pan with cooking spray. Add chopped onion and next 3 ingredients (through shallots) to pan; coat vegetables with cooking spray. Sauté 4 minutes or just until vegetables are tender. Weigh or lightly spoon 1.1 ounces (about ¼ cup) flour into a dry measuring cup; level with a knife. Sprinkle 1.1 ounces flour over vegetable mixture; cook 1 minute, stirring constantly. Gradually add chicken stock, stirring with a whisk until smooth. Combine cornstarch and cream in a small bowl. Add cornstarch mixture to vegetable mixture; bring to a boil, and cook 3 minutes or until slightly thick, stirring constantly. Reduce heat to low, and stir in chicken.

3. To prepare dumplings, combine milk and egg in a medium bowl. Weigh or lightly spoon 6.75 ounces (about 1½ cups) flour into dry measuring cups; level with a knife. Combine 6.75 ounces flour and next 6 ingredients (through rind) in a bowl. Add flour mixture to milk mixture, stirring with a fork just until moist.

4. Drop 8 heaping tablespoons of batter onto chicken mixture. Cover and cook over low heat 3 minutes or until dumplings are done (dumplings will float to surface of stew). Do not allow chicken mixture to boil. Remove dumplings with a slotted spoon, and place in a bowl; keep warm. Repeat procedure twice with remaining batter.

5. Divide dumplings among 8 bowls. Ladle stew over dumplings in bowls; sprinkle with pepper and parsley, if desired. Serve immediately.

Serves 8 (serving size: 3 dumplings and 1 cup stew): Calories 324; Fat 6.2g (sat 2.4g, mono 1.8g, poly 1.1g); Protein 33g; Carb 31g; Fiber 2g; Sugars 3g (est. added sugars: 0g); Chol 103mg; Iron 3mg; Sodium 573mg; Calc 116mg

LEMON-GINGER
FRIED CHICKEN

CLASSIC: Calories per serving: 891, Sat Fat: 9.3g, Sodium: 1179mg, Sugars: 21g
MAKEOVER: Calories per serving: 375, Sat Fat: 3.3g, Sodium: 578mg, Sugars: 6g

HANDS-ON: 16 MIN. TOTAL: 3 HR. 30 MIN.

Giving the chicken a double coat of flour mixture creates a golden crust (without the skin) when pan-fried.

1 teaspoon grated lemon rind
1 cup fresh lemon juice (about 4 lemons)
2 teaspoons minced peeled fresh ginger
1 1/2 teaspoons minced fresh garlic
2 bone-in chicken breast halves, skinned
2 bone-in chicken thighs, skinned
2 chicken drumsticks, skinned
4.5 ounces all-purpose flour (about 1 cup)

2 teaspoons ground ginger
1 teaspoon paprika
1/2 teaspoon ground red pepper
1 teaspoon kosher salt
1/2 teaspoon freshly ground black pepper
1/4 cup peanut oil
1/4 cup fat-free, lower-sodium chicken broth
2 tablespoons brown sugar
1 lemon, thinly sliced

1. Place rind, juice, and next 5 ingredients (through drumsticks) in a large zip-top plastic bag; seal bag, and shake to coat chicken. Marinate in refrigerator 1 hour, turning bag occasionally.

2. Sift together flour and next 3 ingredients (through red pepper). Place flour mixture in a large zip-top plastic bag. Remove chicken from marinade bag, reserving marinade. Sprinkle salt and black pepper over chicken. Working with 1 piece at a time, add chicken to flour mixture; seal bag, and shake to coat chicken. Remove chicken from bag, shaking off excess flour mixture. Repeat with remaining chicken. Reserve remaining flour mixture. Place chicken on a wire rack; place rack in a jelly-roll pan. Cover and refrigerate 1 1/2 hours. Let stand at room temperature 30 minutes.

3. Preheat oven to 350°. Working with 1 piece at a time, return chicken to flour mixture; seal bag, and shake to coat. Remove chicken from bag, shaking off excess flour mixture. Repeat with remaining chicken. Discard remaining flour mixture.

4. Heat oil in a large skillet over medium-high heat. Add chicken to pan; cook 3 minutes or until golden, turning once. Arrange chicken in a single layer in a shallow roasting pan. Combine broth and reserved marinade in a small bowl; carefully pour broth mixture into pan. Sprinkle chicken with sugar, and top with lemon slices. Bake at 350° for 45 minutes or until golden and a thermometer registers 165°.

Serves 8 (serving size: 1 breast half, or 1 thigh and 1 drumstick): Calories 375; Fat 15.5g (sat 3.3g, mono 6.6g, poly 4.7g); Protein 31g; Carb 31g; Fiber 2g; Sugars 6g (est. added sugars: 4g); Chol 85mg; Iron 3mg; Sodium 578mg; Calc 48mg

MEXICAN CHICKEN CASSEROLE
WITH CHARRED TOMATO SALSA

CLASSIC: Calories per serving: 510, Sat Fat: 10g, Sodium: 1230mg, Sugars: 8g
MAKEOVER: Calories per serving: 360, Sat Fat: 5.4g, Sodium: 486mg, Sugars: 6g

HANDS-ON: 25 MIN. TOTAL: 1 HR. 10 MIN.

Charring the tomatoes gives a rich flavor to the salsa, which adds flavor to this chicken-and-veggie-packed dish.

SALSA:
8 plum tomatoes, halved and seeded
3 garlic cloves, crushed
1 small onion, chopped
1 seeded jalapeño pepper, quartered

Cooking spray
⅓ cup chopped fresh cilantro
3 tablespoons fresh lime juice
⅛ teaspoon black pepper

CASSEROLE:
1 cup chopped onion
1 cup fresh or frozen corn kernels
1 cup diced zucchini
1 cup chopped red bell pepper
3 cups shredded cooked chicken
  breast
1 tablespoon minced garlic
2 teaspoons chili powder
1 teaspoon ground cumin

1 (10-ounce) can green chile enchilada
  sauce
1 (4-ounce) can chopped green chiles
12 (6-inch) corn tortillas
4 ounces Monterey Jack cheese,
  shredded (about 1 cup)
4 ounces feta cheese, crumbled
  (about 1 cup)

SNEAK ATTACK
Pumping up the amount of veggies while reducing the cheese keeps the dish satisfying and filling.

1. Preheat broiler.

2. To prepare salsa, combine first 4 ingredients on a baking sheet coated with cooking spray. Broil 20 minutes or until charred, stirring once. Remove from oven; cool slightly. Place tomato mixture in a food processor; add cilantro, lime juice, and black pepper. Process until smooth. Set aside.

3. Preheat oven to 350°. To prepare casserole, heat a large nonstick skillet over medium-high heat. Lightly coat pan with cooking spray. Add 1 cup onion, corn, zucchini, and bell pepper; sauté 6 minutes or until tender. Add chicken and next 5 ingredients (through green chiles); sauté 2 minutes or until thoroughly heated. Remove from heat. Spread ½ cup salsa over the bottom of a 13 x 9–inch baking dish coated with cooking spray. Arrange half of tortillas over salsa. Spoon 2 cups chicken mixture over tortillas. Top with ¾ cup salsa. Sprinkle with ½ cup of each cheese. Repeat layers, starting with remaining tortillas and ending with remaining cheeses. Bake at 350° for 25 minutes or until bubbly.

Serves 8: Calories 360; Fat 12g (sat 5.4g, mono 2.6g, poly 1.4g); Protein 26g; Carb 39g; Fiber 5g; Sugars 6g (est. added sugars: 0g); Chol 70mg; Iron 1mg; Sodium 486mg; Calc 232mg

CHICKEN CORDON BLEU

CLASSIC: Calories per serving: 720, Sat Fat: 17.6g, Sodium: 1000mg, Sugars: 1g
MAKEOVER: Calories per serving: 414, Sat Fat: 5.5g, Sodium: 513mg, Sugars: 0g

HANDS-ON: 16 MIN. TOTAL: 41 MIN.

Panko is a Japanese-style crumb that stays crispy, even during cooking. Blended with robust seasoning and cheese, it browns to a golden crisp in the oven.

4 (6-ounce) skinless, boneless chicken breast halves
½ teaspoon black pepper
¼ teaspoon salt
¾ cup panko (Japanese breadcrumbs)
2.25 ounces all-purpose flour (about ½ cup)
1 tablespoon water

1 large egg
2.5 ounces shredded Gruyère cheese, divided (about ⅔ cup)
1 tablespoon chopped fresh thyme
2 garlic cloves, minced
4 pancetta slices (about 1¼ ounces)
Cooking spray

1. Preheat oven to 350°.

2. Place each chicken piece between 2 sheets of plastic wrap; pound to ¼-inch thickness. Sprinkle chicken with pepper and salt.

3. Heat a skillet over medium heat. Add panko; cook 2 minutes or until toasted, stirring often. Remove from heat. Place flour in a shallow dish. Combine 1 tablespoon water and egg in a bowl; beat lightly. Pour egg mixture into a shallow dish. Combine panko, 2 tablespoons cheese, thyme, and garlic in another shallow dish.

4. Working with 1 chicken piece at a time, dredge in flour. Dip in egg mixture; dredge in panko mixture. Top with 1 pancetta slice and 2 tablespoons cheese. Roll up; secure with a wooden pick. Place roll, seam side down, on a wire rack coated with cooking spray. Place rack on a baking sheet. Repeat procedure with remaining ingredients. Bake at 350° for 25 minutes or until chicken is done.

Serves 4 (serving size: 1 roll): Calories 414; Fat 12.4g (sat 5.5g, mono 2.8g, poly 1g); Protein 51g; Carb 21g; Fiber 1g; Sugars 0g (est. added sugars: 0g); Chol 169mg; Iron 2mg; Sodium 513mg; Calc 213mg

CREAMY CHICKEN AND
BROCCOLI CASSEROLE

CLASSIC: Calories per serving: 610, Sat Fat: 17.2g, Sodium: 710mg, Sugars: 3g
MAKEOVER: Calories per serving: 277, Sat Fat: 3.6g, Sodium: 547mg, Sugars: 6g

HANDS-ON: 20 MIN. TOTAL: 20 MIN.

A traditional creamy chicken casserole can have more than 600 calories per serving. Canola mayonnaise and fat-free yogurt provide extra creaminess in this lightened version, without the yogurt tang.

1 (12-ounce) package steam-in-bag broccoli florets
1 tablespoon canola oil
1 cup prechopped onion
2 (8-ounce) packages presliced mushrooms
3 tablespoons all-purpose flour
1½ cups fat-free milk
12 ounces chopped skinless, boneless rotisserie chicken breast (about 3 cups)

½ cup plain fat-free Greek yogurt
¼ cup canola mayonnaise
½ teaspoon freshly ground black pepper
¼ teaspoon salt
2 ounces sharp cheddar cheese, shredded (about ½ cup)
1 ounce Parmesan cheese, grated (about ¼ cup)

1. Preheat broiler.

2. Prepare broccoli in microwave according to package directions.

3. Heat a large ovenproof skillet over medium-high heat. Add oil to pan; swirl to coat. Add onion and mushrooms; sauté 12 minutes or until mushrooms brown and liquid evaporates. Sprinkle mushroom mixture with flour; cook 1 minute, stirring constantly. Stir in milk. Bring to a boil; cook 3 minutes or until thick and bubbly. Stir in broccoli and chicken; cook 1 minute. Remove pan from heat. Stir in yogurt, mayonnaise, pepper, and salt. Top with cheeses; broil 2 minutes.

Serves 6 (serving size: 1½ cups): Calories 277; Fat 11.9g (sat 3.6g, mono 5.1g, poly 2.2g); Protein 29g; Carb 15g; Fiber 3g; Sugars 6g (est. added sugars: 1g); Chol 66mg; Iron 2mg; Sodium 547mg; Calc 253mg

TUNA NOODLE CASSEROLE

CLASSIC: Calories per serving: 841, Sat Fat: 26.8g, Sodium: 791mg, Sugars: 0g
MAKEOVER: Calories per serving: 403, Sat Fat: 5.8g, Sodium: 608mg, Sugars: 9g

HANDS-ON: 22 MIN. TOTAL: 38 MIN.

Although the recipe calls for egg noodles, you can use any short pasta to make this dish. Fat-free milk and less-fat cream cheese drastically reduces the saturated fat, without losing creaminess.

8 ounces wide egg noodles
2 tablespoons olive oil
1/2 cup chopped yellow onion
1/3 cup chopped carrot
2 tablespoons all-purpose flour
2 3/4 cups fat-free milk
4 ounces 1/3-less-fat cream cheese, softened (about 1/2 cup)
2 tablespoons Dijon mustard

1/2 teaspoon salt
1/2 teaspoon freshly ground black pepper
1 cup frozen green peas, thawed
2 ounces grated Parmigiano-Reggiano cheese, divided (about 1/2 cup)
2 (5-ounce) cans albacore tuna in water, drained and flaked
Cooking spray

SECRET TO SUCCESS
For a rich and thick sauce, use less-fat cream cheese instead of a cream base.

1. Preheat broiler.

2. Cook noodles according to package directions, omitting salt and fat. Drain. Heat a large skillet over medium heat. Add oil to pan; swirl to coat. Add onion and carrot; cook 6 minutes or until carrot is almost tender, stirring occasionally. Sprinkle with flour; cook 1 minute, stirring constantly. Gradually stir in milk; cook, stirring constantly with a whisk, 5 minutes or until slightly thick. Stir in cream cheese, mustard, salt, and pepper; cook 2 minutes, stirring constantly.

3. Remove pan from heat. Stir in noodles, peas, 1/4 cup Parmigiano-Reggiano cheese, and tuna. Spoon mixture into a shallow broiler-safe 2-quart glass or ceramic baking dish coated with cooking spray; top with 1/4 cup Parmigiano-Reggiano cheese. Broil 3 minutes or until golden and bubbly. Let stand 5 minutes before serving.

Serves 6 (serving size: 1 1/3 cups): Calories 403; Fat 14.2g (sat 5.8g, mono 4.4g, poly 1.6g); Protein 27g; Carb 42g; Fiber 3g; Sugars 9g (est. added sugars: 1g); Chol 81mg; Iron 2mg; Sodium 608mg; Calc 293mg

CHICKEN TETRAZZINI

CLASSIC: Calories per serving: 516, Sat Fat: 8.9g, Sodium: 1625mg, Sugars: 7g
MAKEOVER: Calories per serving: 435, Sat Fat: 4.9g, Sodium: 573mg, Sugars: 8g

HANDS-ON: 35 MIN. TOTAL: 65 MIN.

Our chicken tetrazzini is a hearty, stick-to-your-ribs kind of meal that will leave you feeling lighter.

10 ounces uncooked linguine
2 tablespoons butter
1.1 ounces all-purpose flour (about ¼ cup)
2½ cups unsalted chicken stock
1 (12-ounce) can evaporated low-fat milk
2.5 ounces grated Parmigiano-Reggiano cheese, divided
1 ounce ⅓-less-fat cream cheese (about 2 tablespoons)
1 teaspoon kosher salt
½ teaspoon black pepper
4 teaspoons olive oil, divided
2 (8-ounce) packages sliced mushrooms
1 cup chopped onion
1½ tablespoons minced garlic
2 teaspoons fresh thyme
½ cup dry white wine
3 cups shredded cooked chicken breast
1 cup frozen green peas
Cooking spray
1½ ounces French bread baguette, torn
¼ cup chopped fresh flat-leaf parsley

> ## SECRET TO SUCCESS
> Create a crunchy finishing touch with crusty baguette crumbs instead of sodium-laden packaged breadcrumbs.

1. Preheat oven to 375°.

2. Cook pasta according to package directions, omitting salt and fat; drain.

3. Melt butter in a medium saucepan over medium heat. Stir in flour; cook 2 minutes, stirring constantly with a whisk. Gradually add stock and milk; bring to a boil. Reduce heat, and simmer 5 minutes. Remove from heat; stir in 2 ounces Parmigiano-Reggiano cheese, cream cheese, salt, and pepper.

4. Heat a large skillet over medium-high heat. Add 1 tablespoon oil to pan; swirl to coat. Add mushrooms; sauté 3 minutes, stirring occasionally. Add onion, garlic, and thyme; sauté 3 minutes. Add wine; cook 1 minute. Combine milk mixture, mushroom mixture, pasta, chicken, and peas; toss to combine. Spoon pasta mixture into a 13 x 9–inch glass or ceramic baking dish coated with cooking spray.

5. Place bread in a food processor; drizzle with 1 teaspoon oil. Process until coarse crumbs form. Combine breadcrumbs and remaining Parmigiano-Reggiano; sprinkle over pasta. Bake at 375° for 30 minutes or until browned and bubbly. Sprinkle with chopped parsley.

Serves 8 (serving size: about 1¼ cups): Calories 435; Fat 12.2g (sat 4.9g, mono 4.1g, poly 1.3g); Protein 33g; Carb 45g; Fiber 4g; Sugars 8g (est. added sugars: 0g); Chol 69mg; Iron 3mg; Sodium 573mg; Calc 249mg

ENCHILADA CASSEROLE

CLASSIC: Calories per serving: 712, Sat Fat: 24.3g, Sodium: 1138mg, Sugars: 4g
MAKEOVER: Calories per serving: 377, Sat Fat: 7g, Sodium: 650mg, Sugars: 4g

HANDS-ON: 14 MIN. TOTAL: 30 MIN.

Perfect for any weeknight, this dish drastically reduces the amount of fat and sodium found in traditional enchiladas.

1 pound ground sirloin
1 cup chopped onion
1 tablespoon butter
1 tablespoon minced garlic
1 1/2 tablespoons all-purpose flour
1 cup fat-free, lower-sodium beef broth
1 tablespoon 40%-less-sodium taco
  seasoning mix

1 (8-ounce) can unsalted tomato sauce
4 (8-inch) whole-wheat flour tortillas
1.5 ounces Monterey Jack cheese with
  jalapeño peppers, shredded (about
  1/3 cup)

1. Heat a large nonstick skillet over medium-high heat. Add beef and onion to pan; cook 6 minutes, stirring to crumble beef.

2. Preheat oven to 400°.

3. Melt butter in a medium saucepan over medium-high heat. Add garlic; sauté 1 minute. Sprinkle with flour; cook 30 seconds, stirring constantly. Add broth, taco seasoning mix, and tomato sauce to pan. Bring to a boil; cook 2 minutes, stirring occasionally. Add 1 1/2 cups tomato mixture to beef mixture, reserving 1/2 cup tomato mixture.

4. Place 1 tortilla in a 9-inch pie plate. Top with 1 cup beef mixture. Repeat layers, ending with tortilla. Spread reserved tomato mixture over tortilla. Top with cheese. Bake at 400° for 10 minutes or until cheese melts. Cool slightly. Cut into 4 wedges.

Serves 4 (serving size: 1 wedge): Calories 377; Fat 14.6g (sat 7g, mono 5.3g, poly 1.6g); Protein 30g; Carb 32g; Fiber 5g; Sugars 4g (est. added sugars: 0g); Chol 76mg; Iron 3mg; Sodium 650mg; Calc 91mg

BEEF AND BLACK BEAN
ENCHILADAS

CLASSIC: Calories per serving: 712, Sat Fat: 24.3g, Sodium: 1138mg, Sugars: 5g
MAKEOVER: Calories per serving: 343, Sat Fat: 5.8g, Sodium: 540mg, Sugars: 5g

HANDS-ON: 60 MIN. TOTAL: 1 HR. 30 MIN.

Make all of the components ahead and simply assemble the enchiladas just before baking.

SAUCE:
2 dried ancho chiles, stemmed
3 cups fat-free, lower-sodium chicken broth
1 (6-inch) corn tortilla, torn into small pieces
1/3 cup fresh cilantro leaves
2 teaspoons minced fresh garlic
2 green onions, coarsely chopped

ENCHILADAS:
8 ounces ground sirloin
2 teaspoons olive oil
2 cups chopped onion
4 teaspoons minced fresh garlic
1 teaspoon dried Mexican oregano
1/2 teaspoon ground cumin
1/4 teaspoon kosher salt
1 tablespoon unsalted tomato paste
2/3 cup rinsed and drained organic black beans
1/2 cup fat-free, lower-sodium chicken broth
1 tablespoon fresh lime juice
4 cups water
12 (6-inch) corn tortillas, at room temperature
Cooking spray
2.5 ounces sharp cheddar cheese, shredded (about 2/3 cup)
2 ounces Monterey Jack cheese, shredded (about 1/2 cup)
3 green onions, thinly sliced and divided
6 tablespoons Mexican crema

1. Preheat oven to 400°.

2. To prepare sauce, place ancho chiles in a medium saucepan. Add 3 cups broth; bring to a boil. Reduce heat, and simmer 5 minutes. Stir in 1 torn tortilla; simmer 5 minutes, stirring occasionally. Pour chile mixture into a blender; let stand 10 minutes. Add cilantro, 2 teaspoons garlic, and 2 coarsely chopped green onions to blender; process until smooth. Return mixture to pan; bring to a boil over medium heat. Cook until reduced to 2 cups (about 7 minutes), stirring occasionally. Remove from heat.

3. To prepare enchiladas, heat a large skillet over medium-high heat. Add beef; sauté 5 minutes or until browned. Remove beef from pan using a slotted spoon; drain on paper towels. Wipe pan with paper towels. Return pan to medium heat. Add oil to pan; swirl to coat. Add onion; cook 8 minutes or until tender,

stirring occasionally. Add garlic and next 3 ingredients; cook 2 minutes, stirring constantly. Stir in tomato paste; cook 1 minute, stirring frequently. Stir in beef, beans, and ½ cup broth; bring to a boil, scraping pan to loosen browned bits. Cook 1 minute, stirring occasionally. Remove from heat; stir in lime juice.

4. Place 4 cups water in a saucepan over medium-high heat; bring to a simmer. Working with 1 tortilla at a time, dip tortillas in simmering water 2 to 3 seconds each or until softened. Place 1 tortilla on a flat work surface; spoon 3 tablespoons beef mixture onto 1 end of each tortilla. Roll up, jelly-roll style. Repeat procedure with remaining tortillas and beef mixture. Spread ½ cup sauce in bottom of a 13 x 9–inch glass or ceramic baking dish coated with cooking spray. Arrange enchiladas, seam sides down, in prepared dish. Pour remaining sauce over enchiladas. Top with cheeses. Bake at 400° for 20 minutes or until lightly browned and bubbly. Let stand 10 minutes. Sprinkle with 3 sliced green onions; serve with crema.

Serves 6 (serving size: 2 enchiladas and 1 tablespoon crema): Calories 343; Fat 15.4g (sat 5.8g, mono 5.1g, poly 1.4g); Protein 18g; Carb 36g; Fiber 7g; Sugars 5g (est. added sugars: 0g); Chol 48mg; Iron 3mg; Sodium 540mg; Calc 236mg

MEATBALLS
WITH SPICED TOMATO SAUCE

CLASSIC: Calories per serving: 684, Sat Fat: 13.7g, Sodium: 1258mg, Sugars: 10g
MAKEOVER: Calories per serving: 339, Sat Fat: 5.2g, Sodium: 708mg, Sugars: 5g

HANDS-ON: 18 MIN. TOTAL: 50 MIN.

It'll be hard for your family to resist the comforting aroma wafting from the kitchen. A combination of lean ground beef and lamb cuts saturated fat without losing richness.

1 tablespoon olive oil
2 tablespoons finely chopped onion
1 teaspoon minced fresh garlic
1/2 cup fresh breadcrumbs
1/4 cup chopped fresh mint
1/2 pound ground lamb
1/2 pound ground sirloin
1 teaspoon kosher salt, divided
1/2 teaspoon black pepper, divided
1 large egg, lightly beaten

1/2 cup chopped onion
1 teaspoon ground ginger
1 teaspoon ground cumin
1 teaspoon ground cinnamon
1 (15-ounce) can crushed tomatoes
1/4 cup water
Small mint leaves
3 (6-inch) whole-wheat pitas, halved
   and warmed

1. Heat olive oil in a large skillet over medium-high heat. Add 2 tablespoons onion and garlic to pan; cook 1 minute, stirring constantly. Cool slightly. Combine onion mixture, breadcrumbs, and mint. Add lamb, beef, 1/2 teaspoon salt, 1/4 teaspoon pepper, and egg; stir gently. Shape mixture into 30 (1-inch) meatballs.

2. Return pan to medium-high heat; add meatballs to pan. Cook 4 minutes. Remove meatballs from pan. Add 1/2 cup onion to pan; sauté 2 minutes. Add ginger and next 3 ingredients (through tomatoes); simmer 5 minutes. Stir in 1/4 cup water, 1/2 teaspoon salt, and 1/4 teaspoon pepper. Return meatballs to pan; simmer 20 minutes or until done. Sprinkle with mint leaves. Serve with pitas.

Serves 6 (serving size: 1 pita half and 5 meatballs): Calories 339; Fat 14.9g (sat 5.2g, mono 6.4g, poly 1.7g); Protein 21g; Carb 32g; Fiber 5g; Sugars 5g (est. added sugars: 0g); Chol 78mg; Iron 4mg; Sodium 708mg; Calc 55mg

SLOW-COOKED RAGÙ

CLASSIC: Calories per serving: 527, Sat Fat: 5.9g, Sodium: 2116mg, Sugars: 21g
MAKEOVER: Calories per serving: 197, Sat Fat: 3.8g, Sodium: 393mg, Sugars: 3g

HANDS-ON: 30 MIN. TOTAL: 6 HR. 30 MIN.

We use a small amount of richly flavored pancetta and hot turkey sausage to keep the flavor of our sauce robust.

2 ounces pancetta, chopped
1 pound ground sirloin
12 ounces lean ground pork
1 (4-ounce) link hot turkey Italian
  sausage, casing removed
1 tablespoon canola oil
1 1/3 cups diced onion
2/3 cup diced carrot
2/3 cup diced celery

1/4 cup unsalted tomato paste
2 tablespoons minced fresh garlic
1/2 cup dry white wine
2 cups unsalted chicken stock
1 (15-ounce) can unsalted crushed
  tomatoes, undrained
1 teaspoon salt, divided
1 teaspoon freshly ground black pepper
1 bay leaf

SECRET TO SUCCESS
This meaty sauce is great ladled over whole-grain pasta, and leftovers freeze well.

1. Place pancetta in a large skillet over medium-high heat; cook 4 minutes or until beginning to brown, stirring occasionally. Add beef, and cook 3 minutes or until browned, stirring to crumble beef. Place beef mixture in a 6-quart electric slow cooker. Return skillet to medium-high heat. Add ground pork and sausage; cook 5 minutes or until browned, stirring to crumble. Add pork mixture to slow cooker.

2. Return skillet to medium-high heat. Add oil; swirl to coat. Add onion, carrot, and celery; sauté 4 minutes. Add tomato paste and garlic; cook 2 minutes, stirring frequently. Add wine; bring to a boil. Cook 2 minutes or until wine mostly evaporates, scraping pan to loosen browned bits. Add stock, tomatoes, 3/4 teaspoon salt, pepper, and bay leaf; bring to a boil. Carefully pour stock mixture into slow cooker; cover and cook on LOW for 6 hours. Discard bay leaf. Stir in 1/4 teaspoon salt.

Serves 12 (serving size: about 2/3 cup): Calories 197; Fat 10.8g (sat 3.8g, mono 4.2g, poly 1.1g); Protein 16g; Carb 7g; Fiber 1g; Sugars 3g (est. added sugars: 1g); Chol 52mg; Iron 2mg; Sodium 393mg; Calc 32mg

CLASSIC MEAT LOAF

CLASSIC: Calories per serving: 410, Sat Fat: 6.2g, Sodium: 888mg, Sugars: 16g
MAKEOVER: Calories per serving: 253, Sat Fat: 3g, Sodium: 389mg, Sugars: 8g

HANDS-ON: 55 MIN. TOTAL: 55 MIN.

Baking meat loaf as a free-form shape instead of in a pan allows for extra fat to drain.

1 pound cremini mushrooms
1 tablespoon canola oil
1¼ cups finely chopped onion
6 garlic cloves, minced
2 tablespoons dry sherry
2 teaspoons chopped fresh thyme
8 ounces ground sirloin

½ cup panko (Japanese breadcrumbs)
⅝ teaspoon kosher salt
½ teaspoon black pepper
1 large egg, lightly beaten
Cooking spray
¼ cup lower-sodium ketchup, divided

SNEAK ATTACK
Bulking up the meat loaf with sautéed cremini mushrooms adds deep, earthy flavor and lightens the dish.

1. Preheat oven to 375°.

2. Place half of mushrooms in a food processor; process until minced. Place minced mushrooms in a bowl. Repeat procedure with remaining mushrooms. Rinse and wipe processor clean.

3. Heat a large skillet over medium-high heat. Add oil to pan; swirl to coat. Add onion; sauté 3 minutes. Add garlic; sauté 1 minute. Add mushrooms; cook 7 minutes or until liquid evaporates and mushrooms begin to brown. Add sherry; cook 1 minute, stirring frequently. Remove from heat; stir in thyme. Cool slightly.

4. Combine mushroom mixture, beef, and next 4 ingredients (through egg), mixing until well combined. Shape mixture into a 7 x 3–inch free-form loaf on a foil-lined baking sheet coated with cooking spray. Bake at 375° for 20 minutes. Remove from oven; brush with half of ketchup. Bake an additional 10 to 15 minutes or until a thermometer registers 160°. Remove from oven; brush with remaining ketchup. Cut into 8 slices.

Serves 4 (serving size: 2 slices): Calories 253; Fat 10.9g (sat 3g, mono 5.2g, poly 1.5g); Protein 18g; Carb 20g; Fiber 2g; Sugars 8g (est. added sugars: 2g); Chol 83mg; Iron 2mg; Sodium 389mg; Calc 59mg

ALL-AMERICAN
MEAT LOAF

CLASSIC: Calories per serving: 390, Sat Fat: 9.4g, Sodium: 725mg, Sugars: 11g
MAKEOVER: Calories per serving: 258, Sat Fat: 5.8g, Sodium: 557mg, Sugars: 7g

HANDS-ON: 15 MIN. TOTAL: 1 HR. 20 MIN.

We updated the classic recipe by adding cheddar cheese and tangy buttermilk, all while keeping it healthful.

1 1/2 ounces French bread, torn into pieces
1 pound ground sirloin
1 cup coarsely chopped onion
2 ounces sharp cheddar cheese, diced (about 1/2 cup)
1/2 cup ketchup, divided
5 tablespoons chopped fresh flat-leaf parsley, divided

1/4 cup nonfat buttermilk
1 tablespoon minced fresh garlic (about 3 cloves)
1 tablespoon Dijon mustard
1/2 teaspoon freshly ground black pepper
1/4 teaspoon kosher salt
2 large eggs, lightly beaten
Cooking spray

1. Preheat oven to 350°.

2. Place bread in a food processor; pulse 10 times or until coarse crumbs measure 1 cup. Arrange breadcrumbs in an even layer on a baking sheet. Bake at 350° for 6 minutes or until lightly toasted; cool. Combine toasted breadcrumbs, beef, onion, cheese, 1/4 cup ketchup, 3 tablespoons parsley, and remaining ingredients except cooking spray in a bowl; gently mix just until combined.

3. Transfer mixture to a 9 x 5-inch loaf pan coated with cooking spray; do not pack. Bake at 350° for 30 minutes. Brush top of loaf with 1/4 cup ketchup. Bake an additional 25 minutes or until a thermometer registers 160°. Let stand 10 minutes; cut into 6 slices. Sprinkle with 2 tablespoons parsley, if desired.

Serves 6 (serving size: 1 slice): Calories 258; Fat 12.6g (sat 5.8g, mono 4g, poly 0.6g); Protein 21g; Carb 14g; Fiber 1g; Sugars 7g (est. added sugars: 3g); Chol 119mg; Iron 3mg; Sodium 557mg; Calc 104mg

BEEF AND MUSHROOM
SLOPPY JOES

CLASSIC: Calories per serving: 610, Sat Fat: 9.1g, Sodium: 1220mg, Sugars: 21g
MAKEOVER: Calories per serving: 439, Sat Fat: 4.6g, Sodium: 618mg, Sugars: 15g

HANDS-ON: 20 MIN. TOTAL: 20 MIN.

Cremini mushrooms offer deeper, richer flavor, but you can also use regular button mushrooms. They boost umami flavor without adding more salt.

1 tablespoon olive oil
12 ounces ground sirloin
2 (8-ounce) packages presliced
  cremini mushrooms
1 cup prechopped onion
3 garlic cloves, minced
½ cup unsalted tomato paste
1 tablespoon minced fresh oregano
2 tablespoons red wine vinegar

2 tablespoons Worcestershire sauce
1 tablespoon molasses
¼ teaspoon salt
¾ teaspoon freshly ground black
  pepper
½ teaspoon hot sauce
4 (2-ounce) Kaiser rolls or hamburger
  buns, toasted

CRAZY TRICK
Whirling mushrooms in a food processor creates a fine texture that closely resembles ground beef.

1. Heat a large nonstick skillet over medium-high heat. Add oil; swirl to coat. Add beef; cook 4 minutes or until browned, stirring to crumble.

2. While beef cooks, place mushrooms in a food processor; pulse 10 times or until finely chopped. Add mushrooms, onion, and garlic to pan; cook 3 minutes or until onion is tender. Add tomato paste and next 5 ingredients (through salt) to pan; cook 5 minutes or until mushrooms are tender and liquid evaporates. Stir in pepper and hot sauce. Spoon about 1 cup beef mixture onto bottom half of each bun; top with top halves of buns.

Serves 4 (serving size: 1 sandwich): Calories 439; Fat 14.7g (sat 4.6g, mono 6.8g, poly 1.9g); Protein 27g; Carb 49g; Fiber 4g; Sugars 15g (est. added sugars: 7g); Chol 55mg; Iron 6mg; Sodium 618mg; Calc 160mg

SAUSAGE AND CHEESE
BREAKFAST CASSEROLE

CLASSIC: Calories per serving: 328, Sat Fat: 10.5g, Sodium: 736mg, Sugars: 3g
MAKEOVER: Calories per serving: 251, Sat Fat: 3.7g, Sodium: 574mg, Sugars: 5g

HANDS-ON: 18 MIN. TOTAL: 9 HR. 43 MIN.

Prep this the night before for an easy breakfast or brunch. Turkey sausage is leaner than ground pork sausage. Find turkey sausage in the freezer section of the supermarket with other breakfast meats.

1 teaspoon canola oil
12 ounces turkey breakfast sausage
2 cups 1% low-fat milk
2 cups egg substitute
1 teaspoon dry mustard
½ teaspoon freshly ground black pepper
¼ teaspoon salt
¼ teaspoon ground red pepper
3 large eggs
16 (1-ounce) slices whole grain bread
4 ounces finely shredded reduced-fat extra-sharp cheddar cheese (about 1 cup)
Cooking spray
Paprika

CRAZY TRICK
Egg substitute offers a fluffy egg texture and taste without all the fat and cholesterol.

1. Heat oil a large nonstick skillet over medium-high heat. Add sausage to pan; cook 5 minutes or until browned, stirring to crumble. Remove from heat; cool.

2. Combine milk and next 6 ingredients (through eggs) in a large bowl, stirring with a whisk.

3. Trim crusts from bread. Cut bread into 1-inch cubes. Add bread cubes, sausage, and cheese to milk mixture, stirring to combine. Pour bread mixture into a 13 x 9–inch glass or ceramic baking dish or 3-quart casserole coated with cooking spray, spreading evenly. Cover and refrigerate 8 hours or overnight.

4. Preheat oven to 350°.

5. Remove casserole from refrigerator; let stand 30 minutes. Sprinkle casserole with paprika. Bake at 350° for 45 minutes or until set and lightly browned. Let stand 10 minutes.

Serves 12 (serving size: about 1 cup): Calories 251; Fat 9.6g (sat 3.7g, mono 2.3g, poly 2.1g); Protein 20g; Carb 20g; Fiber 3g; Sugars 5g (est. added sugars: 0g); Chol 78mg; Iron 3mg; Sodium 574mg; Calc 196mg

BEEF and PINTO BEAN
CHILI

CLASSIC: Calories per serving: 540, Sat Fat: 12.2g, Sodium: 1054mg, Sugars: 8g
MAKEOVER: Calories per serving: 421, Sat Fat: 6.8g, Sodium: 565mg, Sugars: 10g

HANDS-ON: 20 MIN. TOTAL: 2 HR. 20 MIN.

For a three-alarm chili, leave the seeds and membranes in the jalapeños. The sour cream has a cooling effect, but you can seed the peppers or use less for a milder result.

Cooking spray

1 pound boneless chuck roast, trimmed and cut into 1-inch pieces

3/8 teaspoon salt, divided

2 tablespoons canola oil

4 cups chopped onion (about 2 medium)

1/4 cup minced jalapeño peppers (about 2 large)

10 garlic cloves, minced

1 (12-ounce) bottle beer

1 tablespoon paprika

1 tablespoon ground cumin

2 tablespoons tomato paste

3 cups fat-free, lower-sodium beef broth

1 (28-ounce) can whole peeled tomatoes, drained and chopped

1 (15-ounce) can pinto beans, rinsed and drained

1/2 cup thinly sliced radish

1 avocado, peeled, seeded, and chopped

6 tablespoons small cilantro leaves

6 tablespoons sour cream

6 lime wedges

1. Heat a Dutch oven over high heat. Coat pan with cooking spray. Sprinkle beef with 1/8 teaspoon salt. Add beef to pan; sauté 5 minutes, turning to brown on all sides. Remove from pan. Add oil to pan; swirl to coat. Add onion and jalapeño; sauté 8 minutes or until lightly browned, stirring occasionally. Add garlic; sauté 1 minute, stirring constantly. Stir in beer, scraping pan to loosen browned bits; bring to a boil. Cook until liquid almost evaporates (about 10 minutes), stirring occasionally. Stir in paprika, cumin, and tomato paste; cook 1 minute, stirring frequently. Add broth, tomatoes, beans, and beef; bring to a boil. Reduce heat, and simmer 1 1/2 hours or until mixture is thick and beef is very tender, stirring occasionally. Stir in 1/4 teaspoon salt.

2. Ladle 1 cup chili into each of 6 bowls. Divide radish and avocado among bowls. Top each serving with 1 tablespoon cilantro and 1 tablespoon sour cream. Serve with lime wedges.

Serves 6: Calories 421; Fat 23g (sat 6.8g, mono 10.9g, poly 2.6g); Protein 22g; Carb 30g; Fiber 9g; Sugars 10g (est. added sugars: 1g); Chol 53mg; Iron 4mg; Sodium 565mg; Calc 123mg

BEEF FLORENTINE PENNE

CLASSIC: Calories per serving: 553, Sat Fat: 15.3g, Sodium: 1136mg, Sugars: 6g
MAKEOVER: Calories per serving: 309, Sat Fat: 2.7g, Sodium: 295mg, Sugars: 3g

HANDS-ON: 58 MIN. TOTAL: 58 MIN.

The sauce for this satisfying pasta dish is deceptively silky. The rich mouthfeel is a result of the starch released by the pasta during the cooking process.

2 tablespoons olive oil, divided
8 ounces uncooked penne (tube-shaped pasta; about 2 cups)
½ cup vertically sliced Vidalia or other sweet onion
¼ teaspoon kosher salt
1 (8-ounce) package sliced cremini mushrooms
Cooking spray
12 ounces ground sirloin
2 garlic cloves, minced
6 cups unsalted beef stock
1 tablespoon fresh lemon juice
¼ teaspoon freshly ground black pepper
1 (6-ounce) package baby spinach, coarsely chopped
1 ounce grated fresh Parmigiano-Reggiano cheese (about ¼ cup)

1. Heat a large Dutch oven over medium heat. Add 1 tablespoon oil to pan; swirl to coat. Add pasta; cook 5 minutes or until toasted, stirring frequently. Remove pasta from pan.

2. Increase heat to medium-high. Heat 1 tablespoon oil in pan. Add onion, salt, and mushrooms to pan; coat mushroom mixture with cooking spray. Sauté 6 minutes or until mushrooms are browned and onions are lightly caramelized. Add beef and garlic; cook 5 minutes or until beef is browned, stirring to crumble. Remove beef mixture from pan.

3. While beef mixture cooks, place stock in a 2-quart glass measure or medium glass bowl. Microwave at HIGH 2 to 3 minutes or until hot; keep warm.

4. Reduce heat to medium. Add toasted pasta and 1 cup stock to pan. Cook 8 to 9 minutes or until liquid is nearly absorbed, stirring constantly. Add 4 cups stock, 1 cup at a time, stirring constantly until each portion of stock is absorbed before adding the next (about 35 minutes total). Add 1 cup stock, beef mixture, lemon juice, pepper, and spinach, stirring until spinach wilts (pasta should be al dente). Stir in cheese, and serve immediately.

Serves 6 (serving size: 1⅓ cups): Calories 309; Fat 9.1g (sat 2.7g, mono 4.7g, poly 1g); Protein 38g; Carb 23g; Fiber 3g; Sugars 3g (est. added sugars: 0g); Chol 139mg; Iron 5mg; Sodium 295mg; Calc 91mg

CHILI CORN CHIP PIE

CLASSIC: Calories per serving: 583, Sat Fat: 13.2g, Sodium: 973mg, Sugars: 2g
MAKEOVER: Calories per serving: 414, Sat Fat: 7g, Sodium: 682mg, Sugars: 7g

HANDS-ON: 40 MIN. TOTAL: 40 MIN.

This recipe is a healthy version of Chili Pie. Often served from concession stands at fairs, festivals, and sporting events, this crowd-pleaser usually involves splitting the bag of chips open, ladling chili into the bag, and then topping with cheese, onions, and other garnishes. Our version saves calories by using a small amount of corn chips on top as a crunchy garnish.

Cooking spray
1 pound ground sirloin
1¼ cups chopped onion
6 garlic cloves, minced
½ teaspoon ground cumin
½ teaspoon ground red pepper
⅛ teaspoon kosher salt
1 tablespoon unsalted tomato paste
1 cup fat-free, lower-sodium beef broth
⅓ cup water
1 (10-ounce) can diced tomatoes and green chiles, undrained
4 ounces lightly salted corn chips (such as Fritos)
1.5 ounces shredded sharp cheddar cheese (about ⅓ cup)
¼ cup fat-free sour cream
½ cup diagonally sliced green onion tops

1. Heat a large skillet over medium-high heat. Coat pan with cooking spray. Add beef to pan; sauté 5 minutes, stirring to crumble. Remove beef; drain. Wipe pan clean with paper towels. Add onion to pan; sauté 4 minutes, stirring occasionally. Add garlic; sauté 1 minute, stirring constantly. Stir in beef, cumin, pepper, and salt.

2. Stir in tomato paste; cook 1 minute, stirring occasionally. Add broth, ⅓ cup water, and tomatoes; bring to a boil. Reduce heat to medium, and simmer 15 minutes or until slightly thick, stirring occasionally. Remove from heat.

3. Place 1 ounce chips in each of 4 bowls, and top each serving with about ⅔ cup beef mixture, about 1 tablespoon cheese, and 1 tablespoon sour cream. Sprinkle each serving with 2 tablespoons green onions.

Serves 4: Calories 414; Fat 21.9g (sat 7g, mono 7.6g, poly 5.5g); Protein 25g; Carb 29g; Fiber 3g; Sugars 7g (est. added sugars: 0g); Chol 68mg; Iron 3mg; Sodium 682mg; Calc 160mg

BEEF AND BEAN TACO SALAD

CLASSIC: Calories per serving: 847, Sat Fat: 15.4g, Sodium: 1023mg, Sugars: 7g
MAKEOVER: Calories per serving: 384, Sat Fat: 5.4g, Sodium: 607mg, Sugars: 8g

HANDS-ON: 25 MIN. TOTAL: 25 MIN.

Instead of frying the tortillas, we lightly coat them with cooking spray and broil until crisp–a method that produces the crispiest shells while saving about 10g fat per serving.

¾ pound ground sirloin

¾ cup refrigerated fresh salsa

1 (15-ounce) can unsalted black beans, rinsed and drained

Cooking spray

4 (8-inch) 100% whole-wheat soft taco flour tortillas

1 cup chopped tomato

¾ cup chopped ripe avocado

¼ cup chopped fresh cilantro

2 teaspoons fresh lime juice

1 teaspoon olive oil

¼ cup fat-free sour cream

2 teaspoons adobo sauce (from canned chipotle chiles in adobo sauce)

1 (8-ounce) package presliced iceberg lettuce

1.5 ounces preshredded reduced-fat Mexican blend cheese (about ⅓ cup)

1. Preheat broiler.

2. Heat a large nonstick skillet over medium-high heat. Add beef to pan; sauté 5 minutes or until browned, stirring to crumble. Add salsa and beans; cook 5 minutes or until liquid almost evaporates.

3. Place 4 (7-ounce) ramekins upside down on a large jelly-roll pan; coat ramekins with cooking spray. Place 1 tortilla over each ramekin; fold down sides to form upside-down cups. Lightly coat tortillas with cooking spray. Broil 2 to 3 minutes on middle oven rack or until tortillas brown in spots. Remove pan from oven; let stand 1 minute. Invert tortillas, propping against ramekins and sides of pan to keep their shape; lightly coat with cooking spray. Broil an additional 2 minutes on middle rack or until browned. Remove from heat; cool slightly.

4. Place tomato, avocado, cilantro, lime juice, and oil in a small bowl; toss gently to combine. Combine sour cream and adobo sauce in a small bowl, stirring well.

5. Divide lettuce among tortilla bowls. Top with beef mixture; sprinkle with cheese. Divide avocado mixture over top; dollop 1 tablespoon sour cream mixture over each serving.

Serves 4 (serving size: 1 salad): Calories 384; Fat 16.7g (sat 5.4g, mono 7.7g, poly 1.7g); Protein 30g; Carb 43g; Fiber 10g; Sugars 8g (est. added sugars: 1g); Chol 56mg; Iron 5mg; Sodium 607mg; Calc 307mg

MEAT AND CHEESE
LASAGNA

CLASSIC: Calories per serving: 1183, Sat Fat: 30.9g, Sodium: 1407mg, Sugars: 9g
MAKEOVER: Calories per serving: 395, Sat Fat: 7.3g, Sodium: 540mg, Sugars: 7g

HANDS-ON: 20 MIN. TOTAL: 1 HR. 12 MIN.

Trim saturated fat and calories by using fat-free ricotta cheese, part-skim mozzarella, and extra-lean beef. Bump up the beef with finely chopped mushrooms.

3 cups fat-free ricotta cheese
12 ounces part-skim mozzarella cheese, shredded (about 3 cups)
6 tablespoons chopped fresh parsley, divided
3 tablespoons unsalted butter, melted
2 tablespoons chopped fresh oregano
6 cloves garlic, minced and divided
2 large eggs, lightly beaten
1 1/4 pounds ground sirloin
1 (8-ounce) package cremini mushrooms, chopped
1 teaspoon freshly ground black pepper
1/2 teaspoon crushed red pepper
4 1/2 cups lower-sodium marinara sauce
1/2 teaspoon salt
Cooking spray
12 lasagna noodles, cooked
2 ounces grated fresh Parmigiano-Reggiano cheese (about 1/2 cup)

CRAZY TRICK
Stir in butter to the fat-free ricotta to add richness. It's still lighter than part-skim ricotta.

1. Preheat oven to 375°.

2. Combine ricotta, 4 ounces (about 1 cup) mozzarella, 4 tablespoons parsley, butter, oregano, 2 garlic cloves, and eggs; set aside.

3. Place beef and mushrooms in a large nonstick skillet over medium-high heat; sprinkle with peppers and 4 garlic cloves. Cook 6 minutes or until beef is browned and mushrooms are tender, stirring to crumble; drain. Return beef mixture to pan; stir in marinara sauce and salt; remove from heat.

4. Spread 1 cup meat sauce in bottom of a broiler-safe 13 x 9–inch glass or ceramic baking dish coated with cooking spray. Top with 3 noodles; spread with 1 1/2 cups meat sauce, and dollop with one-third of ricotta mixture (about 1 1/4 cups). Repeat layers twice, beginning with noodles and ending with ricotta mixture. Top with 3 noodles and 1 1/2 cups meat sauce. Sprinkle with 8 ounces (2 cups) mozzarella cheese and Parmigiano-Reggiano cheese. Cover with foil coated with cooking spray. Bake at 375° for 30 minutes. Uncover and bake an additional 10 minutes or until bubbly.

5. Preheat broiler (keep lasagna in oven).

6. Broil lasagna 1 to 2 minutes or until cheese is golden brown and sauce is bubbly. Remove from oven; let stand 10 minutes. Sprinkle with 2 tablespoons parsley; cut into 12 pieces.

Serves 12 (serving size: 1 piece): Calories 395; Fat 14.8g (sat 7.3g, mono 4g, poly 0.7g); Protein 30g; Carb 32g; Fiber 2g; Sugars 7g (est. added sugars 2g); Chol 99mg; Iron 3mg; Sodium 540mg; Calc 391mg

CLASSIC BACON
CHEESEBURGER SLIDERS

CLASSIC: Calories per serving: 830, Sat Fat: 24.8g, Sodium: 1500mg, Sugars: 5g
MAKEOVER: Calories per serving: 406, Sat Fat: 5.4g, Sodium: 803mg, Sugars: 9g

HANDS-ON: 22 MIN. TOTAL: 22 MIN.

Though we usually shy away from processed foods, we do love American cheese here for that old-school burger-joint flavor; you can certainly substitute cheddar, if you prefer. Rinsing the onion removes some of its harsh bite; use a fine sieve.

4 center-cut bacon slices, cut in half
  crosswise
1 pound ground sirloin
1 1/2 teaspoons olive oil
1/2 teaspoon garlic powder
1/2 teaspoon freshly ground black
  pepper
1/8 teaspoon kosher salt

Cooking spray
2 slices 2% reduced-fat American
  cheese, quartered
8 teaspoons ketchup
8 slider buns, split and toasted
4 teaspoons minced fresh onion, rinsed
  and drained
8 green-leaf lettuce leaves

1. Cook bacon in a skillet over medium heat until crisp; drain.

2. Place beef in a medium bowl. Drizzle with oil, and sprinkle with garlic powder, pepper, and salt; mix well to combine. Divide mixture into 8 equal portions, shaping each into a 3-inch patty.

3. Heat a grill pan or cast-iron skillet over medium-high heat. Coat pan with cooking spray. Add patties; cook 3 minutes or until seared. Turn patties over; top each with 1 piece of cheese. Cover and cook 2 minutes or until beef is done and cheese melts.

4. Spread 1 teaspoon ketchup on top half of each bun; top each with 1/2 teaspoon onion. Layer bottom half of each bun with 1 lettuce leaf, 1 patty, 1 bacon piece, and top half of bun.

Serves 4 (serving size: 2 sliders): Calories 406; Fat 15g (sat 5.4g, mono 4.4g, poly 3.4g); Protein 32g; Carb 38g; Fiber 2g; Sugars 9g (est. added sugars: 3g); Chol 66mg; Iron 4mg; Sodium 803mg; Calc 215mg

GYROS

CLASSIC: Calories per serving: 510, Sat Fat: 12g, Sodium: 1120mg, Sugars: 6g
MAKEOVER: Calories per serving: 375, Sat Fat: 4.4g, Sodium: 627mg, Sugars: 6g

HANDS-ON: 20 MIN. TOTAL: 32 MIN.

A Greek specialty, gyros are traditionally made from spiced, spit-roasted lamb. Here, we lighten lamb with sirloin, and shape the mixture into loaves. The yogurt dressing is a variation on traditional tzatziki.

LOAVES:

6 ounces ground lamb
6 ounces ground sirloin
1 teaspoon onion powder
1 teaspoon garlic powder
1 teaspoon dried oregano

2 teaspoons fresh lemon juice
¼ teaspoon salt
3 garlic cloves, minced
Cooking spray
⅛ teaspoon ground red pepper

SAUCE:

1 cup shredded peeled cucumber
¼ cup vertically sliced red onion
1 tablespoon chopped fresh mint
½ teaspoon garlic powder
½ teaspoon fresh lemon juice

⅛ teaspoon salt
⅛ teaspoon black pepper
1 (8-ounce) carton plain fat-free yogurt
4 pocketless pitas

1. Preheat broiler.

2. To prepare loaves, combine first 8 ingredients, stirring well. Divide mixture in half, forming each half into a 6 x 3–inch loaf. Place loaves on a broiler pan coated with cooking spray; broil 7 minutes on each side or until done.

3. Sprinkle loaves with red pepper. Cut each loaf crosswise into ⅛-inch slices.

4. To prepare sauce, place cucumber and onion on several layers of heavy-duty paper towels. Cover with additional paper towels; let stand 5 minutes.

5. Combine cucumber mixture, mint, and next 5 ingredients (through yogurt), stirring well. Divide meat slices among pitas; top each serving with about ¼ cup sauce.

Serves 4 (serving size: 1 gyro): Calories 375; Fat 11.6g (sat 4.4g, mono 4.7g, poly 1g); Protein 25g; Carb 42g; Fiber 2g; Sugars 6g (est. added sugars: 0g); Chol 61mg; Iron 4mg; Sodium 627mg; Calc 158mg

MUSHROOM AND PROVOLONE
PATTY MELTS

CLASSIC: Calories per serving: 1014, Sat Fat: 35.8g, Sodium: 1230mg, Sugars: 6g
MAKEOVER: Calories per serving: 407, Sat Fat: 4.4g, Sodium: 770mg, Sugars: 5g

HANDS-ON: 27 MIN. TOTAL: 27 MIN.

Your family won't believe this comforting sandwich is light. For the kids, use beef broth instead of beer, and try mild whole-wheat bread.

1/4 cup thinly sliced onion, divided
1 pound ground sirloin
1/4 teaspoon salt, divided
1/4 teaspoon freshly ground black pepper, divided
1 tablespoon olive oil, divided
1 (8-ounce) package presliced cremini mushrooms

1 1/2 teaspoons all-purpose flour
1/4 cup dark lager beer
8 (1.1-ounce) slices rye bread
Cooking spray
4 (0.67-ounce) slices reduced-fat provolone cheese

1. Chop enough of the sliced onion to measure 1/4 cup. Combine chopped onion, beef, 1/8 teaspoon salt, and 1/8 teaspoon pepper in a medium bowl. Divide beef mixture into 4 equal portions with moist hands, shaping each into a 4-inch oval patty. Press thumb in center of each patty, leaving a nickel-sized indentation.

2. Heat a large nonstick skillet over medium-high heat. Add 1 teaspoon oil to pan, swirling to coat. Add patties; cook 4 minutes on each side or until done.

3. Heat 2 teaspoons oil in a medium skillet over medium-high heat. Add mushrooms, remaining onion, 1/8 teaspoon salt, and 1/8 teaspoon pepper; sauté 3 minutes. Sprinkle flour over mushroom mixture; cook 1 minute, stirring constantly. Stir in beer; cook 30 seconds or until thick. Remove from heat; keep warm.

4. When patties are done, remove from large pan. Wipe pan clean; heat over medium-high heat. Coat 1 side of each bread slice with cooking spray. Place 4 bread slices, coated sides down, in pan. Top each with 1 patty, 1 cheese slice, and one-fourth of mushroom mixture. Top with remaining bread slices; coat with cooking spray. Cook 2 minutes on each side or until browned.

Serves 4 (serving size: 1 sandwich): Calories 407; Fat 13g (sat 4.4g, mono 5.8g, poly 1.5g); Protein 36g; Carb 37g; Fiber 5g; Sugars 5g (est. added sugars: 0g); Chol 70mg; Iron 4mg; Sodium 770mg; Calc 213mg

VEGGIE BURGERS

CLASSIC: Calories per serving: 623, Sat Fat: 6.9g, Sodium: 1169mg, Sugars: 10g
MAKEOVER: Calories per serving: 384, Sat Fat: 3.4g, Sodium: 649mg, Sugars: 5g

HANDS-ON: 42 MIN. TOTAL: 54 MIN.

A mix of golden beets and chewy whole-grain brown rice boosts the flavor, while chopped toasted walnuts and blue cheese add subtle crunch and rich flavor.

6 (1½-ounce) artisanal sandwich rolls
Cooking spray
3 cups grated cooked golden beet (about 3 medium)
⅓ cup chopped walnuts, toasted
⅓ cup panko (Japanese breadcrumbs)
3 tablespoons grated fresh horseradish
3 tablespoons minced fresh chives
¼ teaspoon freshly ground black pepper
1 (8.8-ounce) package precooked brown rice

2 teaspoons Dijon mustard
2 large eggs
1 large egg white
⅜ teaspoon kosher salt, divided
2 tablespoons canola oil
2 ounces blue cheese, crumbled (about ½ cup)
¼ cup canola mayonnaise
1 teaspoon fresh lemon juice
1½ cups arugula

1. Preheat broiler.

2. Place rolls, cut sides up, on a baking sheet; coat with cooking spray. Broil 2 minutes or until toasted. Set aside.

3. Reduce oven temperature to 400°; place a baking sheet in oven.

4. Combine beet and next 6 ingredients (through rice). Combine mustard, eggs, and egg white. Add ¼ teaspoon salt and mustard mixture to beet mixture; stir well. Spoon about ⅔ cup rice mixture into a (4-inch) round biscuit cutter; pack mixture down. Remove mixture from mold; repeat 5 times to form 6 patties.

5. Heat a large skillet over medium-high heat. Add 1 tablespoon oil; swirl to coat. Carefully add 3 patties to pan; cook 3 minutes. Carefully transfer patties to a preheated baking sheet coated with cooking spray, turning patties over. Repeat procedure with 1 tablespoon oil and 3 patties. Return baking sheet to oven; bake patties at 400° for 12 minutes.

6. Combine cheese, mayonnaise, juice, and ⅛ teaspoon salt. Place bottom half of each roll on a plate. Divide mayonnaise mixture among roll bottoms; top each with 1 patty. Arrange ¼ cup arugula on each patty; top with roll tops.

Serves 6 (serving size: 1 burger): Calories 384; Fat 17.8g (sat 3.4g, mono 6.9g, poly 6.3g); Protein 13g; Carb 43g; Fiber 4g; Sugars 5g (est. added sugars: 0g); Chol 69mg; Iron 3mg; Sodium 649mg; Calc 111mg

LOUISVILLE HOT BROWNS
WITH CAULIFLOWER MORNAY

CLASSIC: Calories per serving: 828, Sat Fat: 25.7g, Sodium: 2556mg, Sugars: 15g
MAKEOVER: Calories per serving: 331, Sat Fat: 5.5g, Sodium: 640mg, Sugars: 5g

HANDS-ON: 32 MIN. TOTAL: 37 MIN.

A Kentucky classic gets a modern twist with a light but creamy cauliflower puree that stands in for the traditional cheese sauce.

1½ cups chopped cauliflower
1 cup unsalted chicken stock
⅓ cup 2% reduced-fat milk
1 ounce fresh pecorino Romano
  cheese, grated (about ¼ cup)
1½ tablespoons unsalted butter
½ teaspoon freshly ground black
  pepper, divided
¼ teaspoon kosher salt

4 (1½-ounce) slices multigrain bread
4 center-cut bacon slices, chopped
12 ounces turkey breast cutlets (about
  ¼ inch thick)
4 (½-inch-thick) slices heirloom
  beefsteak tomatoes
1 tablespoon chopped fresh flat-leaf
  parsley
1 tablespoon chopped fresh chives

1. Preheat broiler.

2. Combine cauliflower and stock in a medium saucepan. Bring to a boil; cook 10 minutes or until tender. Place cauliflower mixture in a blender. Add milk, cheese, butter, ¼ teaspoon pepper, and salt. Remove center piece of blender lid (to allow steam to escape); secure blender lid on blender. Place a clean towel over opening in blender lid (to avoid splatters); process until smooth.

3. Place bread on a baking sheet. Broil 2 minutes or until toasted on one side.

4. Cook bacon in a large ovenproof skillet over medium-high heat until crisp. Remove bacon with a slotted spoon. Sprinkle turkey with ¼ teaspoon pepper. Add turkey to pan; cook 2 minutes on each side or until done. Remove turkey from pan; let stand 5 minutes. Shred turkey into large pieces. Arrange bread slices in a single layer, toasted side down, in pan. Top bread slices with turkey. Pour cauliflower mixture over turkey; broil 3 minutes or until sauce begins to bubble. Top each serving with 1 tomato slice, one-fourth of bacon, and herbs.

Serves 4 (serving size: 1 sandwich): Calories 331; Fat 11.7g (sat 5.5g, mono 3.4g, poly 1.4g); Protein 33g; Carb 24g; Fiber 5g; Sugars 5g (est. added sugars: 0g); Chol 78mg; Iron 3mg; Sodium 640mg; Calc 162mg

GRILLED HAM, CHICKEN, AND GRUYÈRE
SANDWICHES

CLASSIC: Calories per serving: 1007, Sat Fat: 15.5g, Sodium: 1702mg, Sugars: 9g
MAKEOVER: Calories per serving: 371, Sat Fat: 6g, Sodium: 750mg, Sugars: 6g

HANDS-ON: 28 MIN. TOTAL: 28 MIN.

This is a perfect sandwich for watching the big game. Serve it with an amber beer, whose toasty malt and bitter hops complement the sweet pears and nutty cheese.

2 (6-ounce) skinless, boneless chicken
  breast halves
Cooking spray
¼ teaspoon freshly ground black
  pepper
1½ ounces prosciutto, cut into 4 thin
  slices
8 (¾-ounce) slices sourdough bread
4 teaspoons butter, softened and
  divided

2 ounces Gruyère cheese, shredded
  (about ½ cup)
2 tablespoons Dijon mustard
2 cups arugula
3 tablespoons thinly sliced shallots
2 teaspoons fresh lemon juice
1 large red-skinned pear, sliced

1. Cut each chicken breast in half horizontally to form 4 cutlets. Heat a large skillet over medium-high heat. Coat pan with cooking spray. Sprinkle chicken with pepper. Add chicken to pan; cook 4 minutes on each side or until done. Remove chicken from pan. Wrap 1 prosciutto slice around each cutlet.

2. Return pan to medium heat. Coat pan with cooking spray. Spread 1 side of each bread slice with ½ teaspoon butter. Place 4 bread slices, buttered sides down, in pan. Top each bread slice in pan with 2 tablespoons cheese; toast bread for 2 minutes or until underside is toasted and cheese melts. Remove bread from pan. Recoat pan with cooking spray. Place 4 bread slices, buttered sides down, in pan; toast 2 minutes or until toasted. Remove from pan.

3. Top each cheese-topped bread slice with 1 chicken cutlet. Spread 1½ teaspoons mustard over untoasted side of each remaining bread slice. Combine arugula, shallots, and juice in a bowl; toss. Divide arugula mixture among sandwiches; top each sandwich with 1 bread slice, mustard side down. Serve with pear slices.

Serves 4 (serving size: 1 sandwich and ¼ pear): Calories 371; Fat 11.5g (sat 6g, mono 3.3g, poly 1.2g); Protein 32g; Carb 34g; Fiber 3g; Sugars 6g (est. added sugars: 0g); Chol 81mg; Iron 3mg; Sodium 750mg; Calc 197mg

CHEESY VEGETABLE AND BEAN
QUESADILLAS

CLASSIC: Calories per serving: 557, Sat Fat: 8.8g, Sodium: 1317mg, Sugars: 11g
MAKEOVER: Calories per serving: 253, Sat Fat: 2.8g, Sodium: 631mg, Sugars: 6g

HANDS-ON: 29 MIN. TOTAL: 29 MIN.

The ooey-gooey cheese in a quesadilla is what makes it everyone's favorite, but the calories certainly do not. Try this flip on your favorite treat by using beans to hold it all together instead of the traditional mountain of cheese. Mixing shredded cheese with a low-fat creamy cheese also adds to the goodness of this recipe.

1 red bell pepper, cut into strips
1 yellow bell pepper, cut into strips
1 small Vidalia or other sweet onion, vertically sliced
1 small zucchini, thinly sliced
Cooking spray
1 tablespoon ground cumin
2 tablespoons chopped fresh cilantro
½ teaspoon grated lime rind
2 tablespoons fresh lime juice
1 (15-ounce) can fat-free refried beans
6 ounces shredded queso fresco (about 1½ cups)
3 (0.75-ounce) wedges spreadable Swiss cheese
6 (8-inch) fat-free flour tortillas

1. Combine first 4 ingredients in a large bowl; coat vegetable mixture with cooking spray. Heat a large nonstick skillet over medium-high heat. Add vegetable mixture to pan; sauté 6 to 8 minutes or until vegetables are lightly browned. Add cumin and next 3 ingredients (through lime juice); cook 30 seconds, stirring constantly. Transfer vegetable mixture to a bowl; cool slightly. Wipe pan clean with a paper towel.

2. Place beans in a bowl; stir until smooth. Combine queso fresco and cheese wedges in another bowl; stir until smooth.

3. Place tortillas on a large cutting board or work surface. Spread ¼ cup beans over half of each tortilla. Spread about 3 tablespoons cheese mixture over other half of each tortilla. Spoon ½ cup vegetable mixture over cheese mixture; fold tortillas in half.

4. Reheat pan over medium-high heat. Coat quesadillas with cooking spray. Place 2 quesadillas in pan; cook 1 to 2 minutes on each side or until cheese melts and tortillas are golden brown. Remove from pan; keep warm. Repeat procedure twice with remaining quesadillas. Cut each quesadilla into 4 wedges, and serve immediately.

Serves 6 (serving size: 1 quesadilla): Calories 253; Fat 5.5g (sat 2.8g, mono 0.7g, poly 0.1g); Protein 11g; Carb 40g; Fiber 4g; Sugars 6g (est. added sugars: 0g); Chol 17mg; Iron 2mg; Sodium 631mg; Calc 143mg

CREAMY GRILLED CHEESE
SKILLET PANINI

CLASSIC: Calories per serving: 487, Sat Fat: 16.9g, Sodium: 728mg, Sugars: 6g
MAKEOVER: Calories per serving: 242, Sat Fat: 4.5g, Sodium: 567mg, Sugars: 3g

HANDS-ON: 11 MIN. TOTAL: 11 MIN.

A meltingly delicious grilled cheese sandwich is just perfect some days to chase away the winter blues or accommodate the best bowl of soup ever. Here's how to satisfy your craving without blowing your calories for the day. Keep your sandwich interesting by experimenting with different low-fat cheeses to find the flavor profile that suits you best.

4 ounces 2% reduced-fat extra-sharp
   cheddar cheese, shredded (about
   1 cup
1 tablespoon canola mayonnaise
1 teaspoon Dijon mustard

Dash of freshly ground black pepper
8 (1-ounce) slices hearty whole-grain
   wheat bread
Cooking spray

1. Combine first 4 ingredients in a medium bowl; mix well (mixture will be very thick). Spread 3 tablespoons cheese mixture on 1 side of each of 4 bread slices. Top each with 1 bread slice. Lightly coat sandwiches with cooking spray.

2. Heat a large nonstick skillet over medium-low heat. Add sandwiches to pan; top sandwiches with foil coated with cooking spray. Place a smaller skillet on top of foil; cook 2 to 3 minutes. Remove small skillet and foil; turn sandwiches, and replace foil and skillet. Cook 2 to 3 minutes or until sandwiches are golden brown and cheese mixture melts. Serve immediately.

Serves 4 (serving size: 1 sandwich): Calories 242; Fat 8.9g (sat 4.5g, mono 1.5g, poly 0.7g); Protein 14g; Carb 25g; Fiber 4g; Sugars 3g (est. added sugars: 0g); Chol 20mg; Iron 1mg; Sodium 567mg; Calc 263mg

CREAMY, LIGHT
MACARONI AND CHEESE

CLASSIC: Calories per serving: 654, Sat Fat: 18g, Sodium: 734mg, Sugars: 8g
MAKEOVER: Calories per serving: 390, Sat Fat: 6.1g, Sodium: 589mg, Sugars: 7g

HANDS-ON: 1 HR. TOTAL: 1 HR. 25 MIN.

A trio of bold cheeses packs more flavor than a one-cheese approach, while grooved pasta ensures full sauce coverage.

3 cups cubed peeled butternut squash (about 1 [1-pound] squash)
1½ cups fat-free milk
1¼ cups fat-free, lower-sodium chicken broth
2 garlic cloves, peeled
2 tablespoons plain fat-free Greek yogurt
1 teaspoon kosher salt
½ teaspoon freshly ground pepper
5 ounces shredded Gruyère cheese (about 1¼ cups)
4 ounces grated pecorino Romano cheese (about 1 cup)
1 ounce finely grated fresh Parmigiano-Reggiano cheese, divided (about ¼ cup)
1 pound uncooked macaroni
Cooking spray
1 teaspoon olive oil
½ cup panko (Japanese breadcrumbs)
2 tablespoons chopped fresh parsley (optional)

SNEAK ATTACK
We turned to butternut squash, which adds color, creaminess, and a boost of veggies to cheddar cheese sauce.

1. Preheat oven to 375°.

2. Combine squash, milk, broth, and garlic in a medium saucepan; bring to a boil over medium-high heat. Reduce heat to medium; simmer until squash is tender when pierced with a fork, about 25 minutes. Remove from heat.

3. Place squash mixture in a blender. Add yogurt, salt, and pepper. Remove center piece of blender lid (to allow steam to escape); secure blender lid on blender. Place a clean towel over opening in blender lid (to avoid splatters). Blend until smooth. Place squash mixture in a bowl; stir in Gruyère, pecorino Romano, and 2 tablespoons Parmigiano-Reggiano. Stir until combined.

4. Cook pasta according to package directions, omitting salt and fat; drain well. Add pasta to squash mixture; stir until combined. Spread mixture into a 13 x 9–inch glass or ceramic baking dish coated with cooking spray.

5. Heat oil in a medium skillet over medium heat. Add panko; cook 2 minutes or until golden brown. Remove from heat; stir in 2 tablespoons Parmigiano-Reggiano cheese. Sprinkle panko mixture over hot pasta mixture. Lightly coat topping with cooking spray. Bake at 375° for 25 minutes or until bubbly. Sprinkle with parsley, if desired, and serve immediately.

Serves 8 (serving size: 1⅓ cups): Calories 390; Fat 10.9g (sat 6.1g, mono 2.1g, poly 0.4g); Protein 19g; Carb 54g; Fiber 3g; Sugars 7g (est. added sugars: 0g); Chol 31mg; Iron 2mg; Sodium 589mg; Calc 403mg

SMOKY SHRIMP AND CHICKEN
GUMBO

CLASSIC: Calories per serving: 552, Sat Fat: 5.9g, Sodium: 772mg, Sugars: 3g
MAKEOVER: Calories per serving: 334, Sat Fat: 1.6g, Sodium: 539mg, Sugars: 3g

HANDS-ON: 58 MIN. TOTAL: 3 HR. 13 MIN.

Making homemade stock drastically reduces the sodium. Freeze leftover stock up to three months, and use for chowder or risotto.

STOCK:
1 pound unpeeled medium shrimp
8 cups water
1 teaspoon black peppercorns
4 garlic cloves, crushed
3 large celery stalks, chopped
3 bay leaves
3 medium carrots, coarsely chopped
1 large onion, coarsely chopped

GUMBO:
6 tablespoons canola oil, divided
2.25 ounces all-purpose flour (about ½ cup)
6 skinless, boneless chicken thighs, cut into bite-sized pieces
2 cups finely chopped white onion
1 tablespoon Creole seasoning
3 garlic cloves, minced
2 medium celery stalks, chopped
2 medium tomatoes, finely chopped
1 large green bell pepper, seeded and finely chopped
3 cups fat-free, lower-sodium chicken broth
2 bay leaves
1 cup frozen cut okra
2 teaspoons Worcestershire sauce
2 teaspoons hot pepper sauce (such as Tabasco)
½ teaspoon black pepper
½ teaspoon smoked paprika
2 cups hot cooked brown rice

1. To prepare stock, peel and devein shrimp, reserving shells. Cut each shrimp in half lengthwise; cover shrimp, and refrigerate.

2. Combine reserved shrimp shells, 8 cups water, and next 6 ingredients (through coarsely chopped onion) in a large Dutch oven; bring to a boil. Reduce heat, and simmer 1 hour. Strain through a sieve into a bowl; discard solids. Set aside 3 cups stock; keep warm. Reserve remaining stock for another use.

3. To prepare gumbo, heat a large cast-iron skillet over low heat; add ¼ cup canola oil. Cook 2 minutes, swirling to coat pan. Weigh or lightly spoon flour into a dry measuring cup. Gradually add flour to oil, stirring constantly with a whisk until smooth. Increase heat to medium; cook 8 minutes or until flour mixture is caramel-colored, stirring frequently. Cook 2 minutes or until mixture is chestnut-colored, stirring constantly. Remove from heat; slowly add warm shrimp stock, stirring until smooth. Pour stock mixture into a large bowl.

4. Heat 1 tablespoon oil in a large Dutch oven over medium heat. Add chicken; cook 7 minutes, turning to brown on all sides. Add onion and next 5 ingredients (through bell pepper); sauté 3 minutes. Return stock mixture to pan; add broth and bay leaves. Bring to a boil; reduce heat, and simmer 45 minutes.

5. Add okra and next 3 ingredients (through black pepper). Simmer 30 minutes.

6. Combine shrimp and paprika; toss to coat shrimp. Heat a large nonstick skillet over medium-high heat. Add 1 tablespoon oil to pan; swirl to coat. Add shrimp; sauté 2 minutes or until shrimp are done. Stir shrimp into okra mixture. Discard bay leaves. Serve over rice.

Serves 8 (serving size: 1 cup gumbo and ¼ cup rice): Calories 334; Fat 14.3g (sat 1.6g, mono 7.6g, poly 4.1g); Protein 26g; Carb 25g; Fiber 3g; Sugars 3g (est. added sugars: 0g); Chol 130mg; Iron 3mg; Sodium 539mg; Calc 76mg

SHRIMP BISQUE

HANDS-ON: 1 HR. 23 MIN. TOTAL: 1 HR. 58 MIN.

This take on a usually high-fat favorite uses a deceptively healthy substitute for cream that you will find indispensable in your kitchen repertoire from now on.

BROWN RICE CREAM:
2 cups water
½ cup uncooked instant brown rice

1 cup 2% reduced-fat milk

SHRIMP BISQUE:
1 pound unpeeled medium shrimp
4 teaspoons canola oil, divided
2 carrots, peeled and coarsely
   chopped
2 celery stalks, coarsely chopped
1 leek, trimmed and chopped

2 tablespoons tomato paste
1 bay leaf
4 cups water
⅓ cup dry sherry
3 tablespoons all-purpose flour
¼ teaspoon salt

1. To prepare brown rice cream, bring 2 cups water and rice to a boil in a medium saucepan; cover, reduce heat, and simmer 30 minutes. Remove from heat; let stand, covered, 5 minutes. Pour mixture into a blender; add milk. Remove center piece of blender lid (to allow steam to escape); secure blender lid on blender. Place a clean towel over opening in blender lid (to avoid splatters). Blend 2 minutes or until smooth. Set aside.

2. To prepare bisque, peel shrimp, reserving shells. Cover and refrigerate shrimp. Heat 2 teaspoons oil in a large Dutch oven over medium heat. Add shrimp shells, carrot, celery, and leek; cook 8 minutes or until shells are bright pink and vegetables are lightly caramelized, stirring frequently. Stir in tomato paste and bay leaf. Add 4 cups water and sherry, scraping pan to loosen browned bits. Bring to a boil; reduce heat to medium-low, and simmer 30 minutes, stirring occasionally. Strain mixture through a sieve into a large bowl, reserving stock. Discard solids.

3. Return Dutch oven to medium-high heat; add 2 teaspoons oil to pan. Add shrimp; cook 3 minutes or until shrimp are done. Remove shrimp from pan; keep warm. Add flour to drippings in pan; cook 1 minute, stirring constantly. Gradually add 1 cup reserved stock, stirring until smooth and slightly thick. Stir in remaining stock, salt, and 2 cups brown rice cream. Bring to a simmer; reduce heat to medium-low, and cook 10 minutes, stirring occasionally.

Serves 12 (serving size: ½ cup): Calories 98; Fat 2.6g (sat 0.4g, mono 1.1g, poly 0.6g); Protein 7g; Carb 10g; Fiber 1g; Sugars 2g (est. added sugars: 0g); Chol 49mg; Iron 1mg; Sodium 90mg; Calc 60mg

BROCCOLI-CHEESE SOUP

CLASSIC: Calories per serving: 429, Sat Fat: 17.9g, Sodium: 720mg, Sugars: 8g
MAKEOVER: Calories per serving: 210, Sat Fat: 5.5g, Sodium: 520mg, Sugars: 3g

HANDS-ON: 45 MIN. TOTAL: 45 MIN.

We like our version extra chunky, so we only puree about a third of the broccoli mixture in step 3. For a thinner, smoother consistency, add more soup to the blender.

4 cups unsalted chicken stock, divided
½ cup uncooked instant brown rice
1 cup 1% low-fat milk
2 teaspoons extra-virgin olive oil
1 cup chopped onion
3 garlic cloves, minced

1¼ pounds broccoli florets, coarsely chopped
¾ teaspoon kosher salt
½ teaspoon freshly ground black pepper
5 ounces extra-sharp cheddar cheese, shredded and divided (about 1¼ cups)

1. Combine 2 cups stock and rice in a small saucepan over medium-high heat; bring to a boil. Cover, reduce heat, and simmer 25 minutes. Remove from heat; let stand 5 minutes. Place rice mixture and milk in a blender. Remove center piece of blender lid (to allow steam to escape); secure blender lid on blender. Place a clean towel over opening in blender lid (to avoid splatters). Blend until smooth.

2. Heat a large saucepan over medium heat. Add oil to pan; swirl to coat. Add onion; sauté 4 minutes, stirring occasionally. Add garlic; cook 30 seconds. Add broccoli and salt; cook 5 minutes, stirring frequently. Add 2 cups stock; bring to a boil. Reduce heat, and simmer 5 minutes or just until broccoli is tender. Add rice mixture; simmer 2 minutes, stirring occasionally.

3. Place 2 cups soup in blender; process until smooth. Return pureed soup to pan. Add pepper and 4 ounces cheese; stir until cheese melts. Divide soup among 6 bowls; sprinkle with 1 ounce cheese.

Serves 6 (serving size: about 1 cup): Calories 210; Fat 10.3g (sat 5.5g, mono 3.5g, poly 0.6g); Protein 14g; Carb 17g; Fiber 4g; Sugars 3g (est. added sugars: 0g); Chol 27mg; Iron 1mg; Sodium 520mg; Calc 290mg

CRAZY TRICK

A nifty little trick with instant brown rice made our cheesy wishes come true. When overcooked in chicken stock, the rice becomes silky, savory, and soft—perfect for a puree when blended with low-fat milk. The result is a thick, nutty, whole-grain "cream" that eliminates the need for heavy cream, butter, or refined white flour, leaving room for plenty of cheese.

CREAMY, LIGHT
POTATO SOUP

CLASSIC: Calories per serving: 525, Sat Fat: 16g, Sodium: 1143mg, Sugars: 7g
MAKEOVER: Calories per serving: 223, Sat Fat: 2.7g, Sodium: 478mg, Sugars: 5g

HANDS-ON: 35 MIN. TOTAL: 1 HR. 10 MIN.

Combining baking potatoes with Yukon gold potatoes adds richness in flavor and thickness in texture.

1 1/2 tablespoons extra-virgin olive oil, divided
1 cup chopped onion
1 teaspoon chopped fresh thyme
5 garlic cloves, chopped
1 pound cubed peeled baking potato
1 pound cubed Yukon gold potato
5 cups unsalted chicken stock
1 teaspoon kosher salt, divided
1 bay leaf
1 pound cauliflower, cut into florets

3/4 teaspoon freshly ground black pepper, divided
Cooking spray
1 1/2 cups 2% reduced-fat milk
3/4 cup chopped green onions, divided
1/2 cup fat-free fromage blanc or sour cream
2 ounces sharp cheddar cheese, grated (about 1/2 cup)
4 center-cut bacon slices, cooked and crumbled

SNEAK ATTACK
Because cauliflower has two-thirds fewer calories per ounce than the starchy potato, swapping some in is both wise and tasty. Roasting the cauliflower adds a nutty flavor.

1. Preheat oven to 450°.

2. Heat a large Dutch oven over medium-high heat. Add 1 1/2 teaspoons oil to pan; swirl to coat. Add onion, thyme, and garlic; sauté 5 minutes or until tender, stirring occasionally. Add potatoes, stock, 1/2 teaspoon salt, and bay leaf; bring to a boil. Cover, reduce heat, and simmer 35 minutes or until potatoes are very tender, stirring occasionally. Remove from heat; discard bay leaf.

3. While potatoes simmer, combine 1 tablespoon oil, cauliflower, 1/4 teaspoon salt, and 1/4 teaspoon pepper on a jelly-roll pan coated with cooking spray; toss to coat. Roast at 450° for 30 minutes or until browned, turning once.

4. Place cauliflower mixture and milk in a blender. Remove center piece of blender lid (to allow steam to escape); secure blender lid on blender. Place a clean towel over opening (to avoid splatters). Blend until smooth. Pour cauliflower mixture into a large bowl. Add half of potato mixture to blender; pulse 5 to 6 times or until coarsely chopped. Pour into bowl with cauliflower mixture. Repeat with remaining potato mixture. Place cauliflower-potato mixture in Dutch oven over medium heat. Stir in 1/4 teaspoon salt, 1/2 teaspoon pepper, 1/2 cup green onions, and fromage blanc; stir until fromage blanc melts. Ladle soup into 8 bowls. Top with remaining green onions, cheddar cheese, and bacon.

Serves 8 (serving size: about 1 1/4 cups soup, 1 1/2 teaspoons green onions, 1 tablespoon cheese, and 1 1/2 teaspoons bacon): Calories 223; Fat 6.7g (sat 2.7g, mono 2.8g, poly 0.5g); Protein 13g; Carb 30g; Fiber 4g; Sugars 5g (est. added sugars: 0g); Chol 15mg; Iron 2mg; Sodium 478mg; Calc 185mg

Pan-Fried Egg Rolls,
page 110

TAKEOUT FAVORITES

REUBEN SANDWICHES

HANDS-ON: 18 MIN. TOTAL: 18 MIN.

With sauerkraut, corned beef, and rye bread, a delicatessen Reuben sandwich has a serious sodium issue. Add salad dressing and cheese, and the saturated fat and calories start to climb, too. Our solution: Use shaved Swiss cheese and lower-sodium corned beef.

DRESSING:

1/4 cup canola mayonnaise

1 tablespoon chili sauce

2 teaspoons finely minced dill pickle

1 teaspoon Worcestershire sauce

1/2 teaspoon grated onion

SANDWICHES:

8 (3/4-ounce) slices whole-grain rye bread

3 ounces Swiss cheese, shaved (about 3/4 cup)

4 ounces lower-sodium corned beef, thinly sliced

1 cup organic sauerkraut, drained well

1. Preheat broiler.

2. To prepare dressing, combine first 5 ingredients in a small bowl, stirring well.

3. To prepare sandwiches, place bread slices in a single layer on a heavy baking sheet. Broil 1 1/2 minutes or until toasted. Turn bread over, and broil 1 minute or until lightly toasted. Remove 4 slices from pan. Divide cheese among 4 slices, sprinkling it over lightly toasted sides. Broil 1 minute or until cheese melts. Spread about 1 1/2 tablespoons dressing over cheese-coated side of each bread slice; top each serving with 1 ounce corned beef, 1/4 cup sauerkraut, and 1 bread slice. Serve immediately.

Serves 4 (serving size: 1 sandwich): Calories 336; Fat 19.9g (sat 5.6g, mono 8.1g, poly 3.6g); Protein 15g; Carb 24g; Fiber 3g; Sugars 3g (est. added sugars: 0g); Chol 40mg; Iron 2mg; Sodium 790mg; Calc 212mg

DIJON CROQUE MONSIEUR

CLASSIC: Calories per serving: 510, Sat Fat: 13g, Sodium: 1200mg, Sugars: 7g
MAKEOVER: Calories per serving: 314, Sat Fat: 4.8g, Sodium: 706mg, Sugars: 5g

HANDS-ON: 20 MIN. TOTAL: 20 MIN.

Instead of your usual grilled ham and cheese, try this French-style sandwich that's enhanced by the zip of whole-grain mustard and lower-sodium ham.

1 tablespoon whole-grain Dijon
  mustard
1 tablespoon canola mayonnaise
8 (1-ounce) slices whole-grain bread
4 ounces lower-sodium ham, thinly
  sliced

2 ounces shredded Gruyère cheese
  (about $\frac{1}{2}$ cup)
$\frac{1}{4}$ teaspoon freshly ground black
  pepper
$\frac{1}{4}$ cup fat-free milk
2 large eggs, lightly beaten
Cooking spray

1. Combine mustard and mayonnaise in a small bowl. Spread $\frac{3}{4}$ teaspoon mustard mixture over each bread slice. Layer each of 4 bread slices with 1 ounce ham and 2 tablespoons cheese. Sprinkle with pepper; top with remaining bread slices.

2. Combine milk and eggs in a shallow dish. Dip both sides of each sandwich into egg mixture. Heat a large skillet over medium heat. Coat pan with cooking spray. Add sandwiches to pan; cook 3 minutes on each side or until lightly browned and cheese melts.

Serves 4 (serving size: 1 sandwich): Calories 314; Fat 13g (sat 4.8g, mono 4.5g, poly 2.4g); Protein 22g; Carb 26g; Fiber 4g; Sugars 5g (est. added sugars: 1g); Chol 125mg; Iron 2mg; Sodium 706mg; Calc 240mg

SOUTHWEST CRISPY
CHICKEN SLIDERS

CLASSIC: Calories per serving: 886, Sat Fat: 9.3g, Sodium: 1514mg, Sugars: 14g
MAKEOVER: Calories per serving: 402, Sat Fat: 5.7g, Sodium: 576mg, Sugars: 2g

HANDS-ON: 32 MIN. TOTAL: 32 MIN.

Chicken breasts and panko crisp up nicely without a deep fryer.

MUFFINS:

3 ounces all-purpose flour (about 1 cup)
$2/3$ cup yellow cornmeal
$3/4$ teaspoon baking soda
$1/4$ teaspoon baking powder
$1/4$ teaspoon kosher salt
$3/4$ cup nonfat buttermilk

2 tablespoons butter, melted
1 large egg, lightly beaten
1.5 ounces sharp cheddar cheese, shredded (about $1/3$ cup)
1 jalapeño pepper, seeded and minced
Cooking spray

CHICKEN:

$2/3$ cup panko (Japanese breadcrumbs)
$1/4$ cup fat-free milk
1 large egg, lightly beaten
3 (6-ounce) skinless, boneless chicken breast halves
2 tablespoons canola oil, divided
2 teaspoons fresh lime juice

1 ripe peeled avocado
2 applewood-smoked bacon slices, cooked and crumbled
12 ($1/2$-inch-thick) slices ripe tomato
$1/4$ teaspoon kosher salt
$1/4$ teaspoon freshly ground black pepper

1. Preheat oven to 350°. To prepare muffins, combine flour, cornmeal, baking soda, baking powder, and $1/4$ teaspoon salt in a medium bowl, stirring well with a whisk. Combine buttermilk, butter, and 1 egg, stirring well. Add buttermilk mixture to flour mixture, stirring just until combined. Stir in cheese and jalapeño. Spoon batter into 12 muffin cups coated with cooking spray. Bake at 350° for 17 minutes or until a wooden pick comes out clean. Remove from pan; cool on a wire rack. Cut muffins in half crosswise.

2. To prepare chicken, place panko in a shallow dish. Combine fat-free milk and 1 egg in a shallow dish. Split each chicken breast in half lengthwise to form 6 cutlets; cut each cutlet in half crosswise to form 12 pieces. Heat 1 tablespoon oil in a large skillet over medium-high heat. Dip chicken in egg mixture; dredge in panko. Coat panko lightly with cooking spray. Add 6 chicken pieces to pan; cook 3 minutes on each side or until golden and done. Repeat procedure with remaining oil and chicken.

3. Combine lime juice and avocado; mash to desired consistency. Stir in bacon. Divide mixture among muffins; top each slider with 1 chicken piece and 1 tomato slice. Sprinkle with $1/4$ teaspoon salt and black pepper.

Serves 6 (serving size: 2 sliders): Calories 402; Fat 18g (sat 5.7g, mono 8.3g, poly 2.6g); Protein 25g; Carb 34g; Fiber 3g; Sugars 2g (est. added sugars: 0g); Chol 106mg; Iron 2mg; Sodium 576mg; Calc 129mg

CHICKEN VERDE
ENCHILADAS

CLASSIC: Calories per serving: 943, Sat Fat: 27.1g, Sodium: 1155mg, Sugars: 6g
MAKEOVER: Calories per serving: 453, Sat Fat: 6.5g, Sodium: 627mg, Sugars: 5g

HANDS-ON: 25 MIN. TOTAL: 25 MIN.

Adding flavor to the sauce thickens it without all the extra cheese. Boost the flavor of the chicken with salsa verde, fresh cilantro, pickled jalapeños, and cumin. By mixing in fresh tomato, mashed avocado, and reduced-fat sour cream, we were able to cut back on the amount of cheese.

3/4 cup prechopped onion
3/4 cup unsalted chicken stock
1/2 cup salsa verde
1/3 cup finely chopped cilantro stems
2 tablespoons sliced pickled jalapeño pepper
5 teaspoons all-purpose flour
1/2 teaspoon ground cumin
2 garlic cloves, thinly sliced
8 ounces shredded skinless, boneless rotisserie chicken breast (about 2 cups)

3/4 cup chopped tomato
3 tablespoons reduced-fat sour cream
1 ripe peeled avocado, coarsely mashed
8 (6-inch) corn tortillas
4 ounces reduced-fat sharp cheddar cheese, shaved (about 1 cup)
2 tablespoons cilantro leaves

CRAZY TRICK
How do you shred chicken quickly? Pull apart the meat with two forks while it's warm.

1. Place oven rack in lower third of oven; preheat broiler.

2. Combine first 8 ingredients in a medium saucepan. Bring to a boil; reduce heat, and simmer 4 minutes. Stir in chicken; cook 1 minute or until heated. Remove from heat. Stir in tomato, sour cream, and avocado.

3. Stack tortillas; wrap stack in damp paper towels, and microwave at HIGH for 45 seconds. Spoon 1 cup chicken mixture into an 11 x 7–inch glass or ceramic baking dish. Spoon 1/3 cup chicken mixture in center of each tortilla; roll up. Arrange tortillas, seam sides down, in baking dish. Top with cheese. Broil 3 minutes or until cheese melts. Sprinkle with cilantro leaves.

Serves 4 (serving size: 2 enchiladas): Calories 453; Fat 18.6g (sat 6.5g, mono 6.1g, poly 2.1g); Protein 30g; Carb 45g; Fiber 8g; Sugars 5g (est. added sugars: 0g); Chol 75mg; Iron 1mg; Sodium 627mg; Calc 280mg

CHICKEN PARMESAN

CLASSIC: Calories per serving: 850, Sat Fat: 14.1g, Sodium: 3355mg, Sugars: 11g
MAKEOVER: Calories per serving: 503, Sat Fat: 5.4g, Sodium: 659mg, Sugars: 16g

HANDS-ON: 20 MIN. TOTAL: 1 HR. 30 MIN.

Reducing the cheeses and the oil used to brown the chicken and in the tomato sauce shaves off 300 calories and about 10g fat per serving.

TOMATO SAUCE:

1 ounce sun-dried tomatoes, packed without oil (about ¼ cup)
1 cup boiling water
1 teaspoon olive oil
2 cups chopped red bell pepper
1 cup chopped onion
2 pints cherry tomatoes

¼ cup chopped fresh parsley
2 tablespoons chopped fresh basil
1 tablespoon balsamic vinegar
¼ teaspoon salt
¼ teaspoon freshly ground black pepper
2 garlic cloves, minced

CHICKEN:

¼ cup panko (Japanese breadcrumbs)
1 ounce grated fresh Parmesan cheese (about ¼ cup)
¼ teaspoon black pepper
4 (4-ounce) skinless, boneless chicken breast halves

1 large egg white, lightly beaten
1 tablespoon olive oil
Cooking spray
4 ounces part-skim mozzarella cheese, shredded (about 1 cup)
2 cups hot cooked fettuccine

1. To prepare tomato sauce, combine sun-dried tomatoes and 1 cup boiling water in a bowl; cover and let stand 30 minutes or until soft. Drain and finely chop tomatoes. Heat 1 teaspoon olive oil in a large saucepan over medium-high heat. Add sun-dried tomatoes, bell pepper, and onion; sauté 7 minutes. Stir in canned tomatoes; bring to a boil. Cover, reduce heat, and simmer 10 minutes. Remove from heat; stir in parsley, basil, vinegar, salt, ¼ teaspoon black pepper, and garlic.

2. Preheat oven to 350°.

3. To prepare chicken, combine panko, Parmesan, and ¼ teaspoon black pepper in a shallow dish. Place each breast half between 2 sheets of heavy-duty plastic wrap; flatten to ¼-inch thickness using a meat mallet or small heavy skillet. Dip each breast half in egg white; dredge in panko mixture. Heat 1 tablespoon oil in a large nonstick skillet over medium-high heat. Add chicken; cook 5 minutes on each side or until golden. Arrange in a 13 x 9–inch glass or ceramic baking dish coated with cooking spray. Pour tomato sauce over chicken. Sprinkle with mozzarella. Bake at 350° for 15 minutes. Serve over fettuccine, if desired.

Serves 4 (serving size: 1 chicken breast half, 1 cup sauce, ¼ cup cheese, and ½ cup pasta): Calories 503; Fat 15.3g (sat 5.4g, mono 4.6g, poly 1.2g); Protein 43g; Carb 48g; Fiber 8g; Sugars 16g (est. added sugars: 0g); Chol 92mg; Iron 3mg; Sodium 659mg; Calc 337mg

NASHVILLE HOT CHICKEN

HANDS-ON: 20 MIN. TOTAL: 20 MIN.

This simple recipe is a revelation: It tastes as good as the old-school, super-savory chicken you'd get in a bucket, but without the saturated fat.

8 (3-ounce) skinless, boneless chicken thighs
1 large egg, lightly beaten
1.5 ounces all-purpose flour (about ⅓ cup)
1 teaspoon garlic powder
1 teaspoon onion powder
1 teaspoon freshly ground black pepper
½ teaspoon ground red pepper
½ teaspoon kosher salt, divided
1½ tablespoons canola oil
1½ tablespoons hot sauce

1. Combine chicken and egg in a shallow dish; toss to coat. Combine flour, garlic powder, onion powder, peppers, and ¼ teaspoon salt in a shallow dish; dredge chicken in flour mixture. Heat a large nonstick skillet over medium-high heat. Add oil to pan; swirl to coat. Add chicken; cook 5 minutes on each side or until browned and done. Drain chicken on a plate lined with paper towels. Sprinkle with ¼ teaspoon salt; top with hot sauce.

Serves 4 (serving size: 2 thighs): Calories 312; Fat 13.6g (sat 2.6g, mono 6.2g, poly 3.4g); Protein 36g; Carb 10g; Fiber 1g; Sugars 0g (est. added sugars: 0g); Chol 208mg; Iron 2mg; Sodium 444mg; Calc 30mg

PAN-FRIED CHICKEN FINGERS
WITH SPICY DIPPING SAUCE

CLASSIC: Calories per serving: 686, Sat Fat: 3.8g, Sodium: 1202mg, Sugars: 27g
MAKEOVER: Calories per serving: 414, Sat Fat: 1.5g, Sodium: 495mg, Sugars: 4g

HANDS-ON: 25 MIN. TOTAL: 25 MIN.

Instead of batter-coated, deep-fried chicken drowning in fatty sauce, our chicken gets a crunchy exterior from cereal and is served with just enough spicy mayo for dipping.

DIPPING SAUCE:
1/4 cup canola mayonnaise
2 teaspoons Sriracha

1 teaspoon fresh lime juice
1/2 teaspoon lower-sodium soy sauce

CHICKEN:
1/4 cup all-purpose flour
1 1/2 teaspoons freshly ground black pepper
1 1/2 teaspoons paprika
1 tablespoon water
2 large eggs, lightly beaten

3 cups whole-grain flake cereal (such as Kashi 7-Grain Flakes), finely crushed (about 2 1/2 cups crushed)
1 pound chicken breast tenders
1/4 teaspoon salt
1 1/2 tablespoons canola oil

1. To prepare dipping sauce, combine canola mayonnaise, Sriracha, lime juice, and soy sauce in a small bowl, stirring with a whisk. Cover and chill.

2. To prepare chicken, combine flour, black pepper, and paprika. Place flour mixture in a shallow dish. Combine 1 tablespoon water and eggs; place in another shallow dish. Place crushed cereal in a third shallow dish.

3. Sprinkle chicken with salt. Working with 1 piece at a time, dredge chicken in flour mixture. Dip in egg mixture; dredge in cereal. Repeat procedure with remaining chicken pieces.

4. Heat a large skillet over medium-high heat. Add oil to pan; swirl to coat. Add chicken pieces to pan; cook 2 minutes on each side or until done. Serve immediately with sauce.

Serves 4 (serving size: about 3 ounces chicken fingers and 1 tablespoon sauce): Calories 414; Fat 14g (sat 1.5g, mono 7g, poly 4.2g); Protein 34g; Carb 38g; Fiber 5g; Sugars 4g (est. added sugars: 1g); Chol 156mg; Iron 3mg; Sodium 495mg; Calc 38mg

SWEET AND SOUR CHICKEN

CLASSIC: Calories per serving: 1003, Sat Fat: 2.1g, Sodium: 1341mg, Sugars: 90g
MAKEOVER: Calories per serving: 474, Sat Fat: 1.8g, Sodium: 523mg, Sugars: 9g

HANDS-ON: 23 MIN. TOTAL: 23 MIN.

Powdered peanut butter (which you'll find on the nut butters aisle) adds richness and depth for very few calories here; if you'd rather not use it, substitute more flour.

¼ cup mirin (sweet rice wine) or ¼ cup dry sherry mixed with 2 teaspoons sugar
1 large egg, lightly beaten
1 pound skinless, boneless chicken breast tenders, cut into 2-inch pieces
¼ cup powdered peanut butter
3 tablespoons quick-mixing flour (such as Wondra)
3 tablespoons cornstarch
1 tablespoon sugar
3 tablespoons canola oil
¾ cup sliced green onions
1 red bell pepper, chopped
5 tablespoons water
3 tablespoons ketchup
2 tablespoons Sriracha
1 tablespoon plum sauce
1 teaspoon Worcestershire sauce
1 (8.8-ounce) package precooked white rice
¼ cup cilantro leaves
2 tablespoons toasted sesame seeds

1. Combine mirin and egg in a medium bowl. Add chicken; toss to coat. Let stand 5 minutes; drain well.

2. Combine powdered peanut butter and next 3 ingredients (through sugar) in a bowl. Add chicken; toss well to coat. Heat a large skillet over medium-high heat. Add oil to pan; swirl to coat. Add chicken; cook 3 minutes on each side or until done. Remove chicken from pan; keep warm.

3. Heat pan over high heat. Add onions and bell pepper; stir-fry 1 minute. Combine 5 tablespoons water and next 4 ingredients (through Worcestershire) in a bowl. Add chicken and ketchup mixture to pan; cook 1 minute, tossing to coat.

4. Divide rice among 4 plates; top with chicken mixture. Sprinkle with cilantro leaves and sesame seeds.

Serves 4 (serving size: ½ cup rice, about 1 cup chicken mixture, 1 tablespoon cilantro, and 1½ teaspoons sesame seeds): Calories 474; Fat 16.6g (sat 1.8g, mono 8.4g, poly 4.4g); Protein 31g; Carb 50g; Fiber 3g; Sugars 9g (est. added sugars: 5g); Chol 77mg; Iron 2mg; Sodium 523mg; Calc 34mg

OVEN-FRIED SHRIMP AND OKRA
LOUISIANA PO'BOY

CLASSIC: Calories per serving: 830, Sat Fat: 5.2g, Sodium: 2031mg, Sugars: 6g
MAKEOVER: Calories per serving: 396, Sat Fat: 1.4g, Sodium: 754mg, Sugars: 5g

HANDS-ON: 33 MIN. TOTAL: 33 MIN.

Yellow cornmeal provides a crunchy exterior to this Southern classic.

2 tablespoons finely chopped green onions
1 tablespoon drained chopped capers
2 tablespoons canola mayonnaise
1½ teaspoons fresh lemon juice
1 teaspoon Creole mustard
⅛ teaspoon ground red pepper
1 small garlic clove, grated
½ cup nonfat buttermilk, divided
15 small okra pods, trimmed and halved lengthwise (about 6 ounces)
½ teaspoon kosher salt, divided

10 ounces medium shrimp, peeled and deveined
1 tablespoon all-purpose flour
⅔ cup yellow cornmeal
1½ teaspoons salt-free Cajun/Creole seasoning
3 tablespoons canola oil
4 top-split hot dog buns, toasted
½ cup thinly sliced iceberg lettuce
1 medium tomato, cut in half lengthwise and thinly sliced

1. Place a jelly-roll pan in oven. Preheat oven to 450° (leave pan in oven as it preheats).

2. Combine first 7 ingredients in a small bowl, stirring well. Chill.

3. Combine 2 tablespoons buttermilk and okra; toss to coat. Sprinkle with ¼ teaspoon salt; toss to coat.

4. Place shrimp in a medium bowl. Sprinkle with flour; toss well to coat. Drizzle with 6 tablespoons buttermilk, and sprinkle with ¼ teaspoon salt; toss to coat. Drain okra and shrimp through a sieve; discard liquid.

5. Combine cornmeal and Cajun/Creole seasoning in a large zip-top plastic bag. Add okra and shrimp; seal bag, and shake well to coat.

6. Carefully remove pan from oven; drizzle with oil, tilting pan to spread oil. Remove shrimp and okra from cornmeal, shaking off excess; arrange in a single layer on pan. Bake at 450° for 5 minutes; carefully stir and turn over. Bake 4 minutes or until done.

7. Spread about 1 tablespoon sauce on 1 side of each hot dog bun; divide lettuce and tomato among buns. Divide shrimp and okra mixture among buns.

Serves 4 (serving size: 1 sandwich): Calories 396; Fat 15.7g (sat 1.4g, mono 8.5g, poly 4.8g); Protein 18g; Carb 46g; Fiber 4g; Sugars 5g (est. added sugars: 0g); Chol 90mg; Iron 3mg; Sodium 754mg; Calc 194mg

CASHEW CHICKEN

CLASSIC: Calories per serving: 677, Sat Fat: 8g, Sodium: 1539mg, Sugars: 10g
MAKEOVER: Calories per serving: 340, Sat Fat: 3.4g, Sodium: 435mg, Sugars: 9g

HANDS-ON: 60 MIN. TOTAL: 4 HR. 20 MIN.

A take on the Indian dish murgh makhani, this recipe features a thick sauce flavored with Indian spices and spice blends such as garam masala, coriander, ginger, and ground red pepper. Serve over brown basmati rice or with naan flatbread.

²/₃ cup cashews, toasted
²/₃ cup plain fat-free Greek yogurt
¼ cup tomato paste
2 tablespoons white vinegar
1¼ teaspoons garam masala
1 teaspoon ground coriander
1 teaspoon grated peeled fresh ginger
¼ teaspoon ground red pepper
2 garlic cloves, chopped
4 skinless, boneless chicken thighs, cut into bite-sized pieces (about 14 ounces)
2 (8-ounce) skinless, boneless chicken breasts, cut into bite-sized pieces

Cooking spray
2 ¾ cups finely chopped onion (2 large)
2 green cardamom pods, lightly crushed
1 (2-inch) cinnamon stick
2 cups fat-free, lower-sodium chicken broth
1 cup organic tomato puree
1 teaspoon Hungarian sweet paprika
¼ teaspoon salt
3 tablespoons half-and-half
Chopped fresh cilantro (optional)

1. Combine first 9 ingredients in a blender or food processor; process until smooth. Combine nut mixture and chicken in a large bowl; cover and refrigerate 3 hours or overnight.

2. Heat a large Dutch oven over medium-low heat. Coat pan with cooking spray. Add onion, cardamom, and cinnamon stick to pan; cover and cook 10 minutes or until onion is golden, stirring often.

3. Add chicken mixture to pan; cook 10 minutes, stirring frequently. Stir in broth, tomato puree, paprika, and salt, scraping pan to loosen browned bits. Cook 1 hour or until thick. Stir in half-and-half; cook 1 minute, stirring occasionally. Remove from heat. Discard cinnamon stick. Garnish with fresh cilantro, if desired.

Serves 6 (serving size: about 1 cup): Calories 340; Fat 13.6g (sat 3.4g, mono 5.8g, poly 2.6g); Protein 37g; Carb 19g; Fiber 4g; Sugars 9g (est. added sugars: 1g); Chol 91mg; Iron 3mg; Sodium 435mg; Calc 83mg

PAN-FRIED SHRIMP

CLASSIC: Calories per serving: 686, Sat Fat: 5.6g, Sodium: 1805mg, Sugars: 4g
MAKEOVER: Calories per serving: 435, Sat Fat: 2g, Sodium: 610mg, Sugars: 1g

HANDS-ON: 25 MIN. TOTAL: 25 MIN.

Shrimp are coated in a thin tempura-style batter and dredged in a breadcrumb coating to pump up the crunch.

1 cup panko (Japanese breadcrumbs)
1 tablespoon finely chopped fresh
  flat-leaf parsley leaves
$1/4$ teaspoon kosher salt
3.5 ounces rice flour (about $3/4$ cup)
2.25 ounces all-purpose flour (about
  $1/2$ cup)

$1/2$ teaspoon baking soda
12 ounces chilled pilsner beer
6 tablespoons canola oil
$1 1/2$ pounds large shrimp, peeled and
  deveined

1. Combine first 3 ingredients in a shallow baking dish; toss to combine. Weigh or lightly spoon rice flour and all-purpose flour into dry measuring cups; level with a knife. Combine flours and baking soda in a large bowl, stirring with a whisk. Gradually add beer, stirring with a whisk until smooth.

2. Heat a large skillet over medium-high heat. Add 3 tablespoons oil to pan; swirl to coat. Dip half of shrimp in batter; shake off excess. Dredge shrimp lightly in panko mixture. Place shrimp in a single layer in pan; cook $2 1/2$ minutes on each side or until golden brown. Remove shrimp from pan; drain on paper towels. Repeat procedure with remaining oil, shrimp, batter, and panko mixture.

Serves 4: Calories 435; Fat 23.1g (sat 2g, mono 13.6g, poly 6.5g); Protein 30g; Carb 23g; Fiber 1g; Sugars 1g (est. added sugars: 0g); Chol 252mg; Iron 4mg; Sodium 610mg; Calc 52mg

CHICKEN NUGGETS
WITH CRISPY POTATO CHIPS

CLASSIC: Calories per serving: 440, Sat Fat: 14g, Sodium: 890mg, Sugars: 1g
MAKEOVER: Calories per serving: 241, Sat Fat: 0.7, Sodium: 386mg, Sugars: 5g

HANDS-ON: 34 MIN. TOTAL: 1 HR. 24 MIN.

The kids will love this recipe, and thanks to our oven-frying method you won't feel guilty serving it to them.

CHICKEN NUGGETS:

4 (6-ounce) skinless, boneless chicken breast halves, cut into 1-inch pieces
1/3 cup low-fat buttermilk
1/3 cup dill pickle juice

1 1/2 cups panko (Japanese breadcrumbs)
1/4 teaspoon kosher salt
2 tablespoons water
1 large egg, lightly beaten

POTATO CHIPS:

1 tablespoon extra-virgin olive oil
1/4 teaspoon salt
1 medium purple sweet potato, cut crosswise into 1/8-inch-thick slices

1 medium baking potato, cut crosswise into 1/8-inch-thick slices

HONEY MUSTARD:

1/4 cup canola mayonnaise
1/4 cup plain fat-free Greek yogurt
1 tablespoon honey

1 tablespoon prepared mustard
1 teaspoon Dijon mustard

CRAZY TRICK
Crisp the potato chips by using your microwave.

1. To prepare chicken nuggets, combine first 3 ingredients in a large zip-top plastic bag. Refrigerate 1 hour, turning bag occasionally. Place panko in a large skillet; cook over medium heat 3 minutes or until toasted, stirring frequently. Preheat oven to 400°. Remove chicken from marinade; discard marinade. Sprinkle chicken with 1/4 teaspoon kosher salt. Place panko in a zip-top plastic bag. Combine 2 tablespoons water and egg in a shallow dish; dip half of chicken in egg mixture. Add chicken to bag; seal bag, and shake to coat. Remove chicken from bag; arrange in a single layer on a baking sheet. Repeat procedure with remaining egg mixture, panko, and chicken. Bake chicken at 400° for 12 minutes or until done.

2. To prepare chips, combine oil, 1/4 teaspoon salt, and potatoes in a large bowl; toss to coat. Cut a piece of parchment paper to fit a microwave-safe plate. Place paper on plate; arrange purple potato slices in a single layer on paper. Microwave at HIGH for 4 minutes or until crisp. Repeat with baking potato slices.

3. To prepare honey mustard, combine mayonnaise and next 4 ingredients (through mustard).

Serves 8 (serving size: about 6 nuggets, about 13 chips, and 1 tablespoon honey mustard): Calories 241; Fat 6.1g (sat 0.7g, mono 3g, poly 1.3g); Protein 24g; Carb 21g; Fiber 2g; Sugars 5g (est. added sugars: 2g); Chol 76mg; Iron 1mg; Sodium 386mg; Calc 31mg

LOBSTER ROLLS
WITH SHAVED FENNEL AND CITRUS

CLASSIC: Calories per serving: 450, Sat Fat: 2g, Sodium: 720mg, Sugars: 3g
MAKEOVER: Calories per serving: 238, Sat Fat: 0.8g, Sodium: 699mg, Sugars: 3g

HANDS-ON: 18 MIN. TOTAL: 22 MIN.

Bright citrus and licorice notes from the fennel complement the sweet, tarragon-flecked lobster meat. We used New England-style hot dog buns, which are top-split and have an open crumb on the sides.

3 cups coarsely chopped cooked lobster meat (about 3 [1¼-pound] lobsters)
3 tablespoons canola mayonnaise
2 teaspoons chopped fresh tarragon
½ teaspoon kosher salt, divided
2 cups thinly sliced fennel bulb (about 1 medium)
½ teaspoon grated orange rind
1 tablespoon fresh orange juice
1 tablespoon fresh lemon juice
1 tablespoon rice wine vinegar
2 teaspoons extra-virgin olive oil
¼ teaspoon freshly ground black pepper
Cooking spray
6 (1½-ounce) hot dog buns

1. Combine lobster, mayonnaise, 2 teaspoons tarragon, and ¼ teaspoon salt; cover and refrigerate.

2. Combine fennel, ¼ teaspoon salt, orange rind, and next 5 ingredients (through pepper).

3. Heat a large skillet over medium heat. Coat pan with cooking spray. Add buns to pan; cook 2 minutes on each side or until lightly browned. Place ⅓ cup fennel salad in each bun. Top each serving with ½ cup lobster salad.

Serves 6 (serving size: 1 lobster roll): Calories 238; Fat 6.2g (sat 0.8g, mono 3g, poly 1.9g); Protein 19g; Carb 25g; Fiber 2g; Sugars 3g (est. added sugars: 0g); Chol 52mg; Iron 2mg; Sodium 699mg; Calc 120mg

CRAB CAKES

CLASSIC: Calories per serving: 722, Sat Fat: 12.6g, Sodium: 815mg, Sugars: 0g
MAKEOVER: Calories per serving: 292, Sat Fat: 1.6g, Sodium: 571mg, Sugars: 1g

HANDS-ON: 22 MIN. TOTAL: 32 MIN.

We load up on meaty crab to keep fillers to a minimum with this fresh take on crab cakes.

CRAB CAKES:

2 tablespoons finely chopped fresh chives
1 tablespoon chopped fresh flat-leaf parsley
1½ tablespoons canola mayonnaise
½ teaspoon grated lemon rind
1 tablespoon fresh lemon juice
¼ teaspoon freshly ground black pepper
⅛ teaspoon ground red pepper
1 large egg
1 pound lump crabmeat, drained and shell pieces removed
⅓ cup panko (Japanese breadcrumbs)
1 tablespoon olive oil

REMOULADE:

¼ cup canola mayonnaise
1 tablespoon chopped shallots
1½ tablespoons drained chopped capers
2 teaspoons Creole mustard
1 teaspoon fresh lemon juice
¼ teaspoon ground red pepper
⅛ teaspoon kosher salt

> **SECRET TO SUCCESS**
> A streamlined remoulade (there are no gherkins, anchovies, or green olives) is best made one day ahead.

1. To prepare crab cakes, combine first 8 ingredients. Add crab and panko, tossing gently to combine. Cover and refrigerate 30 minutes.

2. Fill a ⅓-cup dry measuring cup with crab mixture. Invert onto work surface; gently pat into a ¾-inch-thick patty. Repeat procedure with remaining crab mixture, forming 8 cakes.

3. Heat 1½ teaspoons oil in a large skillet over medium-high heat. Add 4 crab cakes to pan; cook 4 minutes or until bottoms are golden. Carefully turn cakes; cook 4 minutes or until bottoms are golden and crab cakes are thoroughly heated. Remove cakes from pan; keep warm. Wipe pan dry with paper towels. Heat 1½ teaspoons oil in pan. Repeat procedure with 4 crab cakes.

4. To prepare remoulade, combine ¼ cup mayonnaise and next 6 ingredients (through salt) in a small bowl; stir with a whisk. Serve with crab cakes.

Serves 4 (serving size: 2 crab cakes): Calories 292; Fat 22g (sat 1.6g, mono 7.8g, poly 10.2g); Protein 19g; Carb 5g; Fiber 1g; Sugars 1g (est. added sugars: 0g); Chol 161mg; Iron 1mg; Sodium 571mg; Calc 53mg

NEW ENGLAND
CLAM CHOWDER

CLASSIC: Calories per serving: 730, Sat Fat: 17g, Sodium: 530mg, Sugars: 1g
MAKEOVER: Calories per serving: 336, Sat Fat: 5.1g, Sodium: 629mg, Sugars: 3g

HANDS-ON: 30 MIN. TOTAL: 30 MIN.

We didn't skimp on the clams, so every bite is full of flavor.

2 cups refrigerated diced potatoes
  with onion
2¼ cups water, divided
50 littleneck clams, scrubbed
2 thyme sprigs
1 bay leaf
1 applewood-smoked bacon slice,
  finely chopped
½ cup finely chopped celery

3 tablespoons all-purpose flour
1 (8-ounce) bottle clam juice
1 teaspoon chopped fresh thyme
1 cup half-and-half
¼ teaspoon kosher salt
1 tablespoon chopped fresh chives
¼ teaspoon freshly ground black
  pepper
½ cup oyster crackers

> **SECRET TO SUCCESS**
> Bring the half-and-half as close to room temperature as possible before adding to the chowder to help keep it from breaking.

1. Combine potato mixture and 1¼ cups water in a microwave-safe dish. Microwave at HIGH 8 minutes or until potatoes are tender. Set aside.

2. While potatoes cook, combine 1 cup water, clams, thyme sprigs, and bay leaf in a Dutch oven; bring to a boil over medium-high heat. Cover, reduce heat, and simmer 6 minutes or until shells open. Remove clams from pan using a slotted spoon; discard any unopened shells. Strain cooking liquid through a fine sieve over a bowl; discard solids. Cool clams slightly. Remove meat from shells; chop. Discard shells.

3. Heat a medium saucepan over medium heat. Add bacon to pan; cook 4 minutes or until browned and crisp, stirring occasionally. Remove bacon from pan using a slotted spoon. Increase heat to medium-high. Add celery to drippings in pan; sauté 3 minutes or until tender, stirring occasionally.

4. Combine flour and bottled clam juice in a small bowl, stirring with a whisk until smooth. Add clam juice mixture and reserved cooking liquid to pan. Bring mixture to a boil; cook 1 minute, stirring constantly with a whisk. Add reserved potato mixture and chopped thyme to pan; reduce heat, and simmer 5 minutes, stirring occasionally. Remove from heat. Stir in chopped clams, half-and-half, and salt. Divide chowder among 4 bowls; sprinkle with bacon, chives, and pepper. Serve with oyster crackers.

Serves 4 (serving size: about 1½ cups chowder and 2 tablespoons crackers): Calories 336; Fat 10.4g (sat 5.1g, mono 2.8g, poly 1.2g); Protein 29g; Carb 30g; Fiber 2g; Sugars 3g (est. added sugars: 0g); Chol 88mg; Iron 27mg; Sodium 629mg; Calc 164mg

FISH SANDWICHES
WITH MINT-CAPER TARTAR SAUCE

CLASSIC: Calories per serving: 770, Sat Fat: 9g, Sodium: 1920mg, Sugars: 16g
MAKEOVER: Calories per serving: 413, Sat Fat: 1.8g, Sodium: 678mg, Sugars: 8g

HANDS-ON: 21 MIN. TOTAL: 28 MIN.

Breading the fish fillets in panko and baking them instead of frying keeps crunch and quickly cuts fat and calories.

2 tablespoons canola mayonnaise
2 tablespoons low-fat sour cream
1 tablespoon capers, chopped
1 tablespoon finely chopped fresh mint
2 teaspoons finely chopped fresh flat-leaf parsley
1/2 teaspoon red wine vinegar
3/8 teaspoon freshly ground black pepper, divided
1 medium Vidalia onion, thinly sliced
3 cups ice water
1/4 teaspoon salt
4 (6-ounce) square-cut mahimahi fillets
1.1 ounces all-purpose flour (about 1/4 cup)
2 large egg whites, lightly beaten
1 cup panko (Japanese breadcrumbs)
1 1/2 tablespoons olive oil
4 (1 1/2-ounce) Kaiser rolls, toasted
8 thin tomato slices

1. Preheat oven to 350°.

2. Combine first 6 ingredients in a small bowl; stir in 1/8 teaspoon pepper. Set tartar sauce aside.

3. Combine onion and 3 cups ice water; soak 20 minutes. Drain on paper towels.

4. Sprinkle 1/4 teaspoon pepper and salt over fish. Place flour in a shallow dish; place egg whites in another dish. Place panko in another. Dredge both sides of fish in flour; dip in egg white, and dredge in panko. Heat a large nonstick skillet over medium-high heat. Add oil to pan; swirl to coat. Add fish to pan; cook 2 minutes on each side or until browned. Place fish on a baking sheet. Bake at 350° for 6 minutes or until fish flakes easily when tested with a fork.

5. Spread about 4 teaspoons tartar sauce on bottom half of each bun. Top each with 1 fish fillet. Arrange onion over fish; top with 2 tomato slices and top half of bun.

Serves 4 (serving size: 1 sandwich): Calories 413; Fat 11.4g (sat 1.8g, mono 5.9g, poly 2.4g); Protein 39g; Carb 36g; Fiber 2g; Sugars 8g (est. added sugars: 0g); Chol 127mg; Iron 4mg; Sodium 678mg; Calc 99mg

FRIED CATFISH
WITH HUSH PUPPIES AND TARTAR SAUCE

CLASSIC: Calories per serving: 714, Sat Fat: 7.1g, Sodium: 1179mg, Sugars: 8g
MAKEOVER: Calories per serving: 507, Sat Fat: 4.1g, Sodium: 709mg, Sugars: 2g

HANDS-ON: 20 MIN. TOTAL: 45 MIN.

Adding cornmeal to the flour reduces oil absorption, resulting in a lighter, crisper deep fry.

TARTAR SAUCE:

¼ cup organic canola mayonnaise
1 tablespoon dill pickle relish
1 tablespoon chopped flat-leaf parsley
1 teaspoon prepared horseradish
¾ teaspoon fresh lemon juice
⅛ teaspoon salt

CATFISH:

8 cups peanut oil
6 (6-ounce) catfish fillets
⅛ teaspoon salt
9 ounces all-purpose flour, divided
1¼ cups cornmeal
1 teaspoon freshly ground black pepper
2 cups buttermilk
2 large eggs

HUSH PUPPIES:

3.4 ounces all-purpose flour (¾ cup)
⅓ cup cornmeal
⅓ cup buttermilk
3 tablespoons grated fresh onion
1 teaspoon baking powder
¼ teaspoon ground red pepper
⅛ teaspoon salt
1 large egg, lightly beaten

1. To prepare tartar sauce, combine first 6 ingredients. Cover and chill.

2. To prepare catfish, clip a candy/fry thermometer to a Dutch oven; add oil to pan. Heat oil to 385°. Sprinkle fillets with ⅛ teaspoon salt. Place 4.5 ounces flour in a shallow dish. Combine 4.5 ounces flour, cornmeal, and black pepper in another shallow dish. Combine 2 cups buttermilk and 2 eggs in a third dish. Dredge fillets in flour; dip in buttermilk mixture. Dredge in cornmeal mixture; shake off excess breading. Place 2 fillets in hot oil; cook 5 minutes or until done, turning occasionally. Keep oil temperature at 375°. Remove fillets from pan using a slotted spoon; drain on paper towels. Return oil temperature to 385°. Repeat procedure with remaining fillets.

3. To prepare hush puppies, weigh or lightly spoon 3.4 ounces (about ¾ cup) flour into a dry measuring cup; level with a knife. Combine 3.4 ounces flour and next 7 ingredients (through 1 beaten egg). Drop batter 1 tablespoonful at a time into pan; fry at 375° for 5 minutes or until browned, turning frequently. Remove hush puppies from pan using a slotted spoon; drain on paper towels.

Serves 6 (serving size: 1 fillet, 2 hush puppies, and 4 teaspoons tartar sauce): Calories 507; Fat 23.8g (sat 4.1g, mono 8.4g, poly 9.4g); Protein 29g; Carb 43g; Fiber 3g; Sugars 2g (est. added sugars: 0g); Chol 153mg; Iron 4mg; Sodium 709mg; Calc 171mg

FISH TACOS
WITH TOMATILLO SAUCE

CLASSIC: Calories per serving: 530, Sat Fat: 1.5g, Sodium: 550mg, Sugars: 0g
MAKEOVER: Calories per serving: 291, Sat Fat: 1.3g, Sodium: 375mg, Sugars: 4g

HANDS-ON: 26 MIN. TOTAL: 26 MIN.

Tilapia is a sustainable freshwater fish that's widely available and offers mild flavor. You can use a more assertively flavored fish, such as mackerel, if you prefer.

3 garlic cloves
2 medium tomatillos, husked and rinsed
½ medium jalapeño pepper
½ cup cilantro stems
3 tablespoons canola mayonnaise
½ teaspoon sugar
³/₈ teaspoon salt, divided
2 cups very thinly sliced red cabbage

1 tablespoon fresh lime juice
1 tablespoon extra-virgin olive oil
4 (6-ounce) tilapia fillets
¼ teaspoon freshly ground black pepper
Cooking spray
8 (6-inch) corn tortillas
¼ cup fresh cilantro leaves

SECRET TO SUCCESS
A flavor-packed tomatillo crema replaces heavy sour cream.

1. Preheat broiler.

2. Arrange garlic, tomatillos, and jalapeño in a single layer on a foil-lined jelly-roll pan. Broil 3 minutes on each side or until blackened. Combine tomatillo mixture, cilantro stems, mayonnaise, sugar, and ⅛ teaspoon salt in a mini food processor or blender; blend until smooth.

3. Combine cabbage, juice, and oil in a medium bowl; toss to coat.

4. Heat a large skillet over medium-high heat. Sprinkle fish with ¼ teaspoon salt and black pepper. Coat pan with cooking spray. Add fish to pan; cook 2 minutes. Turn fish over; cook 1 minute.

5. Working with 1 tortilla at a time, heat tortillas over medium-high heat directly on the eye of a burner for about 15 seconds on each side or until lightly charred. Arrange half of a tilapia fillet in center of each tortilla; top each with ¼ cup cabbage mixture, about 1½ tablespoons tomatillo mixture, and about 1½ teaspoons cilantro leaves.

Serves 4 (serving size: 2 tacos): Calories 291; Fat 10.3g (sat 1.3g, mono 5g, poly 2.6g); Protein 29g; Carb 23g; Fiber 3g; Sugars 4g (est. added sugars: 1g); Chol 64mg; Iron 1mg; Sodium 375mg; Calc 55mg

FANCY FISH STICKS

CLASSIC: Calories per serving: 750, Sat Fat: 9g, Sodium: 1212mg, Sugars: 10g
MAKEOVER: Calories per serving: 361, Sat Fat: 1.9g, Sodium: 611mg, Sugars: 1g

HANDS-ON: 25 MIN. TOTAL: 40 MIN.

Capture the crunch appeal of super-convenient frozen fish sticks, but get them out of the nutrition doghouse.

¼ cup reduced-fat mayonnaise
¼ cup fat-free sour cream
1 tablespoon Creole mustard
2 teaspoons fresh lime juice
½ teaspoon Cajun seasoning
Cooking spray
1 tablespoon canola oil
½ cup all-purpose flour
¼ teaspoon freshly ground black pepper
½ cup lager-style beer
1½ tablespoons creamy mustard blend (such as Dijonnaise)

1 tablespoon fresh lime juice
2 large egg whites
1 large egg
⅔ cup panko (Japanese breadcrumbs)
⅓ cup unsalted pumpkinseed kernels, toasted
1 teaspoon ground cumin
½ teaspoon chipotle chile powder
1 pound halibut or other lean white fish fillets, cut into 4 x 1–inch pieces (about 12 pieces)
¼ teaspoon kosher salt
4 lime wedges

CRAZY TRICK
Grinding panko and pumpkinseeds creates an extra-crunchy coating that doesn't need to be deep-fried, saving tons of calories and fat.

1. Combine first 5 ingredients in a small bowl, stirring with a whisk. Cover and chill.

2. Preheat oven to 425°.

3. Coat a baking sheet with cooking spray, and spread with oil; heat in oven 12 minutes.

4. Combine flour and black pepper in a shallow dish. Combine beer, mustard blend, lime juice, egg whites, and egg in another shallow dish; stir with a whisk until foamy. Place panko, pumpkinseeds, cumin, and chipotle powder in a food processor; pulse 20 times or until coarse crumbs form. Place panko mixture in a shallow dish.

5. Sprinkle fish with salt. Working with 1 piece at a time, dredge fish in flour mixture. Dip in egg mixture, and dredge in panko mixture until completely covered.

6. Remove preheated baking sheet from oven; place fish on pan, and return to oven. Bake at 425° for 15 minutes or until fish flakes easily with a fork, turning once. Serve immediately with sauce and lime wedges.

Serves 4 (serving size: about 3 fish sticks, 2 tablespoons sauce, and 1 lime wedge): Calories 361; Fat 12.7g (sat 1.9g, mono 4.8g, poly 4.1g); Protein 31g; Carb 28g; Fiber 2g; Sugars 1g (est. added sugars: 0g); Chol 104mg; Iron 2mg; Sodium 611mg; Calc 51mg

CHEDDAR CHEESEBURGERS
WITH CARAMELIZED SHALLOTS

CLASSIC: Calories per serving: 740, Sat Fat: 16g, Sodium: 930mg, Sugars: 6g
MAKEOVER: Calories per serving: 370, Sat Fat: 6.1g, Sodium: 654mg, Sugars: 1g

HANDS-ON: 38 MIN. TOTAL: 38 MIN.

Tender, golden shallots lend sweetness to the classic cheeseburger. Lean ground beef and light mayonnaise quickly cut the fat and calories.

1 tablespoon olive oil, divided
2 cups thinly sliced shallots
½ teaspoon kosher salt, divided
1 tablespoon white wine vinegar
1 pound ground sirloin
2 garlic cloves, minced

2 ounces sharp cheddar cheese,
  shredded (about ½ cup)
1 cup baby arugula
4 (1½-ounce) hamburger buns,
  toasted
3 tablespoons light mayonnaise

1. Heat a nonstick skillet over medium-low heat. Add 2 teaspoons oil; swirl to coat. Add shallots and ¼ teaspoon salt; cook 15 minutes or until golden brown, stirring occasionally. Stir in vinegar; cook 1 minute. Remove from heat; keep warm.

2. Gently combine beef and garlic. Divide meat mixture into 4 equal portions, gently shaping each into a ½-inch-thick patty. Press a nickel-sized indentation in center of each patty. Sprinkle with ¼ teaspoon salt.

3. Heat a large cast-iron skillet over medium-high heat. Add 1 teaspoon oil; swirl to coat. Add patties; cook 3 minutes on each side or until desired degree of doneness. Top each with 2 tablespoons cheese; cover and cook 1 minute or until cheese melts.

4. Place ¼ cup arugula on bottom half of each bun; top with 1 patty and one-fourth of shallots. Spread about 2 teaspoons mayonnaise on top half of each bun; place on top of burgers.

Serves 4 (serving size: 1 burger): Calories 370; Fat 17.7g (sat 6.1g, mono 5.4g, poly 2.9g); Protein 31g; Carb 32g; Fiber 8g; Sugars 1g (est. added sugars: 0g); Chol 77mg; Iron 2mg; Sodium 654mg; Calc 113mg

QUICK BBQ SANDWICHES
WITH SLAW

HANDS-ON: 30 MIN. TOTAL: 30 MIN.

Pile the slaw on the sandwich for crunch. Pork tenderloin is leaner than Boston butt, with all the flavor.

½ cup unsalted ketchup
3 tablespoons cider vinegar
1 tablespoon lower-sodium soy sauce
2 teaspoons Dijon mustard
¾ teaspoon freshly ground black
   pepper
½ teaspoon onion powder
¼ teaspoon garlic powder
⅛ teaspoon ground ginger

1 (1-pound) pork tenderloin, trimmed
   and halved lengthwise
Cooking spray
4 (1½-ounce) hamburger buns
1½ cups shredded cabbage
½ cup shredded carrot
2 teaspoons sugar
½ teaspoon kosher salt
3 green onions, thinly sliced

1. Preheat grill to high heat.

2. Combine first 8 ingredients in a bowl, stirring well with a whisk. Reserve ¼ cup ketchup mixture. Add pork to remaining ketchup mixture; turn to coat. Place pork on grill rack coated with cooking spray; cover and grill 5 minutes. Turn pork over; grill 6 minutes or until a thermometer registers 150°. Remove pork from grill; let stand 5 minutes. Cut pork diagonally across the grain into thin slices.

3. Arrange buns, cut sides down, in a single layer on grill rack coated with cooking spray; grill 2 minutes or until golden brown and toasted.

4. While pork grills, combine shredded cabbage and next 4 ingredients (through onions) in a medium bowl; toss. Let stand 10 minutes; drain. Place 1 bottom bun half on each of 4 plates; divide sliced pork among buns. Top each serving with 1 tablespoon reserved ketchup mixture and about ½ cup slaw. Place top halves of buns on sandwiches.

Serves 4 (serving size: 1 sandwich): Calories 296; Fat 4.3g (sat 1.2g, mono 1.3g, poly 1.1g); Protein 29g; Carb 35g; Fiber 2g; Sugars 11g (est. added sugars: 2g); Chol 74mg; Iron 3mg; Sodium 695mg; Calc 105mg

PORK AND PINTO BEAN
NACHOS

CLASSIC: Calories per serving: 1258, Sat Fat: 29g, Sodium: 2199mg, Sugars: 12g
MAKEOVER: Calories per serving: 517, Sat Fat: 6.8g, Sodium: 991mg, Sugars: 3g

HANDS-ON: 20 MIN. TOTAL: 57 MIN.

Build smoky flavor with a trifecta of chili powder, chipotle chiles, and bacon.

MEAT:
1 (1-pound) pork tenderloin, trimmed
2 tablespoons olive oil, divided
$\frac{1}{2}$ teaspoon salt, divided
$\frac{1}{4}$ teaspoon black pepper

Cooking spray
2 tablespoons fresh lime juice
1 teaspoon minced garlic

BEANS:
1 can chipotle chiles in adobo sauce
2 tablespoons water
2 teaspoons fresh lime juice
1 teaspoon chili powder
$\frac{1}{4}$ teaspoon salt

2 (15-ounce) cans no salt added pinto
   beans, rinsed
4 applewood-smoked bacon slices,
   cooked and crumbled

TOPPING:
1$\frac{1}{2}$ cups chopped plum tomato
1 cup diced avocado
$\frac{1}{2}$ cup chopped jicama
$\frac{1}{3}$ cup chopped onion
2 tablespoons fresh lime juice
1 tablespoon olive oil
$\frac{1}{4}$ teaspoon salt

Remaining ingredients:
6 ounces sturdy tortilla chips (8 cups)
5 ounces shredded reduced-fat Colby
   and Monterey Jack cheese blend
$\frac{1}{4}$ cup chopped fresh cilantro
1 jalapeño pepper, thinly sliced

1. Preheat oven to 500°. For meat, rub pork with 1 tablespoon oil, $\frac{1}{4}$ teaspoon salt, and black pepper. Place pork in a shallow roasting pan coated with cooking spray. Bake at 500° for 23 minutes or until a thermometer registers 160°. Remove from pan; cool 10 minutes. Shred pork with 2 forks to measure 2 cups; place in a small bowl. Stir in 1 tablespoon oil, $\frac{1}{4}$ teaspoon salt, 2 tablespoons juice, and garlic.

2. For beans, remove 2 chiles and 1 teaspoon adobo sauce from can. Drop chiles through food chute with food processor on; pulse 3 times or until coarsely chopped. Add adobo sauce, 2 tablespoons water, and next 4 ingredients; process 5 seconds or until smooth. Stir in bacon. Preheat broiler. For topping, combine plum tomato and next 6 ingredients; toss. Arrange chips in a single layer on a rimmed baking sheet. Top with beans, meat, and cheese. Broil 4 minutes. Top with cilantro and jalapeño. Serve immediately.

Serves 6 (serving size: 1 ounce chips, $\frac{1}{2}$ cup beans, $\frac{1}{3}$ cup pork, and $\frac{1}{2}$ cup topping): Calories 517; Fat 26.9g (sat 6.8g, mono 12.4g, poly 3.3g); Protein 31g; Carb 38g; Fiber 9g; Sugars 3g (est. added sugars: 0g); Chol 66mg; Iron 3mg; Sodium 991mg; Calc 248mg

PHILLY CHEESESTEAKS

CLASSIC: Calories per serving: 1151, Sat Fat: 27.3g, Sodium: 1480mg, Sugars: 16g
MAKEOVER: Calories per serving: 397, Sat Fat: 4.9g, Sodium: 637mg, Sugars: 5g

HANDS-ON: 35 MIN. TOTAL: 45 MIN.

Meaty, gooey, and delightfully messy, our lightened version of a Philly cheesesteak is the type of sandwich you'll crave all year.

1 (12-ounce) flank steak, trimmed
¼ teaspoon kosher salt
¼ teaspoon freshly ground black pepper
2 (5-inch) portobello mushroom caps
2 teaspoons extra-virgin olive oil, divided
1 cup thinly sliced onion
1½ cups thinly sliced green bell pepper
2 teaspoons minced garlic
½ teaspoon Worcestershire sauce
½ teaspoon lower-sodium soy sauce
2 teaspoons all-purpose flour
½ cup 1% low-fat milk
1 ounce provolone cheese, torn into small pieces
2 tablespoons grated fresh Parmigiano-Reggiano cheese
¼ teaspoon dry mustard
4 (3-ounce) hoagie rolls, toasted

SECRET TO SUCCESS
Forget the artificial cheese sauce: We create a lean white sauce with real cheese–just enough Parm-Regg and provolone to deliver full satisfaction with less sodium and saturated fat.

1. Place beef in freezer 15 minutes. Cut beef across the grain into thin slices. Sprinkle beef with salt and pepper. Remove brown gills from the undersides of mushroom caps using a spoon; discard gills. Remove stems; discard. Thinly slice mushroom caps; cut slices in half crosswise.

2. Heat a large nonstick skillet over medium-high heat. Add 1 teaspoon oil to pan; swirl to coat. Add beef to pan; sauté 2 minutes or until beef loses its pink color, stirring constantly. Remove beef from pan. Add 1 teaspoon oil to pan. Add onion; sauté 3 minutes. Add mushrooms, bell pepper, and garlic; sauté 6 minutes. Return beef to pan; sauté 1 minute or until thoroughly heated and vegetables are tender. Remove from heat. Stir in Worcestershire sauce and soy sauce; keep warm.

3. Place flour in a small saucepan; gradually add milk, stirring with a whisk until blended. Bring to a simmer over medium heat; cook 1 minute or until slightly thick. Remove from heat. Add cheeses and mustard, stirring until smooth. Keep warm (mixture will thicken as it cools).

4. Hollow out top and bottom halves of rolls, leaving a ½-inch-thick shell; reserve torn bread for another use. Divide beef mixture among bottom halves of rolls. Drizzle sauce over beef mixture; replace top halves of rolls.

Serves 4 (serving size: 1 sandwich): Calories 397; Fat 12.4g (sat 4.9g, mono 4.7g, poly 1.6g); Protein 31g; Carb 44g; Fiber 4g; Sugars 5g (est. added sugars: 0g); Chol 37mg; Iron 5mg; Sodium 637mg; Calc 213mg

SPINACH AND ARTICHOKE DIP

CLASSIC: Calories per serving: 227, Sat Fat: 3.9g, Sodium: 569mg, Sugars: 1g
MAKEOVER: Calories per serving: 75, Sat Fat: 2.4g, Sodium: 216mg, Sugars: 2g

HANDS-ON: 13 MIN. TOTAL: 46 MIN.

A go-to appetizer for parties, this recipe has all the creamy-inside, crispy-on-top texture and cheesy taste that make dips like this appealing, but with fewer calories and less fat.

½ cup fat-free sour cream
¼ teaspoon freshly ground black pepper
3 garlic cloves, minced
1 (14-ounce) can artichoke hearts, drained and chopped
1 (10-ounce) package frozen chopped spinach, thawed, drained, and squeezed dry

1 (8-ounce) block ⅓-less-fat cream cheese, softened
1 (8-ounce) block fat-free cream cheese, softened
6 ounces part-skim mozzarella cheese, shredded and divided (about 1½ cups)
1 ounce fresh Parmesan cheese, grated and divided (about ¼ cup)

1. Preheat oven to 350°.

2. Combine first 7 ingredients in a large bowl, stirring until well blended. Add 4 ounces (1 cup) mozzarella and 2 tablespoons Parmesan; stir well. Spoon mixture into a broiler-safe 1½-quart glass or ceramic baking dish. Sprinkle with ½ cup mozzarella and 2 tablespoons Parmesan. Bake at 350° for 30 minutes or until bubbly.

3. Preheat broiler (leave dish in oven). Broil 3 minutes or until cheese is lightly browned.

Serves 22 (serving size: about ¼ cup): Calories 75; Fat 4.2g (sat 2.4g, mono 1.1g, poly 0.2g); Protein 6g; Carb 4g; Fiber 0g; Sugars 2g (est. added sugars: 1g); Chol 15mg; Iron 1mg; Sodium 216mg; Calc 150mg

CRISPY PORK
SPRING ROLLS

HANDS-ON: 45 MIN. TOTAL: 45 MIN.

Serve with spicy Sriracha sauce or sweet red chili sauce.

5 cups peanut oil

1 ounce bean thread noodles

2 medium shallots, peeled and coarsely chopped

2 garlic cloves, chopped

1 stalk peeled fresh lemongrass, coarsely chopped

1 (3.5-ounce) package shiitake mushrooms, stems removed

2 tablespoons dark sesame oil

1 tablespoon fish sauce

1 teaspoon sambal oelek (ground fresh chile paste)

½ teaspoon kosher salt

1 (1-inch) piece fresh ginger, peeled and grated

2 ½ cups grated carrot (about 3 medium)

1 pound lean ground pork

26 frozen square spring roll pastry wrappers, thawed

1. Place peanut oil in a large Dutch oven or deep fryer. Clip a candy/fry thermometer to the side of pot; heat oil to 385°.

2. Place noodles in a bowl, and pour enough boiling water over to cover by 1 inch. Let stand 20 minutes; drain well. Cut noodles with scissors into 1-inch pieces. Set aside.

3. Combine shallots, garlic, and lemongrass in a food processor; process until finely chopped. Add mushrooms; pulse until finely chopped. Add sesame oil and next 4 ingredients (through ginger); process until well combined. Combine noodles, mushroom mixture, carrot, and pork in a large bowl, stirring until well blended. Working with 1 spring roll pastry wrapper at a time (cover remaining wrappers with a damp towel to keep from drying), place wrapper on a smooth work surface in a diamond pattern, with one corner pointing up and another pointing down. Place about 2 tablespoons pork mixture in the middle of pastry. Brush top point of pastry with water. Fold sides of pastry over filling; roll up, jelly-roll fashion, starting from bottom. Gently press seam to seal. Repeat procedure with remaining pastry wrappers and filling to form 26 rolls.

4. Working in batches, place 5 spring rolls in 385° oil; fry 7 minutes or until golden and crisp, turning as necessary. Make sure oil temperature does not drop below 375°. Remove rolls with a slotted spoon; drain on a rack over paper towels. Return oil to 385°. Repeat procedure with remaining spring rolls and oil, making sure oil temperature does not drop below 375°. Serve immediately.

Serves 26 (serving size: 1 roll): Calories 108; Fat 5.5g (sat 1.3g, mono 1.7g, poly 1.4g); Protein 5g; Carb 11g; Fiber 0g; Sugars 0g (est. added sugars: 0g); Chol 13mg; Iron 0mg; Sodium 98mg; Calc 10mg

PAN-FRIED EGG ROLLS

CLASSIC: Calories per serving: 219, Sat Fat: 2g, Sodium: 623mg, Sugars: 5g
MAKEOVER: Calories per serving: 103, Sat Fat: 0.7g, Sodium: 207mg, Sugars: 1g

HANDS-ON: 25 MIN. TOTAL: 25 MIN.

Unlike typical egg rolls with their mishmash of filling, these keep the ingredients more distinct, similar to spring or summer rolls. You'll find sweet chili sauce, made from sun-ripened chile peppers and garlic, in specialty grocery stores or the Asian-foods section of most supermarkets.

12 ounces fresh bean sprouts, chopped
1/4 cup sweet chili sauce, divided
12 (8-inch) egg roll wrappers
12 cooked jumbo shrimp, peeled, deveined, and split in half lengthwise (about 13 ounces)
6 tablespoons chopped fresh cilantro

1/4 cup peanut oil
1 tablespoon rice vinegar
2 teaspoons lower-sodium soy sauce
1/4 teaspoon grated peeled fresh ginger
1/8 teaspoon freshly ground black pepper

1. Combine bean sprouts and 3 tablespoons chili sauce, tossing well to coat.

2. Working with 1 egg roll wrapper at a time (cover remaining wrappers to prevent drying), place wrapper on a work surface with 1 corner pointing toward you (wrapper should look like a diamond). Spoon about 2 heaping tablespoons bean sprout mixture into center of wrapper; top with 2 shrimp halves and 1 1/2 teaspoons cilantro. Fold lower corner of wrapper over filling; fold in side corners. Moisten top corner of wrapper with water; roll up, jelly-roll fashion. Place egg roll, seam side down, on a baking sheet. Repeat procedure with remaining wrappers, bean sprout mixture, shrimp, and cilantro.

3. Heat 2 tablespoons oil in a large nonstick skillet over medium-high heat. Add 6 egg rolls, seam sides down; cook 7 minutes or until golden, turning occasionally. Place on a wire rack. Repeat procedure with 2 tablespoons oil and 6 egg rolls.

4. Combine 1 tablespoon chili sauce, vinegar, and next 3 ingredients (through pepper). Serve sauce with egg rolls.

Serves 12 (serving size: 1 egg roll and 1 1/2 teaspoons sauce): Calories 103; Fat 4g (sat 0.7g, mono 1.7g, poly 1.3g); Protein 8g; Carb 9g; Fiber 1g; Sugars 1g (est. added sugars: 0g); Chol 48mg; Iron 1mg; Sodium 207mg; Calc 23mg

MONGOLIAN BEEF

CLASSIC: Calories per serving: 615, Sat Fat: 6.6g, Sodium: 2388mg, Sugars: 42g
MAKEOVER: Calories per serving: 237, Sat Fat: 3.5g, Sodium: 517mg, Sugars: 4g

HANDS-ON: 20 MIN. TOTAL: 20 MIN.

Cornstarch and lower-sodium soy sauce thicken the sauce, while cutting sodium by almost 2000 mg! Serve this slightly spicy dish over wide rice noodles to catch all the garlic- and ginger-laced sauce.

2 tablespoons lower-sodium soy sauce
1 teaspoon sugar
1 teaspoon cornstarch
2 teaspoons dry sherry
2 teaspoons hoisin sauce
1 teaspoon rice vinegar
1 teaspoon sambal oelek (ground fresh chile paste)
¼ teaspoon salt

2 teaspoons peanut oil
1 tablespoon minced peeled fresh ginger
1 tablespoon minced fresh garlic
1 pound sirloin steak, thinly sliced across the grain
16 medium-sized green onions, cut into 2-inch pieces

1. Combine first 8 ingredients, stirring until smooth.

2. Heat peanut oil in a large nonstick skillet over medium-high heat. Add minced ginger, minced garlic, and beef; sauté 2 minutes or until beef is browned. Add green onion pieces; sauté 30 seconds. Add soy sauce mixture; cook 1 minute or until thick, stirring constantly.

Serves 4 (serving size: 1 cup): Calories 237; Fat 10.5g (sat 3.5g, mono 4.3g, poly 1.1g); Protein 26g; Carb 9g; Fiber 2g; Sugars 4g (est. added sugars: 1g); Chol 60mg; Iron 3mg; Sodium 517mg; Calc 67mg

CLASSIC PAD THAI

CLASSIC: Calories per serving: 695, Sat Fat: 4.2g, Sodium: 2541mg, Sugars: 9g
MAKEOVER: Calories per serving: 432, Sat Fat: 3.6g, Sodium: 640mg, Sugars: 10g

HANDS-ON: 35 MIN. TOTAL: 35 MIN.

This flavor-packed dish cuts sodium and fat with lower-sodium soy sauce and boneless, skinless chicken thighs.

6 ounces uncooked flat rice noodles (pad Thai noodles)
1/4 cup rice vinegar
4 teaspoons sugar, divided
2 tablespoons very thinly sliced banana pepper
3 ounces extra-firm tofu, cut into thin strips
1 tablespoon fresh lime juice
1 tablespoon water
1 tablespoon lower-sodium soy sauce
1 tablespoon fish sauce
1/8 teaspoon salt

2 large eggs, lightly beaten
3 tablespoons peanut oil, divided
3 garlic cloves, minced
1 (2-ounce) skinless, boneless chicken thigh, cut into thin strips
4 cups fresh bean sprouts, divided
3 green onions, trimmed, crushed with the flat side of a knife, and cut into 1 1/2-inch pieces
1 tablespoon small dried shrimp
1/4 cup unsalted, dry-roasted peanuts, chopped
1/4 cup cilantro leaves

1. Prepare noodles according to package directions; drain.

2. Combine vinegar and 1 tablespoon sugar, stirring until sugar dissolves. Add banana pepper; set aside.

3. Place tofu on several layers of heavy-duty paper towels; cover with additional paper towels. Let stand 20 minutes, pressing down occasionally.

4. Combine 1 teaspoon sugar, lime juice, and next 3 ingredients (through fish sauce). Combine salt and eggs, stirring well.

5. Heat a large wok over high heat. Add 1 1/2 tablespoons oil; swirl to coat. Add garlic; stir-fry 15 seconds. Add chicken; stir-fry 2 minutes or until browned. Add tofu; cook 1 minute on each side or until browned. Pour in egg mixture; cook 45 seconds or until egg begins to set around chicken and tofu. Remove egg mixture from pan, and cut into large pieces.

6. Add 1 1/2 tablespoons oil to wok; swirl to coat. Add 2 cups bean sprouts, green onions, and dried shrimp; stir-fry 1 minute. Add noodles and soy sauce mixture; stir-fry 2 minutes, tossing until noodles are lightly browned. Add reserved egg mixture; toss to combine. Arrange 2 cups bean sprouts on a platter; top with noodle mixture. Sprinkle with peanuts and cilantro. Serve with vinegar mixture.

Serves 4 (serving size: 1 1/2 cups noodle mixture and 1 1/2 tablespoons vinegar sauce): Calories 432; Fat 19.1g (sat 3.6g, mono 8.3g, poly 6.1g); Protein 14g; Carb 53g; Fiber 4g; Sugars 10g (est. added sugars: 4g); Chol 110mg; Iron 3mg; Sodium 640mg; Calc 80mg

SPICY CHICKPEA SAMOSAS
WITH RAITA

CLASSIC: Calories per serving: 472, Sat Fat: 12g, Sodium: 1035mg, Sugars: 1g
MAKEOVER: Calories per serving: 156, Sat Fat: 1.7g, Sodium: 369mg, Sugars: 1g

HANDS-ON: 35 MIN. TOTAL: 40 MIN.

Samosas, traditional Indian pastries filled with vegetables, meat, or both, are typically made with homemade dough, then fried. Our samosas remain light and crisp because we enclose the filling in phyllo dough and then bake them.

SAMOSAS:
1½ tablespoons canola oil
½ cup finely chopped carrot
½ cup thinly sliced green onions
2 tablespoons minced peeled fresh ginger
1 tablespoon minced garlic
1 tablespoon tomato paste
1½ teaspoons cumin seeds
1 teaspoon brown mustard seeds
¾ teaspoon kosher salt
¼ teaspoon ground red pepper
¼ teaspoon freshly ground black pepper

1 cup frozen green peas, thawed
1 tablespoon water
1 (15-ounce) can chickpeas (garbanzo beans), rinsed and drained
½ cup chopped fresh cilantro
1 tablespoon fresh lemon juice
24 (14 x 9–inch) sheets frozen phyllo dough, thawed
Cooking spray
2 tablespoons butter, melted

RAITA:
¾ cup plain fat-free Greek yogurt
¾ cup chopped seeded peeled cucumber
2 tablespoons thinly sliced green onions
2 tablespoons chopped fresh cilantro

2 teaspoons fresh lemon juice
¼ teaspoon kosher salt
¼ teaspoon ground cumin
⅛ teaspoon freshly ground black pepper

SNEAK ATTACK
Most samosas are made with potatoes, but instead we use protein-packed chickpeas in the filling.

1. To prepare samosas, heat oil in a skillet over medium heat. Add carrot; cook 3 minutes, stirring frequently. Add ½ cup onions, ginger, and garlic; cook 1 minute, stirring constantly. Add tomato paste and next 5 ingredients (through black pepper); cook 1 minute, stirring constantly. Add peas, 1 tablespoon water, and chickpeas; cook 1 minute. Remove from heat; stir in cilantro and juice. Cool.

2. Preheat oven to 400°.

3. Place 1 phyllo sheet on a large work surface (cover remaining dough to keep from drying); coat with cooking spray. Place another phyllo sheet on coated phyllo; coat with cooking spray. Fold layered sheets in half lengthwise. Spoon 2 tablespoons filling onto bottom end of rectangle, leaving a 1-inch border. Fold bottom corner over mixture, forming a triangle; keep folding back and forth into a triangle to end of phyllo strip. Tuck edges under; place, seam side down, on a baking sheet coated with cooking spray. Brush with melted butter. Repeat procedure with remaining 22 phyllo sheets, cooking spray, filling, and butter. Bake at 400° for 10 minutes or until crisp and golden.

4. To prepare raita, combine Greek yogurt and next 7 ingredients (through ⅛ teaspoon black pepper). Serve with samosas.

Serves 12 (serving size: 1 samosa and 1½ tablespoons raita): Calories 156; Fat 5.8g (sat 1.7g, mono 2.5g, poly 1.1g); Protein 5g; Carb 21g; Fiber 3g; Sugars 1g (est. added sugars: 0g); Chol 5mg; Iron 2mg; Sodium 369mg; Calc 41mg

CHIMICHANGAS

HANDS-ON: 60 MIN. TOTAL: 60 MIN.

The calorie count spikes when this overstuffed cheesy burrito hits the deep fryer. Ours is pan-seared and topped with fresh tomatoes and avocado cream.

2 cups unsalted chicken stock
2 (6-ounce) skinless, boneless chicken
  breast halves
³/₄ cup salsa verde
2 ounces ¹/₃-less-fat cream cheese
  (about ¹/₄ cup)
¹/₂ teaspoon ground cumin
6 tablespoons chopped fresh cilantro,
  divided
1 tablespoon olive oil
1 cup chopped onion
8 ounces presliced cremini mushrooms

4 garlic cloves, minced
2 cups chopped Lacinato kale
¹/₄ teaspoon black pepper
8 (8-inch) flour tortillas
3 ounces preshredded reduced-fat
  4-cheese Mexican blend cheese
  (about ³/₄ cup)
Cooking spray
³/₄ cup ripe peeled avocado, chopped
3 tablespoons 1% low-fat milk
2 tablespoons fresh lime juice, divided
2 cups chopped grape tomatoes

1. Combine stock and chicken in a saucepan over medium heat; bring to a simmer. Cook 8 minutes or until done. Remove chicken with a slotted spoon; let stand 10 minutes. Shred chicken; set aside. Drain cooking liquid through a sieve over a bowl, reserving liquid; discard solids. Set aside 2 tablespoons liquid.

2. Return remaining cooking liquid to pan. Add salsa verde; bring to a boil. Cook until reduced to 1 cup (about 11 minutes). Reduce heat to low. Add cream cheese and cumin; stir with a whisk until smooth. Remove from heat; stir in chicken and ¹/₄ cup cilantro.

3. Heat a large skillet over medium heat. Add oil to pan; swirl to coat. Add onion, mushrooms, and garlic; sauté 8 minutes or until tender. Add kale, black pepper, and reserved 2 tablespoons cooking liquid. Cook 2 minutes or until kale wilts, stirring occasionally. Add kale mixture to chicken mixture. Divide chicken mixture among tortillas. Top each with about 1¹/₂ tablespoons cheese. Fold in edges of tortilla; roll up.

4. Heat a large nonstick skillet over medium-high heat. Coat all sides of each chimichanga with cooking spray. Cook 6 to 8 minutes, turning to brown on all sides.

5. Combine avocado, milk, and 1 tablespoon lime juice in a mini food processor; process until smooth.

6. Combine tomatoes, 2 tablespoons cilantro, and 1 tablespoon lime juice in a bowl; toss. To serve, arrange 1 chimichanga on each of 8 plates. Top each with 1¹/₂ tablespoons avocado cream and about ¹/₄ cup tomato salad.

Serves 8: Calories 296; Fat 10.3g (sat 3g, mono 3.9g, poly 0.9g); Protein 20g; Carb 32g; Fiber 6g; Sugars 4g (est. added sugars: 0g); Chol 39mg; Iron 2mg; Sodium 625mg; Calc 245mg

POUTINE

CLASSIC: Calories per serving: 904, Sat Fat: 21.1g, Sodium: 1231mg, Sugars: 7g
MAKEOVER: Calories per serving: 211, Sat Fat: 3.7g, Sodium: 288mg, Sugars: 1g

HANDS-ON: 22 MIN. TOTAL: 55 MIN.

The fresher the cheese curds, the better they'll be. If you can't find local, fresh curds, substitute Kasseri cheese cubes—a salty Greek cheese with a similar texture. For an even more authentic poutine, substitute duck fat for canola oil (it will add 0.6g sat fat per serving).

1½ tablespoons canola oil
2 pounds baking potatoes, cut into (4 x ¼–inch) strips (about 3 medium potatoes)
¼ teaspoon kosher salt
Cooking spray
6 ounces 50%-less-fat pork sausage
2 tablespoons all-purpose flour
1 tablespoon butter, melted
2 cups unsalted beef stock
2 ounces fresh cheddar cheese curds
Chopped fresh parsley (optional)

1. Place a small roasting pan in oven. Preheat oven to 450°.

2. Carefully remove hot pan from oven. Add canola oil to pan; swirl to coat. Add potatoes. Sprinkle potatoes with salt; toss. Bake at 450° for 45 minutes or until golden, turning once after 30 minutes.

3. Heat a large skillet over medium-high heat. Coat pan with cooking spray. Add sausage; cook 5 minutes or until browned, stirring to crumble. Combine flour and butter, stirring until smooth. Add butter mixture to sausage; cook 1 minute, stirring constantly. Slowly add stock to pan, stirring constantly; bring to a boil. Reduce heat and simmer 3 minutes or until slightly thick, stirring occasionally. Spoon sausage mixture over fries; top with cheese curds. Sprinkle with parsley, if desired.

Serves 8 (serving size: about ½ cup fries, 3 tablespoons gravy, and 1 tablespoon cheese curds): Calories 211; Fat 10.3g (sat 3.7g, mono 2g, poly 0.8g); Protein 8g; Carb 22g; Fiber 2g; Sugars 1g (est. added sugars: 0g); Chol 26mg; Iron 1mg; Sodium 288mg; Calc 67mg

HAM AND VEGGIE
FRIED RICE

CLASSIC: Calories per serving: 503, Sat Fat: 5.6g, Sodium: 644mg, Sugars: 5g
MAKEOVER: Calories per serving: 364, Sat Fat: 1.5g, Sodium: 575mg, Sugars: 5g

HANDS-ON: 10 MIN. TOTAL: 10 MIN.

Tossing in frozen green peas at the end of cooking keeps them bright and lively. Blending sesame oil with vegetable oil cuts saturated fat and boosts flavor.

2 (8.5-ounce) pouches precooked brown rice
2 teaspoons lower-sodium soy sauce
2 teaspoons chili garlic sauce
1 teaspoon toasted sesame oil
2 tablespoons canola oil, divided
1 cup cubed reduced-sodium ham
1 large egg, lightly beaten

1 cup sliced cremini mushrooms
1/2 cup chopped red bell pepper
1/2 cup bean sprouts
1/3 cup sliced green onions
2 large garlic cloves, peeled and sliced
1 (1/2-inch) piece fresh ginger, peeled and thinly sliced
1/2 cup frozen green peas

1. Prepare rice according to package directions; set aside.

2. Combine soy sauce, chili garlic sauce, and sesame oil in a bowl. Heat a wok over high heat. Add 1 tablespoon canola oil. Add ham; cook 2 minutes, stirring frequently. Transfer ham to soy sauce mixture.

3. Add egg to pan; cook 30 seconds. Remove from pan; chop.

4. Add 1 tablespoon canola oil to pan. Add mushrooms and next 5 ingredients (through ginger); stir-fry 2 minutes. Add rice; stir-fry 2 minutes. Add ham mixture and peas; cook 2 minutes. Stir in egg.

Serves 4 (serving size: 1 1/2 cups): Calories 364; Fat 13.9g (sat 1.5g, mono 5.5g, poly 2.8g); Protein 17g; Carb 43g; Fiber 3g; Sugars 5g (est. added sugars: 0g); Chol 69mg; Iron 2mg; Sodium 575mg; Calc 19mg

PORK AND SHIITAKE
POT STICKERS

CLASSIC: Calories per serving: 334, Sat Fat: 3.1g, Sodium: 1611mg, Sugars: 4g
MAKEOVER: Calories per serving: 221, Sat Fat: 2.3g, Sodium: 609mg, Sugars: 4g

HANDS-ON: 20 MIN. TOTAL: 32 MIN.

It's never a bad idea to have a good supply of dumplings on hand for busy nights. Ours taste way better and are much lower in sodium than what you'll find at the store. Plus, they go from freezer to plate in only 10 minutes—what could be easier? Just cook what you need tonight, and stash the rest in the freezer.

2 tablespoons dark sesame oil

$3/4$ cup thinly sliced green onions, divided

4 ounces thinly sliced shiitake mushroom caps

1 tablespoon minced garlic

1 tablespoon grated peeled fresh ginger

14 ounces lean ground pork

5 tablespoons lower-sodium soy sauce, divided

1 tablespoon hoisin sauce

$1/2$ teaspoon freshly ground black pepper

40 gyoza skins or round wonton wrappers

Cornstarch

$1/4$ cup hot water

2 tablespoons brown sugar

2 tablespoons rice wine vinegar

$1 1/2$ tablespoons sambal oelek (ground fresh chile paste)

Cooking spray

1. Heat a large skillet over high heat. Add oil to pan; swirl to coat. Add $1/2$ cup onions, mushrooms, garlic, and ginger; stir-fry 3 minutes. Remove from pan; cool slightly. Combine mushroom mixture, pork, 1 tablespoon soy sauce, hoisin sauce, and pepper in a medium bowl.

2. Arrange 8 gyoza skins on a clean work surface; cover remaining skins with a damp towel to keep them from drying. Spoon about $1 1/2$ teaspoons pork mixture in center of each skin. Moisten edges of skin with water. Fold in half; press edges together with fingertips to seal. Place on a baking sheet sprinkled with cornstarch; cover to prevent drying. Repeat procedure with remaining gyoza skins and pork mixture.

3. Combine $1/4$ cup hot water and brown sugar in a small bowl, stirring until sugar dissolves. Add $1/4$ cup green onions, $1/4$ cup soy sauce, vinegar, and sambal oelek, stirring with a whisk until well combined.

4. Heat a large heavy skillet over high heat. Generously coat pan with cooking spray. Add 10 pot stickers to pan; cook 30 seconds or until browned on one side. Turn pot stickers over; carefully add $1/3$ cup water to pan. Cover tightly; steam 4 minutes. Repeat procedure in batches with remaining pot stickers and more water, or follow freezing instructions. After cooking, serve pot stickers immediately with dipping sauce.

TO FREEZE:

PREPARE recipe through step 3. Freeze dumplings flat on a baking sheet sprinkled with cornstarch 10 minutes or until firm. Place in a large zip-top plastic freezer bag with 1 teaspoon cornstarch; toss. Freeze sauce in a small zip-top plastic freezer bag. Freeze up to 2 months.

TO THAW:

THAW sauce in the microwave at HIGH in 30-second increments. No need to thaw pot stickers.

TO REHEAT:

FOLLOW recipe instructions for cooking, placing frozen dumplings in pan and increasing steaming time by 2 minutes.

Serves 8 (serving size: 5 pot stickers and 1 tablespoon sauce): Calories 221; Fat 8.1g (sat 2.3g, mono 3.7g, poly 1.8g); Protein 11g; Carb 23g; Fiber 1g; Sugars 4g (est. added sugars: 3g); Chol 37mg; Iron 0mg; Sodium 609mg; Calc 13mg

CAESAR SALAD

CLASSIC: Calories per serving: 434, Sat Fat: 4.7g, Sodium: 551mg, Sugars: 4g
MAKEOVER: Calories per serving: 70, Sat Fat: 1.3g, Sodium: 249mg, Sugars: 2g

HANDS-ON: 10 MIN. TOTAL: 25 MIN.

In this remake, traditional egg-based mayonnaise is swapped out for whipped cottage cheese, which takes on the same creaminess and mouthfeel. Anchovies, lemon, and Parmigiano-Reggiano remain for classic flavor.

4 ounces finely grated fresh
  Parmigiano-Reggiano cheese (about
  1 cup)
1 garlic clove
½ cup 1% low-fat cottage cheese
2 tablespoons finely grated fresh
  Parmigiano-Reggiano cheese
1 tablespoon extra-virgin olive oil

2 teaspoons anchovy paste
½ teaspoon Dijon mustard
2 tablespoons fresh lemon juice
1½ teaspoons Worcestershire sauce
¼ teaspoon freshly ground white
  pepper
4 cups torn romaine lettuce

1. Preheat oven to 350°.

2. Line a baking sheet with parchment paper. Arrange 16 tablespoonfuls cheese 2 inches apart on prepared baking sheet to form mounds. Bake at 350° for 6 minutes or until lightly browned. Remove from oven; cool on pan at least 20 minutes. Carefully remove cheese crisps from pan; set aside.

3. Place garlic in a food processor; pulse until minced. Add cottage cheese and next 7 ingredients (through pepper); process until smooth.

4. Place lettuce in a large bowl; add 5 tablespoons dressing, and toss well to coat. Reserve remaining dressing for another use. Divide salad among 4 plates. Garnish each with 1 cheese crisp; reserve remaining cheese crisps for another use.

Serves 4 (serving size: 1 cup salad and 1 cheese crisp): Calories 70; Fat 4.1g (sat 1.3g, mono 1.9g, poly 0.2g); Protein 5g; Carb 3g; Fiber 1g; Sugars 2g (est. added sugars: 0g); Chol 8mg; Iron 1mg; Sodium 249mg; Calc 101mg

Fettuccine Alfredo,
page 135

CLASSICS TAKEOVER

LOBSTER RISOTTO

CLASSIC: Calories per serving: 417, Sat Fat: 6.5g, Sodium: 918mg, Sugars: 4g
MAKEOVER: Calories per serving: 374, Sat Fat: 5.8g, Sodium: 620mg, Sugars: 1g

HANDS-ON: 63 MIN. TOTAL: 63 MIN.

Simmering the shells infuses the broth with lobster flavor and adds elegance to this simple risotto dish.

4 cups fat-free, lower-sodium chicken
  broth
1½ cups water
3 (5-ounce) American lobster tails

3 tablespoons butter, divided
1 cup uncooked Arborio or other
  medium-grain rice
¾ cup frozen green peas, thawed

1. Bring broth and 1½ cups water to a boil in a saucepan. Add lobster; cover and cook 4 minutes. Remove lobster from pan; cool 5 minutes. Remove meat from cooked lobster tails, reserving shells. Chop meat.

2. Place shells in a large zip-top plastic bag. Coarsely crush shells using a meat mallet or heavy skillet. Return crushed shells to broth mixture. Reduce heat to medium-low. Cover and cook 20 minutes. Strain shell mixture through a sieve over a bowl, reserving broth; discard solids. Return broth mixture to pan; keep warm over low heat.

3. Heat 1 tablespoon butter in a medium saucepan over medium-high heat. Add rice to pan; cook 2 minutes, stirring constantly. Stir in 1 cup broth mixture; cook 5 minutes or until liquid is nearly absorbed, stirring constantly. Reserve 2 tablespoons broth mixture. Add remaining broth mixture, ½ cup at a time, stirring constantly until each portion is absorbed before adding the next (about 22 minutes total).

4. Remove from heat; stir in lobster meat, reserved 2 tablespoons broth mixture, 2 tablespoons butter, and peas.

Serves 4 (serving size: 1 cup): Calories 374; Fat 10.7g (sat 5.8g, mono 2.6g, poly 0.9g); Protein 25g; Carb 44g;
Fiber 4g; Sugars 1g (est. added sugars: 0g); Chol 80mg; Iron 2mg; Sodium 620mg; Calc 63mg

PASTA ALLA CARBONARA

CLASSIC: Calories per serving: 814, Sat Fat: 16.3g, Sodium: 1420mg, Sugars: 4g
MAKEOVER: Calories per serving: 398, Sat Fat: 4.8g, Sodium: 671mg, Sugars: 4g

HANDS-ON: 25 MIN. TOTAL: 25 MIN.

Classically, this dish is made using egg yolks and starchy, salty pasta water to make a creamy, rich sauce. Here, we eliminate the extra step and make this a one-pot pasta. The sauce becomes creamy from the natural starches in the pasta. Like a traditional carbonara, this dish needs to be eaten immediately, or the sauce will congeal. We left out peas for the sake of tradition, but by all means add as many veggies as you'd like.

4 ounces diced pancetta
2 cups fat-free, lower-sodium chicken broth
1 teaspoon cracked black pepper
¼ teaspoon kosher salt
1 (16-ounce) package uncooked linguine
1½ cups water, divided
2 ounces grated fresh Parmigiano-Reggiano cheese (about ½ cup)
1 large egg, lightly beaten
Grated lemon rind (optional)
Additional cracked black pepper (optional)

1. Cook pancetta in a large deep skillet over medium heat 5 minutes or until crisp. Remove pancetta from pan, reserving drippings in pan; drain pancetta, and set aside.

2. Add broth and next 3 ingredients (through pasta) to drippings in pan. Bring to a boil; cook 14 minutes or until pasta is al dente, tossing constantly with tongs. Add 1 cup water as needed, ¼ cup at a time, to keep pasta from drying out. Reduce heat to medium-low.

3. Combine cheese, ½ cup water, egg, and lemon rind, if desired; add to pasta, tossing constantly with tongs 2 minutes or until creamy. Sprinkle with pancetta and additional pepper, if desired.

Serves 6 (serving size: ⅙ of pasta and 1½ teaspoons pancetta): Calories 398; Fat 9.8g (sat 4.8g, mono 0.9g, poly 0.2g); Protein 18g; Carb 58g; Fiber 3g; Sugars 4g (est. added sugars: 0g); Chol 50mg; Iron 3mg; Sodium 671mg; Calc 94mg

EGGPLANT PARMESAN

CLASSIC: Calories per serving: 1053, Sat Fat: 30.4g, Sodium: 1965mg, Sugars: 14g
MAKEOVER: Calories per serving: 318, Sat Fat: 8.2g, Sodium: 655mg, Sugars: 3g

HANDS-ON: 25 MIN. TOTAL: 1 HR. 45 MIN.

Save tons of fat and calories by baking the eggplant in whole-wheat panko and using part-skim ricotta and fresh mozzarella.

EGGPLANT:
- 2 large eggs, lightly beaten
- 1 tablespoon water
- 2 cups whole-wheat panko (Japanese breadcrumbs)
- 1 ounce fresh Parmigiano-Reggiano cheese, grated (about 1/4 cup)
- 2 (1-pound) eggplants, peeled and cut crosswise into 1/2-inch-thick slices
- Cooking spray

FILLING:
- 1/2 cup torn fresh basil
- 1 ounce grated fresh Parmigiano-Reggiano cheese (about 1/4 cup)
- 1/2 teaspoon crushed red pepper
- 1 1/2 teaspoons minced garlic
- 1/4 teaspoon salt
- 1 (16-ounce) container part-skim ricotta cheese
- 1 large egg, lightly beaten

REMAINING INGREDIENTS:
- 1 (24-ounce) jar premium pasta sauce
- 1/4 teaspoon salt
- 8 ounces thinly sliced mozzarella cheese
- 3 ounces fontina cheese, finely grated (about 3/4 cup)

1. Preheat oven to 375°. To prepare eggplant, combine 2 eggs and 1 tablespoon water in a shallow dish. Combine panko and 1/4 cup Parmigiano-Reggiano in another dish. Dip eggplant in egg mixture; dredge in panko mixture. Place eggplant slices 1 inch apart on baking sheets coated with cooking spray. Bake at 375° for 30 minutes or until golden, turning slices once and rotating baking sheets after 15 minutes.

2. To prepare filling, combine basil and next 6 ingredients. Spoon 1/2 cup pasta sauce in bottom of a 13 x 9-inch glass or ceramic baking dish coated with cooking spray. Layer half of eggplant slices over pasta sauce. Sprinkle eggplant with 1/8 teaspoon salt. Top with about 3/4 cup pasta sauce; spread half of filling over sauce, and top with one-third of mozzarella and 1/4 cup fontina. Repeat layers, ending with about 1 cup pasta sauce. Cover tightly with foil coated with cooking spray. Bake at 375° for 35 minutes. Remove foil; top with one-third of mozzarella and 1/4 cup fontina. Bake at 375° for 10 minutes. Let stand 10 minutes.

Serves 10 (serving size: 1 slice): Calories 318; Fat 15.1g (sat 8.2g, mono 2.7g, poly 0.6g); Protein 19g; Carb 27g; Fiber 5g; Sugars 3g (est. added sugars: 0g); Chol 99mg; Iron 2mg; Sodium 655mg; Calc 365mg

LOBSTER RISOTTO

CLASSIC: Calories per serving: 417, Sat Fat: 6.5g, Sodium: 918mg, Sugars: 4g
MAKEOVER: Calories per serving: 374, Sat Fat: 5.8g, Sodium: 620mg, Sugars: 1g

HANDS-ON: 63 MIN. TOTAL: 63 MIN.

Simmering the shells infuses the broth with lobster flavor and adds elegance to this simple risotto dish.

4 cups fat-free, lower-sodium chicken broth
1½ cups water
3 (5-ounce) American lobster tails

3 tablespoons butter, divided
1 cup uncooked Arborio or other medium-grain rice
¾ cup frozen green peas, thawed

1. Bring broth and 1½ cups water to a boil in a saucepan. Add lobster; cover and cook 4 minutes. Remove lobster from pan; cool 5 minutes. Remove meat from cooked lobster tails, reserving shells. Chop meat.

2. Place shells in a large zip-top plastic bag. Coarsely crush shells using a meat mallet or heavy skillet. Return crushed shells to broth mixture. Reduce heat to medium-low. Cover and cook 20 minutes. Strain shell mixture through a sieve over a bowl, reserving broth; discard solids. Return broth mixture to pan; keep warm over low heat.

3. Heat 1 tablespoon butter in a medium saucepan over medium-high heat. Add rice to pan; cook 2 minutes, stirring constantly. Stir in 1 cup broth mixture; cook 5 minutes or until liquid is nearly absorbed, stirring constantly. Reserve 2 tablespoons broth mixture. Add remaining broth mixture, ½ cup at a time, stirring constantly until each portion is absorbed before adding the next (about 22 minutes total).

4. Remove from heat; stir in lobster meat, reserved 2 tablespoons broth mixture, 2 tablespoons butter, and peas.

Serves 4 (serving size: 1 cup): Calories 374; Fat 10.7g (sat 5.8g, mono 2.6g, poly 0.9g); Protein 25g; Carb 44g;
Fiber 4g; Sugars 1g (est. added sugars: 0g); Chol 80mg; Iron 2mg; Sodium 620mg; Calc 63mg

PASTA ALLA CARBONARA

CLASSIC: Calories per serving: 814, Sat Fat: 16.3g, Sodium: 1420mg, Sugars: 4g
MAKEOVER: Calories per serving: 398, Sat Fat: 4.8g, Sodium: 671mg, Sugars: 4g

HANDS-ON: 25 MIN. TOTAL: 25 MIN.

Classically, this dish is made using egg yolks and starchy, salty pasta water to make a creamy, rich sauce. Here, we eliminate the extra step and make this a one-pot pasta. The sauce becomes creamy from the natural starches in the pasta. Like a traditional carbonara, this dish needs to be eaten immediately, or the sauce will congeal. We left out peas for the sake of tradition, but by all means add as many veggies as you'd like.

4 ounces diced pancetta
2 cups fat-free, lower-sodium chicken
  broth
1 teaspoon cracked black pepper
1/4 teaspoon kosher salt
1 (16-ounce) package uncooked
  linguine

1 1/2 cups water, divided
2 ounces grated fresh Parmigiano-
  Reggiano cheese (about 1/2 cup)
1 large egg, lightly beaten
Grated lemon rind (optional)
Additional cracked black pepper
  (optional)

1. Cook pancetta in a large deep skillet over medium heat 5 minutes or until crisp. Remove pancetta from pan, reserving drippings in pan; drain pancetta, and set aside.

2. Add broth and next 3 ingredients (through pasta) to drippings in pan. Bring to a boil; cook 14 minutes or until pasta is al dente, tossing constantly with tongs. Add 1 cup water as needed, 1/4 cup at a time, to keep pasta from drying out. Reduce heat to medium-low.

3. Combine cheese, 1/2 cup water, egg, and lemon rind, if desired; add to pasta, tossing constantly with tongs 2 minutes or until creamy. Sprinkle with pancetta and additional pepper, if desired.

Serves 6 (serving size: 1/6 of pasta and 1 1/2 teaspoons pancetta): Calories 398; Fat 9.8g (sat 4.8g, mono 0.9g, poly 0.2g); Protein 18g; Carb 58g; Fiber 3g; Sugars 4g (est. added sugars: 0g); Chol 50mg; Iron 3mg; Sodium 671mg; Calc 94mg

EGGPLANT PARMESAN

CLASSIC: Calories per serving: 1053, Sat Fat: 30.4g, Sodium: 1965mg, Sugars: 14g
MAKEOVER: Calories per serving: 318, Sat Fat: 8.2g, Sodium: 655mg, Sugars: 3g

HANDS-ON: 25 MIN. TOTAL: 1 HR. 45 MIN.

Save tons of fat and calories by baking the eggplant in whole-wheat panko and using part-skim ricotta and fresh mozzarella.

EGGPLANT:

2 large eggs, lightly beaten
1 tablespoon water
2 cups whole-wheat panko (Japanese breadcrumbs)
1 ounce fresh Parmigiano-Reggiano cheese, grated (about ¼ cup)

2 (1-pound) eggplants, peeled and cut crosswise into ½-inch-thick slices
Cooking spray

FILLING:

½ cup torn fresh basil
1 ounce grated fresh Parmigiano-Reggiano cheese (about ¼ cup)
½ teaspoon crushed red pepper
1½ teaspoons minced garlic

¼ teaspoon salt
1 (16-ounce) container part-skim ricotta cheese
1 large egg, lightly beaten

REMAINING INGREDIENTS:

1 (24-ounce) jar premium pasta sauce
¼ teaspoon salt
8 ounces thinly sliced mozzarella cheese

3 ounces fontina cheese, finely grated (about ¾ cup)

1. Preheat oven to 375°. To prepare eggplant, combine 2 eggs and 1 tablespoon water in a shallow dish. Combine panko and ¼ cup Parmigiano-Reggiano in another dish. Dip eggplant in egg mixture; dredge in panko mixture. Place eggplant slices 1 inch apart on baking sheets coated with cooking spray. Bake at 375° for 30 minutes or until golden, turning slices once and rotating baking sheets after 15 minutes.

2. To prepare filling, combine basil and next 6 ingredients. Spoon ½ cup pasta sauce in bottom of a 13 x 9–inch glass or ceramic baking dish coated with cooking spray. Layer half of eggplant slices over pasta sauce. Sprinkle eggplant with ⅛ teaspoon salt. Top with about ¾ cup pasta sauce; spread half of filling over sauce, and top with one-third of mozzarella and ¼ cup fontina. Repeat layers, ending with about 1 cup pasta sauce. Cover tightly with foil coated with cooking spray. Bake at 375° for 35 minutes. Remove foil; top with one-third of mozzarella and ¼ cup fontina. Bake at 375° for 10 minutes. Let stand 10 minutes.

Serves 10 (serving size: 1 slice): Calories 318; Fat 15.1g (sat 8.2g, mono 2.7g, poly 0.6g); Protein 19g; Carb 27g; Fiber 5g; Sugars 3g (est. added sugars: 0g); Chol 99mg; Iron 2mg; Sodium 655mg; Calc 365mg

WILD MUSHROOM PASTITSIO

CLASSIC: Calories per serving: 689, Sat Fat: 16.2g, Sodium: 727mg, Sugars: 11g
MAKEOVER: Calories per serving: 364, Sat Fat: 5.7g, Sodium: 574mg, Sugars: 9g

HANDS-ON: 33 MIN. TOTAL: 1 HR. 18 MIN.

This Greek twist on baked ziti uses low-fat milk in the béchamel, so there's more room for melty mozzarella.

4 teaspoons olive oil, divided
1 cup chopped onion
2 garlic cloves, minced
2 (8-ounce) packages presliced exotic
  mushroom blend, chopped
1 tablespoon chopped fresh oregano
½ teaspoon kosher salt, divided
¼ teaspoon black pepper
⅛ teaspoon ground nutmeg
1 (8-ounce) can tomato sauce

3 tablespoons chopped fresh parsley
2 large eggs, lightly beaten
1 teaspoon unsalted butter
1½ tablespoons all-purpose flour
2 cups 1% low-fat milk
6 ounces shredded part-skim
  mozzarella cheese, divided (about
  1½ cups)
4 cups hot cooked fusilli pasta
Cooking spray

1. Preheat oven to 350°.

2. Heat 1 tablespoon oil in a Dutch oven over medium-high heat; swirl to coat. Add onion and garlic; sauté 3 minutes or until tender. Add mushrooms. Cook 8 minutes or until liquid almost evaporates. Stir in oregano, ¼ teaspoon salt, black pepper, nutmeg, and tomato sauce. Cook 2 minutes, stirring frequently. Remove from heat; set aside.

3. Combine parsley and eggs in a large bowl. Heat 1 teaspoon oil and butter in a medium saucepan over medium heat. Sprinkle flour into pan; cook 2 minutes, stirring constantly. Gradually add milk to flour mixture, stirring with a whisk until smooth. Bring to a boil; cook 2 minutes or until thick, stirring frequently. Remove from heat; let stand 4 minutes. Stir in ¼ teaspoon salt and 1 cup cheese. Gradually add hot milk mixture to egg mixture, stirring constantly with a whisk. Add pasta to milk mixture; toss to combine.

4. Spread 2 cups pasta mixture in an 11 x 7–inch glass or ceramic baking dish coated with cooking spray. Top with mushroom mixture. Top with remaining pasta mixture. Cover with foil coated with cooking spray. Bake at 350° for 30 minutes. Remove foil; sprinkle with ½ cup cheese.

5. Preheat broiler.

6. Broil 5 minutes or until cheese melts. Let stand 15 minutes.

Serves 6 (serving size: 1 piece): Calories 364; Fat 13.1g (sat 5.7g, mono 5g, poly 1.2g); Protein 20g; Carb 42g; Fiber 4g; Sugars 9g (est. added sugars: 0g); Chol 92mg; Iron 3mg; Sodium 574mg; Calc 341mg

PORK TENDERLOIN PAPRIKASH

CLASSIC: Calories per serving: 727, Sat Fat: 8.8g, Sodium: 1364mg, Sugars: 8g
MAKEOVER: Calories per serving: 441, Sat Fat: 3.2g, Sodium: 479mg, Sugars: 5g

HANDS-ON: 18 MIN. TOTAL: 32 MIN.

Though not an American classic, paprikash is a Hungarian comfort food staple, similar to beef stroganoff. You can sub sweet paprika for hot paprika, but avoid smoked paprika; it would be too strong. Reduced-fat sour cream knocks the fat back by two-thirds.

6 ounces uncooked egg noodles
1 (1-pound) pork tenderloin, trimmed and cut into 1-inch pieces
$\frac{1}{2}$ teaspoon salt, divided
$\frac{1}{2}$ teaspoon freshly ground black pepper, divided
5 teaspoons olive oil, divided
1$\frac{1}{2}$ cups chopped onion
1 cup chopped green bell pepper
2 teaspoons chopped garlic
2 tablespoons all-purpose flour
2 tablespoons tomato paste
1 teaspoon chopped fresh thyme
1 teaspoon hot paprika
$\frac{1}{2}$ cup dry white wine
1 cup unsalted chicken stock
1 tablespoon cider vinegar
3 tablespoons reduced-fat sour cream

1. Cook noodles according to package directions, omitting salt and fat; drain.

2. Sprinkle pork with $\frac{1}{4}$ teaspoon salt and $\frac{1}{4}$ teaspoon black pepper. Heat a large skillet over medium-high heat. Add 2 teaspoons oil; swirl to coat. Add pork; cook 4 minutes, browning on all sides. Remove pork from pan. Reduce heat to medium. Add 1 tablespoon oil to pan; swirl to coat. Add onion, bell pepper, garlic, $\frac{1}{4}$ teaspoon salt, and $\frac{1}{4}$ teaspoon black pepper; sauté 4 minutes or until vegetables are tender. Add flour, tomato paste, thyme, and paprika; sauté 30 seconds. Add wine; cook 1 minute, scraping pan to loosen browned bits. Add stock and vinegar; bring to a boil. Add pork; reduce heat, and simmer 5 minutes or until pork is tender. Remove pan from heat; stir in sour cream. Serve over noodles.

Serves 4 (serving size: about $\frac{1}{2}$ cup noodles and 1 cup pork mixture): Calories 441; Fat 11.9g (sat 3.2g, mono 5.4g, poly 1.1g); Protein 33g; Carb 44g; Fiber 4g; Sugars 5g (est. added sugars: 1g); Chol 128mg; Iron 4mg; Sodium 479mg; Calc 66mg

MUSHROOM AND ROASTED
GARLIC RISOTTO

CLASSIC: Calories per serving: 445, Sat Fat: 7.7g, Sodium: 1450mg, Sugars: 3g
MAKEOVER: Calories per serving: 381, Sat Fat: 2.5g, Sodium: 589mg, Sugars: 6g

HANDS-ON: 60 MIN. TOTAL: 1 HR. 25 MIN.

Madeira wine and dried porcinis add meaty richness without sodium-laden beef stock.

2 whole garlic heads
2 tablespoons plus 1 teaspoon extra-virgin olive oil, divided
1/2 cup plus 2 tablespoons Madeira wine, divided
5 cups unsalted chicken stock, divided
1/2 cup dried porcini mushrooms (1/2 ounce)
1 3/4 cups chopped onion
3 cups thinly sliced cremini mushrooms (about 8 ounces)

2 1/2 cups thinly sliced shiitake mushroom caps (about 8 ounces)
1 1/2 cups uncooked Arborio rice
2 ounces fresh Parmesan cheese, grated (about 1/2 cup)
1 teaspoon kosher salt
1/2 teaspoon freshly ground black pepper
2 tablespoons chopped fresh sage
Whole sage leaves (optional)

1. Preheat oven to 425°.

2. Cut top off each garlic head; discard. Rub cut side of each garlic head with 1 teaspoon oil. Remove white papery skin from garlic heads (do not peel or separate cloves). Wrap garlic in foil. Bake at 425° for 1 hour or until tender; cool 10 minutes. Separate cloves; squeeze to extract garlic pulp. Discard skins. Combine garlic pulp and 2 tablespoons Madeira in a bowl; mash with a fork.

3. Bring 1 1/2 cups stock to a boil. Add porcini; let stand 30 minutes or until soft. Drain through a colander over a bowl, reserving soaking liquid; chop porcini. Combine porcini liquid and 3 1/2 cups stock; bring to a simmer in a medium saucepan (do not boil). Keep warm.

4. Heat a Dutch oven over medium heat. Add 2 tablespoons oil; swirl to coat. Add onion to pan; sauté 5 minutes or until tender. Add cremini and shiitake mushrooms; cook 5 minutes or until browned, stirring occasionally. Stir in porcini. Add rice; sauté 1 minute, stirring constantly. Add 1/2 cup Madeira; cook 1 minute or until liquid is absorbed. Stir in 1 1/2 cups stock; cook 4 minutes or until liquid is nearly absorbed, stirring constantly. Add remaining stock, 3/4 cup at a time, stirring constantly until each portion of stock is absorbed before adding the next (about 25 minutes total) and reserving 1/3 cup stock from the last addition. Remove pan from heat; stir in garlic mixture, reserved 1/3 cup stock, cheese, salt, pepper, and chopped sage. Spoon into shallow bowls. Garnish with sage leaves, if desired.

Serves 6 (serving size: about 1 cup): Calories 381; Fat 9.4g (sat 2.5g, mono 5.1g, poly 0.8g); Protein 16g; Carb 54g; Fiber 4g; Sugars 6g (est. added sugars: 2g); Chol 6mg; Iron 2mg; Sodium 589mg; Calc 169mg

FETTUCCINE ALFREDO

CLASSIC: Calories per serving: 1002, Sat Fat: 35.3g, Sodium: 1406mg, Sugars: 6g
MAKEOVER: Calories per serving: 461, Sat Fat: 8.2g, Sodium: 715mg, Sugars: 10g

HANDS-ON: 30 MIN. TOTAL: 30 MIN.

Heavy cream, Parmesan cheese, and butter create the regular calorie- and fat-filled Alfredo sauce. Here, we use olive oil instead of butter and nix the cream in favor of a milk-based sauce thickened with flour and cream cheese, leaving plenty of room for a cup of the good stuff–Parmigiano-Reggiano cheese.

1 tablespoon olive oil
2 garlic cloves, minced
1 tablespoon all-purpose flour
1 1/3 cups 1% low-fat milk
5 ounces fresh Parmigiano-Reggiano cheese, shredded and divided (about 1 1/4 cups)
6 tablespoons 1/3-less-fat cream cheese

1/4 teaspoon salt
4 cups hot cooked fettuccine (8 ounces uncooked pasta)
1/2 cup fresh or frozen green peas
1 1/2 cups fresh or frozen asparagus pieces
2 teaspoons chopped fresh flat-leaf parsley
Cracked black pepper (optional)

1. Heat oil in a medium saucepan over medium heat. Add garlic; cook 1 minute, stirring frequently. Stir in flour. Gradually add milk, stirring with a whisk. Cook 6 minutes or until mixture thickens, stirring constantly. Add 1 cup Parmigiano-Reggiano cheese, cream cheese, and salt, stirring with a whisk until cheeses melt. Toss sauce with hot pasta, peas, and asparagus pieces. Sprinkle with 1/4 cup Parmigiano-Reggiano cheese and chopped parsley. Garnish with black pepper, if desired. Serve immediately.

Serves 4 (serving size: about 1 1/2 cups): Calories 461; Fat 14.8g (sat 8.2g, mono 4.8g, poly 0.6g); Protein 24g; Carb 55g; Fiber 4g; Sugars 10g (est. added sugars: 0g); Chol 37mg; Iron 4mg; Sodium 715mg; Calc 475mg

CLASSIC CHICKEN NOODLE SOUP

CLASSIC: Calories per serving: 442, Sat Fat: 3.1g, Sodium: 1064mg, Sugars: 4g
MAKEOVER: Calories per serving: 302, Sat Fat: 1.5g, Sodium: 483mg, Sugars: 3g

HANDS-ON: 28 MIN. TOTAL: 55 MIN.

This is just what the doctor ordered any time of year. Bone-in chicken fortifies commercial stock and adds meaty depth to this classic soup for the soul.

2 tablespoons canola oil
1 bone-in chicken breast half, skinned
1 pound bone-in chicken thighs, skinned
¾ teaspoon kosher salt, divided
½ teaspoon freshly ground black pepper, divided
2 cups chopped onion
1 cup chopped carrot
½ cup (¼-inch-thick) slices celery
1 tablespoon minced fresh garlic
3 fresh parsley sprigs
3 fresh thyme sprigs
1 fresh rosemary sprig
2 bay leaves
1 cup dry white wine
4 cups unsalted chicken stock
1 cup uncooked medium egg noodles
2 tablespoons chopped fresh parsley

1. Heat oil in a Dutch oven over medium-high heat. Sprinkle chicken with ½ teaspoon salt and ¼ teaspoon pepper. Add chicken to pan, flesh side down. Cook 10 minutes, turning thighs after 5 minutes. Cool, and shred. Discard bones.

2. Add onion, carrot, and celery to pan; sauté 10 minutes. Add garlic; sauté 1 minute. Place herb sprigs and bay leaves on cheesecloth. Gather edges; tie securely. Add sachet to pan.

3. Add wine to pan; bring to a boil. Cook 4 minutes. Add chicken and stock. Cover; reduce heat. Cook 7 minutes.

4. Add noodles; cook 6 minutes or until al dente. Discard sachet. Stir in chopped parsley, ¼ teaspoon salt, and ¼ teaspoon pepper.

Serves 6 (serving size: about 1 cup): Calories 302; Fat 9.2g (sat 1.5g, mono 4.2g, poly 2.1g); Protein 31g; Carb 16g; Fiber 2g; Sugars 3g (est. added sugars: 0g); Chol 103mg; Iron 2mg; Sodium 483mg; Calc 54mg

CREAMY ROASTED
TOMATO SOUP

CLASSIC: Calories per serving: 276, Sat Fat: 10.8g, Sodium: 908mg, Sugars: 16g
MAKEOVER: Calories per serving: 91, Sat Fat: 0.6g, Sodium: 289mg, Sugars: 5g

HANDS-ON: 15 MIN. TOTAL: 1 HR. 30 MIN.

Roasting your own tomatoes is preferred, but in a pinch, 1 (28-ounce) can of fire-roasted tomatoes will do; simply omit the chicken stock, and use the whole can. We recommend serving this with the Creamy Grilled Cheese Skillet Panini on page 59.

3 pounds fresh tomatoes, quartered
3 garlic cloves, peeled and crushed
2 medium shallots, peeled and quartered
1 tablespoon coarsely chopped fresh oregano
2 tablespoons extra-virgin olive oil, divided
1 teaspoon kosher salt, divided

½ teaspoon freshly ground black pepper
1 leek, thinly sliced into half-moons (about 1¼ cups)
2 cups unsalted chicken stock
2 ounces fresh basil, leaves and stems separated
1 (1-ounce) Parmigiano-Reggiano cheese rind

CRAZY TRICK
Leeks are natural thickeners in soups and stews. When blended, they act like a roux.

1. Preheat oven to 375°.

2. Combine tomatoes, garlic, shallots, oregano, 1½ teaspoons oil, ½ teaspoon salt, and pepper; toss. Arrange tomato mixture on a large rimmed baking sheet lined with parchment paper. Bake at 375° about 1 hour or until slightly caramelized.

3. Heat a large Dutch oven over medium heat. Add 1½ teaspoons oil to pan; swirl to coat. Add leeks; cover, reduce heat to low, and cook 8 minutes or until tender. Add tomato mixture and any accumulated liquid to pan; cook 2 minutes. Add stock, basil leaves and stems, rind, and ½ teaspoon salt. Simmer, stirring occasionally, about 15 minutes or until liquid is reduced slightly. Remove and discard rind and stems. Place half of soup in a blender. Remove center piece of blender lid (to allow steam to escape); secure blender lid on blender. Place a clean towel over opening in blender lid (to avoid splatters). Blend until smooth. Return pureed soup to pan. Divide among 8 soup bowls; drizzle with 1 tablespoon oil.

Serves 8 (serving size: about ¾ cup): Calories 91; Fat 4.1g (sat 0.6g, mono 2.8g, poly 0.5g); Protein 4g; Carb 12g; Fiber 2g; Sugars 5g (est. added sugars: 0g); Chol 0mg; Iron 1mg; Sodium 289mg; Calc 50mg

BEEF AND MUSHROOM
STROGANOFF

CLASSIC: Calories per serving: 920, Sat Fat: 13.1g, Sodium: 1425mg, Sugars: 11g
MAKEOVER: Calories per serving: 423, Sat Fat: 5.7g, Sodium: 583mg, Sugars: 4g

HANDS-ON: 29 MIN. TOTAL: 29 MIN.

Simply swapping out full-fat for light sour cream drastically lowers the calories and saturated fat.

1 tablespoon canola oil
1 pound beef tenderloin, trimmed and
  cut into 1-inch pieces
3/4 teaspoon salt, divided
1/2 teaspoon freshly ground black
  pepper, divided
1 cup thinly sliced leek
1 tablespoon chopped fresh thyme
2 teaspoons minced garlic

1 (6-ounce) package presliced shiitake
  mushrooms
1 tablespoon all-purpose flour
1/2 teaspoon hot paprika
1 cup unsalted beef stock
1/2 cup light sour cream
2 cups hot cooked wide egg noodles
2 tablespoons chopped fresh parsley

1. Heat oil in a large skillet over high heat; swirl to coat. Add beef; sprinkle with 1/4 teaspoon salt and 1/4 teaspoon pepper. Cook 4 minutes or until browned, turning to brown on all sides. Remove beef from pan.

2. Reduce heat to medium-high. Add leek, thyme, garlic, and mushrooms; sauté 5 minutes or until lightly browned, stirring occasionally. Sprinkle mushroom mixture with flour and paprika; cook 30 seconds, stirring constantly. Add stock; bring to a boil. Reduce heat, and simmer 2 minutes or until sauce is thickened, stirring frequently. Stir in beef, 1/2 teaspoon salt, 1/4 teaspoon pepper, and sour cream. Serve over noodles; sprinkle with parsley.

Serves 4 (serving size: 1/2 cup noodles and 3/4 cup beef mixture): Calories 423; Fat 15.6g (sat 5.7g, mono 5.2g, poly 1.4g); Protein 35g; Carb 35g; Fiber 2g; Sugars 4g (est. added sugars: 0g); Chol 115mg; Iron 4mg; Sodium 583mg; Calc 63mg

SPAGHETTI BOLOGNESE

HANDS-ON: 40 MIN. TOTAL: 40 MIN.

This dish is all about simplicity. We take out the heavy cream and butter without losing the richness of the sauce thanks to blending French bread crumbs with milk.

1 (¾-ounce) slice French bread
¼ cup 1% low-fat milk
2 teaspoons olive oil
1 cup finely chopped onion
½ cup finely chopped carrot
3 garlic cloves, minced
1 tablespoon tomato paste
2 tablespoons red wine vinegar
12 ounces ground sirloin
2 teaspoons dried oregano

½ teaspoon salt
¼ teaspoon black pepper
⅛ teaspoon ground red pepper
1 (14.5-ounce) can diced tomatoes with
   basil, garlic, and oregano, undrained
4 cups hot cooked spaghetti (about
   8 ounces uncooked)
1 ounce shaved fresh Parmigiano-
   Reggiano cheese (about ¼ cup)

1. Place bread in a food processor; pulse until coarse crumbs measure ½ cup. Combine crumbs and milk in a bowl.

2. Heat oil in a large skillet over medium-high heat. Add onion and carrot; sauté 8 minutes. Add garlic and tomato paste; sauté 1 minute, stirring constantly. Add vinegar; cook 30 seconds. Add beef, oregano, salt, and peppers; cook 7 minutes, stirring to crumble. Stir in breadcrumb mixture and tomatoes; bring to a boil. Reduce heat, and simmer 6 minutes, stirring occasionally. Serve over spaghetti; top with cheese.

Serves 4 (serving size: 1 cup spaghetti, about ¾ cup sauce, and 1 tablespoon cheese): Calories 440; Fat 9.6g (sat 3.4g, mono 4g, poly 1.2g); Protein 30g; Carb 59g; Fiber 6g; Sugars 8g (est. added sugars: 0g); Chol 51mg; Iron 5mg; Sodium 682mg; Calc 164mg

WEEKNIGHT "PORCHETTA"

HANDS-ON: 10 MIN. TOTAL: 45 MIN.

No need to add much salt and pepper to this roast–the pancetta wrap both seasons the tenderloin and keeps it moist as it roasts.

1 tablespoon chopped fresh rosemary
1 tablespoon crushed fennel seeds
1 tablespoon olive oil
1 teaspoon minced fresh sage
1 teaspoon crushed red pepper

1 teaspoon grated lemon rind
1/4 teaspoon kosher salt
4 garlic cloves, finely chopped
1 (1 1/2-pound) pork tenderloin, trimmed
4 pancetta slices (about 3 ounces)

1. Preheat oven to 425°.

2. Combine first 8 ingredients in a small bowl. Rub pork with herb mixture; place pork on a jelly-roll pan lined with foil. Arrange pancetta slices over top and sides of pork; secure with wooden picks.

3. Bake at 425° for 25 to 30 minutes or until a thermometer registers 145° (medium). Cover with foil if pancetta begins to brown too quickly. Let stand 10 minutes before slicing.

Serves 6 (serving size: 4 ounces pork): Calories 229; Fat 12.8g (sat 3.5g, mono 4.2g, poly 1.1g); Protein 27g; Carb 1g; Fiber 0g; Sugars 0g (est. added sugars: 0g); Chol 86mg; Iron 1mg; Sodium 348mg; Calc 12mg

PORK CASSOULET

CLASSIC: Calories per serving: 494, Sat Fat: 20.1g, Sodium: 1483mg, Sugars: 4g
MAKEOVER: Calories per serving: 386, Sat Fat: 2.6g, Sodium: 413mg, Sugars: 4g

HANDS-ON: 30 MIN. TOTAL: 11 HR. 15 MIN.

The heartiness of traditional cassoulet is certainly not missed
in this lightened version studded with bacon, pork shoulder, and sausage.

1 pound dried Great Northern beans
3 thick-cut bacon slices, cut into
 1/2-inch pieces
2 cups chopped onion
3/4 cup chopped carrot
3 garlic cloves, minced
12 ounces boneless pork shoulder,
 trimmed and cut into 1-inch pieces
1/2 cup dry white wine
1 tablespoon chopped fresh thyme

1 1/2 teaspoons chopped fresh rosemary
2 bay leaves
1 (14.5-ounce) can unsalted diced
 tomatoes, undrained
2 cups fat-free, lower-sodium chicken
 broth
1 (6-ounce) link sweet Italian sausage
1 cup panko (Japanese breadcrumbs)
2 teaspoons grated lemon rind
Cooking spray

1. Sort and wash beans; place in a large bowl. Cover with water to 2 inches above beans; cover and let
stand 8 hours. Drain beans.

2. Preheat oven to 350°.

3. Cook bacon in a Dutch oven over medium-high heat 6 minutes or until crisp. Remove bacon from pan,
reserving 1 tablespoon drippings in pan.

4. Add onion and carrot to drippings in pan; cook over medium-high heat 5 minutes, stirring frequently.
Add garlic; cook 2 minutes, stirring constantly. Add pork shoulder; cook 3 minutes, turning to brown pork
on all sides. Add wine; cook 1 minute, scraping pan to loosen browned bits. Stir in thyme, rosemary, bay
leaves, and tomatoes; cook 3 minutes. Stir in beans, bacon, and chicken broth; return to a simmer. Cover
and bake at 350° for 45 minutes.

5. Meanwhile, pierce sausage with a fork, and place on a small baking sheet. Bake at 350° for 20 to
25 minutes or until done. Cool sausage 10 minutes; slice into 1/2-inch-thick rounds. Stir sausage into pork
mixture in Dutch oven; cover and bake at 350° for 1 hour 30 minutes. Remove and discard bay leaves.

6. Combine panko and lemon rind in a small bowl. Uncover Dutch oven, and sprinkle panko over pork
mixture; coat with cooking spray. Bake at 350° for 30 minutes or until pork and beans are tender and
topping is lightly browned.

Serves 8 (serving size: 1 1/4 cups): Calories 386; Fat 7.9g (sat 2.6g, mono 2.2g, poly 0.8g); Protein 28g; Carb 48g; Fiber 16g; Sugars 4g
(est. added sugars: 0g); Chol 39mg; Iron 5mg; Sodium 413mg; Calc 132mg

FRENCH ONION SOUP

CLASSIC: Calories per serving: 297, Sat Fat: 9.9g, Sodium: 1885mg, Sugars: 5g
MAKEOVER: Calories per serving: 346, Sat Fat: 5.9g, Sodium: 649mg, Sugars: 12g

HANDS-ON: 1 HR. 20 MIN. TOTAL: 5 HR. 39 MIN.

It's worth the effort to make your own stock, which drastically reduces the sodium in this simple soup.

STOCK:
1 1/2 pounds meaty beef bones
1 pound beef shanks
2 large carrots, peeled and coarsely chopped
2 celery stalks, coarsely chopped
1 medium onion, cut into wedges

3 quarts cold water
3 thyme sprigs
1 tablespoon whole black peppercorns
1 bunch fresh flat-leaf parsley
1 bay leaf

SOUP:
2 tablespoons olive oil
1 tablespoon butter
5 large onions, vertically sliced (about 13 cups)
1 1/8 teaspoons kosher salt
1/2 teaspoon freshly ground black pepper

1 teaspoon chopped fresh thyme
1/4 cup chopped fresh chives
12 (1/2-ounce) slices French bread baguette
4 ounces Gruyère cheese, shredded (about 1 cup)

1. Preheat oven to 450°.

2. To prepare stock, arrange first 5 ingredients in a single layer on a large baking sheet. Bake at 450° for 35 minutes or until browned. Scrape beef mixture and pan drippings into a large Dutch oven. Stir in 3 quarts cold water and next 4 ingredients (through bay leaf); bring to a boil over medium heat. Reduce heat to low, and simmer 2 1/2 hours, skimming surface as necessary. Strain mixture through a fine sieve lined with a double layer of cheesecloth over a bowl; discard solids. Wipe pan clean with paper towels.

3. To prepare soup, return Dutch oven to medium heat. Add oil to pan; swirl to coat. Melt butter in oil. Add sliced onion; cook 5 minutes. Partially cover, reduce heat to medium-low, and cook 15 minutes. Add salt and ground pepper; cook, uncovered, until deep golden brown (about 35 minutes), stirring frequently. Add stock and chopped thyme; bring to a boil. Reduce heat, and simmer until reduced to 8 cups (about 50 minutes). Stir in chives.

4. Preheat broiler. Arrange bread slices on a jelly-roll pan; broil 1 minute on each side or until toasted. Ladle 1 1/3 cups soup into each of 6 broiler-safe bowls on a jelly-roll pan. Top each serving with 2 bread slices, and sprinkle with cheese. Broil 4 minutes or until tops are golden brown and cheese bubbles.

Serves 6: Calories 346; Fat 14.1g (sat 5.9g, mono 6.2g, poly 1.2g); Protein 16g; Carb 41g; Fiber 5g; Sugars 12g (est. added sugars: 0g); Chol 33mg; Iron 2mg; Sodium 649mg; Calc 274mg

SMOKED CHICKEN COBB SALAD
WITH AVOCADO DRESSING

CLASSIC: Calories per serving: 720, Sat Fat: 14.4g, Sodium: 1289mg, Sugars: 5g
MAKEOVER: Calories per serving: 333, Sat Fat: 5.8g, Sodium: 487mg, Sugars: 3g

HANDS-ON: 30 MIN. TOTAL: 48 MIN.

Boost the flavor of the chicken with a clever smoking technique.

AVOCADO DRESSING:
½ cup diced peeled avocado
3 tablespoons water
2 tablespoons extra-virgin olive oil
1 tablespoon fresh lemon juice
¼ teaspoon kosher salt
¼ teaspoon freshly ground black
  pepper
1 garlic clove, minced

SALAD:
3 center-cut bacon slices
1 teaspoon canola oil
2 (6-ounce) skinless, boneless chicken
  breast halves
1 cup hickory wood chips
⅓ cup unsalted chicken stock
4 cups baby spinach
4 cups romaine lettuce, coarsely
  chopped
½ cup chopped fresh basil leaves
⅓ cup diced peeled avocado
2 heirloom tomatoes, cut into ¼-inch-
  thick slices
2 hard-cooked large eggs, chilled and
  quartered lengthwise
1.5 ounces blue cheese, crumbled
  (about ⅓ cup)

1. To prepare dressing, combine first 7 ingredients in a mini food processor; process until smooth.

2. To prepare salad, cook bacon in a nonstick skillet over medium heat until crisp. Remove bacon from pan; crumble. Add canola oil to pan; swirl to coat. Add chicken to pan; sauté 6 minutes on each side or until done. Cool slightly; shred with 2 forks.

3. Pierce 10 holes on one side of the bottom of a 13 x 9–inch disposable aluminum foil pan. Place holes over element on cooktop; place wood chips over holes inside pan. Place a shallow ovenproof bowl on opposite end of pan. Add chicken and stock to bowl. Heat element under holes to medium-high; let stand 1 minute or until chips begin to smoke. Carefully cover pan with foil. Reduce heat to low; smoke chicken 10 minutes. Remove from heat. Drain.

4. Combine spinach, romaine, and basil in a large bowl; toss. Arrange 2 cups spinach mixture on each of 4 plates. Divide bacon, chicken, avocado, tomatoes, eggs, and cheese among plates. Drizzle about 3 tablespoons dressing over each salad.

Serves 4: Calories 333; Fat 21.7g (sat 5.8g, mono 11.1g, poly 2.8g); Protein 27g; Carb 9g; Fiber 5g; Sugars 3g (est. added sugars: 0g); Chol 154mg; Iron 3mg; Sodium 487mg; Calc 146mg

EGG SALAD SANDWICHES

CLASSIC: Calories per serving: 396, Sat Fat: 6.1g, Sodium: 755mg, Sugars: 3g
MAKEOVER: Calories per serving: 297, Sat Fat: 2.6g, Sodium: 591mg, Sugars: 5g

HANDS-ON: 30 MIN. TOTAL: 48 MIN.

Egg salad is a "salad" by name, but a typical homemade version can load on more than 23g fat and almost 900mg sodium.

6 large eggs
3 tablespoons water
3 tablespoons cider vinegar
2 teaspoons sugar
1/4 cup finely chopped celery
1/4 cup mashed ripe avocado
1 tablespoon canola mayonnaise
1 teaspoon fresh lemon juice
3/4 teaspoon Dijon mustard

1/2 teaspoon black pepper
3/8 teaspoon kosher salt
2 tablespoons dry-roasted, salted sunflower seeds
8 (1-ounce) slices whole-grain sunflower bread, toasted (such as Ezekiel)
1 cup baby arugula
4 heirloom tomato slices

SNEAK ATTACK
Mashed avocado replaces heavy mayo and adds creaminess and heart-healthy fat.

1. Add water to a large saucepan to a depth of 1 inch; set a large vegetable steamer in pan. Bring water to a boil over medium-high heat. Add eggs to steamer. Cover and steam eggs 16 minutes. Remove from heat. Place eggs in a large ice water–filled bowl.

2. While eggs cook, combine 3 tablespoons water, vinegar, and sugar in a medium microwave-safe bowl; microwave at HIGH 2 minutes or until boiling. Add celery; let stand 15 minutes. Drain.

3. Meanwhile, combine avocado, mayonnaise, juice, mustard, pepper, and salt in a medium bowl, stirring until smooth.

4. Peel eggs; discard shells. Slice eggs in half lengthwise; reserve 2 yolks for another use. Chop remaining eggs and egg whites. Gently stir eggs, celery, and sunflower seeds into avocado mixture. Top each of 4 bread slices with about 1/2 cup egg mixture, 1/4 cup arugula, 1 tomato slice, and 1 bread slice.

Serves 4 (serving size: 1 sandwich): Calories 297; Fat 12.3g (sat 2.6g, mono 4.7g, poly 4g); Protein 17g; Carb 29g; Fiber 6g; Sugars 5g (est. added sugars: 2g); Chol 186mg; Iron 3mg; Sodium 591mg; Calc 107mg

CREAMY CHICKEN SALAD

CLASSIC: Calories per serving: 748, Sat Fat: 8.1g, Sodium: 1161mg, Sugars: 14g
MAKEOVER: Calories per serving: 339, Sat Fat: 1.9g, Sodium: 525mg, Sugars: 9g

HANDS-ON: 24 MIN. TOTAL: 65 MIN.

Poaching the chicken keeps it moist and succulent, so you'll need less dressing to bind the salad.

2 pounds skinless, boneless chicken
  breast halves
½ cup light mayonnaise
½ cup plain fat-free Greek yogurt
1 tablespoon fresh lemon juice
1 tablespoon white wine vinegar
1 tablespoon Dijon mustard
1 teaspoon honey

½ teaspoon kosher salt
½ teaspoon freshly ground black
  pepper
⅓ cup chopped celery
⅓ cup sweetened dried cranberries
7 tablespoons (about 2 ounces)
  coarsely chopped smoked almonds
6 cups mixed salad greens

SECRET TO SUCCESS
We dress, not drown, the meat so you can actually taste the chicken.

1. Add water to a Dutch oven, filling two-thirds full; bring to a boil.

2. Wrap each chicken breast half completely and tightly in heavy-duty plastic wrap. Add chicken to boiling water. Cover and simmer 20 minutes or until a thermometer registers 165°. Remove from pan; let stand 5 minutes. Unwrap chicken; shred. Refrigerate 30 minutes or until cold.

3. Combine mayonnaise and next 7 ingredients (through black pepper) in a large bowl, stirring with a whisk until combined. Add chicken, celery, cranberries, and almonds; toss well to coat. Cover and refrigerate 1 hour. Serve over salad greens.

Serves 6 (serving size: about 1 cup chicken salad and 1 cup salad greens): Calories 339; Fat 13.6g (sat 1.9g, mono 5.1g, poly 5.1g); Protein 40g; Carb 15g; Fiber 3g; Sugars 9g (est. added sugars: 2g); Chol 95mg; Iron 2mg; Sodium 525mg; Calc 54mg

CHICKEN PICCATA

CLASSIC: Calories per serving: 496, Sat Fat: 13.8g, Sodium: 390mg, Sugars: 0g
MAKEOVER: Calories per serving: 372, Sat Fat: 6.5g, Sodium: 560mg, Sugars: 1g

HANDS-ON: 35 MIN. TOTAL: 35 MIN.

Plenty of white wine and lemon juice makes for a bright and robust sauce without all the butter in this classic Italian dish.

4 (6-ounce) skinless, boneless chicken breast halves
2.25 ounces all-purpose flour (about ½ cup), divided
½ teaspoon kosher salt
½ teaspoon dried Italian seasoning
¼ teaspoon freshly ground black pepper
2½ tablespoons butter, divided
1 tablespoon olive oil

¼ cup minced shallots
4 garlic cloves, thinly sliced
½ cup dry white wine
¾ cup fat-free, lower-sodium chicken broth
2 tablespoons coarsely chopped fresh flat-leaf parsley
2 tablespoons fresh lemon juice
1½ tablespoons drained capers

1. Place each chicken breast half between 2 sheets of heavy-duty plastic wrap; pound to ½-inch thickness using a meat mallet or small heavy skillet. Weigh or lightly spoon flour into a dry measuring cup; level with a knife. Remove 1 teaspoon flour, and place in a small bowl; set aside. Place remaining flour in a shallow dish. Sprinkle chicken with salt, Italian seasoning, and pepper. Dredge chicken in flour in shallow dish; discard remaining flour.

2. Melt 1 tablespoon butter in a large nonstick skillet over medium-high heat. Add oil to pan; swirl to coat. Add chicken to pan; cook 4 minutes on each side or until done. Remove chicken from pan; keep warm.

3. Add ½ tablespoon butter and shallots to drippings in pan; sauté 3 minutes. Add garlic; sauté 1 minute. Add wine; bring to a boil, scraping pan to loosen browned bits. Cook until reduced to 2 tablespoons (about 3 minutes), stirring occasionally. Sprinkle with reserved 1 teaspoon flour, and stir until smooth; stir in broth. Bring to a boil; cook until reduced to ½ cup (about 5 minutes). Remove from heat; stir in 1 tablespoon butter, parsley, lemon juice, and capers. Return chicken to pan, turning to coat with sauce.

Serves 4 (serving size: 1 chicken breast half and 2 tablespoons sauce): Calories 372; Fat 18.7g (sat 6.5g, mono 8.2g, poly 2g); Protein 38g; Carb 7g; Fiber 1g; Sugars 1g (est. added sugars: 0g); Chol 128mg; Iron 1mg; Sodium 560mg; Calc 21mg

EGGS BENEDICT

CLASSIC: Calories per serving: 824, Sat Fat: 42.6g, Sodium: 1108mg, Sugars: 1g
MAKEOVER: Calories per serving: 368, Sat Fat: 4g, Sodium: 610mg, Sugars: 5g

HANDS-ON: 30 MIN. TOTAL: 40 MIN.

The real kicker in this breakfast classic is the buttery, luscious hollandaise sauce. We lighten it up with a mixture of silken tofu and reduced-fat sour cream. When poaching eggs, choose the freshest possible; the whites adhere to the yolk better, making for an easier, cleaner poach.

½ cup white wine
3 tablespoons champagne vinegar, divided
¼ cup minced shallots
¼ teaspoons black peppercorns
6 ounces soft silken tofu
2 tablespoons reduced-fat sour cream
2 tablespoons fresh lemon juice
½ teaspoon Dijon mustard
½ teaspoon honey
¼ teaspoon ground turmeric
⅛ teaspoon ground red pepper
8 large eggs
4 whole-grain English muffins, split and toasted
8 (½-ounce) slices lower-sodium deli ham
¼ teaspoon freshly ground black pepper
⅛ teaspoon paprika

1. In a small skillet, bring wine, 2 tablespoons vinegar, shallots, and peppercorns to a boil; cook about 5 minutes or until liquid is reduced by half. Combine wine mixture, tofu, and next 6 ingredients (through red pepper) in a blender; process until smooth. Return tofu mixture to pan; cook over low heat 3 minutes or until warm, stirring constantly with a whisk.

2. Add water to a large skillet, filling two-thirds full; bring to a simmer. Add 1 tablespoon vinegar to pan. Break each egg into a custard cup, and pour each gently into pan; cook 3 minutes or until desired degree of doneness. Carefully remove eggs from pan using a slotted spoon. Keep warm.

3. Place 2 toasted English muffin halves on each of 4 plates; top each muffin half with 1 ham slice, 1 poached egg, and about 1 tablespoon sauce. Sprinkle with ground black pepper and paprika.

Serves 4 (serving size: 2 muffin halves): Calories 368; Fat 13.3g (sat 4g, mono 4.2g, poly 2.6g); Protein 26g; Carb 31g; Fiber 4g; Sugars 5g (est. added sugars: 2g); Chol 390mg; Iron 4mg; Sodium 610mg; Calc 169mg

SCOTCH EGGS

CLASSIC: Calories per serving: 825, Sat Fat: 16.8g, Sodium: 1208mg, Sugars: 2g
MAKEOVER: Calories per serving: 363, Sat Fat: 4.5g, Sodium: 470mg, Sugars: 3g

HANDS-ON: 25 MIN. TOTAL: 50 MIN.

Normally wrapped in ground pork and breadcrumbs and deep-fried, this recipe was begging for a lightened version.

6 large eggs, divided
1 (14-ounce) can brown or black lentils, drained
8 ounces lean ground pork
1/4 cup grated onion
1 tablespoon chopped fresh chives
2 teaspoons minced fresh sage
2 teaspoons minced fresh thyme
1 teaspoon Worcestershire sauce
1/2 teaspoon salt
1/2 teaspoon dry mustard
1/2 teaspoon freshly ground black pepper
1/8 teaspoon grated whole nutmeg
1 garlic clove, minced
1.1 ounces all-purpose flour (about 1/4 cup)
3/4 cup panko (Japanese breadcrumbs)
Cooking spray

SNEAK ATTACK
Adding mashed lentils to the pork mixture not only cuts down on fat and calories but also adds fiber and protein.

1. Preheat oven to 425°.

2. Place 4 eggs in a medium saucepan. Cover with cold water to 1 inch above eggs; bring just to a boil over medium-high heat. Remove from heat; cover and let stand 1 1/2 to 2 minutes. Remove eggs with a slotted spoon; place in ice water. Remove shells from eggs, and rinse with cold water until cool.

3. Place lentils in a medium bowl; mash with the back of a fork. Add pork and next 10 ingredients (through garlic); mash to desired consistency.

4. Divide pork mixture into 4 portions, shaping each into a 5-inch circle. Weigh or lightly spoon flour into a dry measuring cup; level with a knife. Place flour in a shallow dish. Place 1 cooked egg in flour, turning to coat. Place egg in the center of 1 pork circle. Carefully press pork mixture around egg until it is completely covered; seal well. Dredge in flour, rolling gently to smooth sides, if necessary. Repeat procedure with cooked eggs, flour, and pork mixture.

5. Place 2 eggs in a shallow dish; stir with a whisk. Place panko in a bowl. Dip each coated egg in beaten eggs; dredge in panko. Place coated eggs on a baking sheet, and coat with cooking spray. Bake at 425° for 25 minutes or until golden brown, turning after 12 minutes. Serve eggs hot or at room temperature.

Serves 4 (serving size: 1 Scotch egg): Calories 363; Fat 13g (sat 4.5g, mono 2.8g, poly 1.6g); Protein 31g; Carb 30g; Fiber 8g; Sugars 3g (est. added sugars: 1g); Chol 322mg; Iron 5mg; Sodium 470mg; Calc 68mg

SPINACH-BACON QUICHE

CLASSIC: Calories per serving: 594, Sat Fat: 22.6g, Sodium: 803mg, Sugars: 2g
MAKEOVER: Calories per serving: 317, Sat Fat: 5.6g, Sodium: 435mg, Sugars: 4g

HANDS-ON: 39 MIN. TOTAL: 1 HR. 30 MIN.

This quiche is a slice of heaven that's worthy of a starring role on your spring brunch menu.

5.6 ounces all-purpose flour (about
   1 cup plus 2 tablespoons)
¾ teaspoon kosher salt, divided
½ teaspoon freshly ground black
   pepper, divided
¼ teaspoon baking powder
¼ cup extra-virgin olive oil
3 tablespoons ice water
Cooking spray
3 center-cut bacon slices
¼ cup chopped shallots

2 teaspoons fresh thyme
1 (8-ounce) package presliced
   mushrooms
2 cups packed baby spinach
1 cup 1% low-fat milk
⅓ cup half-and-half
3 large eggs
1 large egg white
2 ounces cave-aged Gruyère cheese,
   grated (about ½ cup)

SECRET TO SUCCESS
A splash of half-and-half adds richness to a base of low-fat milk, without the need for heavy cream.

1. Preheat oven to 425°.

2. Weigh or lightly spoon flour into dry measuring cups; level with a knife. Combine flour, ¼ teaspoon salt, ¼ teaspoon pepper, and baking powder in a food processor; pulse 2 times to combine. Combine oil and 3 tablespoons ice water. With processor on, slowly add oil mixture through food chute; process until dough comes together. Turn dough out onto a lightly floured surface. Knead 1 minute. Press dough into a 5-inch disk; wrap in plastic wrap, and chill 20 minutes.

3. Roll dough into a 12-inch circle. Fit dough into a 9-inch deep-dish pie plate coated with cooking spray. Line dough with foil; arrange pie weights or dried beans on foil. Bake at 425° for 12 minutes or until edges are golden. Remove weights and foil; bake an additional 2 minutes. Cool on a wire rack.

4. Reduce oven temperature to 350°.

5. Cook bacon in a large skillet over medium-high heat until crisp. Remove bacon from pan, reserving drippings; crumble. Return pan to medium-high heat. Add shallots to drippings in pan; sauté 2 minutes. Add thyme and mushrooms; cook 10 minutes, stirring occasionally. Stir in spinach; cook 2 minutes or until spinach wilts. Remove from heat; let stand 10 minutes. Drain any excess liquid. Place milk, half-and-half, eggs, egg white, ½ teaspoon salt, and ¼ teaspoon pepper in a blender; process until smooth.

6. Arrange half of cheese over bottom of crust; top with spinach mixture and half of cheese. Carefully pour milk mixture over cheese. Sprinkle with bacon. Bake at 350° for 45 minutes or until filling is set. Let stand 10 minutes.

Serves 6 (serving size: 1 wedge): Calories 317; Fat 17.5g (sat 5.6g, mono 8.1g, poly 1.7g); Protein 13g; Carb 26g; Fiber 2g; Sugars 4g (est. added sugars: 0g); Chol 111mg; Iron 2mg; Sodium 435mg; Calc 217mg

SHRIMP AND GRITS

CLASSIC: Calories per serving: 615, Sat Fat: 16.6g, Sodium: 1795mg, Sugars: 5g
MAKEOVER: Calories per serving: 236, Sat Fat: 4.1g, Sodium: 583mg, Sugars: 2g

HANDS-ON: 32 MIN. TOTAL: 32 MIN.

No need to coat the shrimp in flour, since it's cooked in bacon and aromatics—
our healthy take on this Southern classic.

3 cups water
1 tablespoon butter
3/4 cup uncooked quick-cooking grits
2 ounces grated Parmesan cheese
  (about 1/2 cup)
5/8 teaspoon kosher salt, divided
3/4 teaspoon freshly ground black
  pepper, divided
2 center-cut bacon slices, chopped
1 cup chopped white onion
1 tablespoon minced garlic
1 (8-ounce) package presliced
  mushrooms
1 pound medium shrimp, peeled and
  deveined
1/2 teaspoon crushed red pepper
1/4 cup half-and-half
1 tablespoon all-purpose flour
3/4 cup fat-free, lower-sodium chicken
  broth
1/3 cup chopped green onions

1. Bring 3 cups water and butter to a boil in a small saucepan. Whisk in grits; cover and cook 5 minutes, stirring frequently. Remove from heat. Stir in cheese, 1/4 teaspoon salt, and 1/2 teaspoon black pepper; cover. Keep warm.

2. Cook bacon in a large nonstick skillet over medium-high heat until crisp. Add white onion, garlic, and mushrooms to pan; cook 8 minutes or until mushrooms begin to brown and give off liquid, stirring frequently. Add shrimp and red pepper; cook 3 minutes. Combine half-and-half and flour in a small bowl, stirring with a whisk until smooth. Add broth, flour mixture, 3/8 teaspoon salt, and 1/4 teaspoon black pepper to pan; bring to a boil. Cook 2 minutes or until slightly thick. Top with green onions. Serve shrimp mixture with grits.

Serves 6 (serving size: 1/2 cup grits and about 1/2 cup shrimp mixture): Calories 236; Fat 7.9g (sat 4.1g, mono 1.4g, poly 0.5g); Protein 18g; Carb 23g; Fiber 2g; Sugars 2g (est. added sugars: 0g); Chol 115mg; Iron 1mg; Sodium 583mg; Calc 173mg

TROUT AMANDINE

CLASSIC: Calories per serving: 479, Sat Fat: 12.9g, Sodium: 227mg, Sugars: 13g
MAKEOVER: Calories per serving: 374, Sat Fat: 5g, Sodium: 435mg, Sugars: 1g

HANDS-ON: 30 MIN. TOTAL: 30 MIN.

Doused in butter and coated in almonds, this classic French dish has been praised for its simplicity, grace in presentation, and flavor. Here, we've lightened it considerably by making the browned butter sauce with almond butter for the nutty richness.

2.25 ounces all-purpose flour (about ½ cup)
⅓ cup 1% low-fat milk
4 (5-ounce) trout fillets
¾ teaspoon kosher salt, divided
½ teaspoon freshly ground black pepper
1 tablespoon plus ½ teaspoon unsalted butter, divided

1 tablespoon olive oil
½ cup water
2 tablespoons unsalted creamy almond butter
1½ tablespoons fresh lemon juice
3 tablespoons sliced almonds, toasted
2 tablespoons minced fresh parsley

1. Place flour in a shallow dish. Place milk in a bowl. Sprinkle fish with ½ teaspoon salt and pepper. Dip fish in milk; dredge in flour. Discard any remaining milk and flour.

2. Heat a large nonstick skillet over medium heat. Add 1½ teaspoons butter and 1½ teaspoons oil to pan; swirl to coat. Add 2 fillets to pan; sauté 2 to 3 minutes on each side or until fish flakes easily when tested with a fork or until desired degree of doneness. Remove from pan, and keep warm. Repeat procedure with 1½ teaspoons butter, 1½ teaspoons oil, and 2 fillets.

3. Combine ½ cup water and almond butter in a small bowl; stir well with a whisk. Add to hot pan, and remove pan from heat. Add ½ teaspoon butter, stirring until butter melts. Stir in lemon juice and ¼ teaspoon salt. Drizzle almond butter sauce over fish; sprinkle with almonds and parsley.

Serves 4 (serving size: 1 fillet and about 2 tablespoons sauce): Calories 374; Fat 21.9g (sat 5g, mono 7.5g, poly 3.3g); Protein 32g; Carb 11g; Fiber 2g; Sugars 1g (est. added sugars: 0g); Chol 93mg; Iron 1mg; Sodium 435mg; Calc 70mg

CLASSIC ITALIAN PANINI WITH
PROSCIUTTO AND FRESH MOZZARELLA

CLASSIC: Calories per serving: 561, Sat Fat: 7.6g, Sodium: 1987mg, Sugars: 11g
MAKEOVER: Calories per serving: 316, Sat Fat: 4.8g, Sodium: 799mg, Sugars: 5g

HANDS-ON: 21 MIN. TOTAL: 21 MIN.

Use this recipe as a panini template, and customize it to your liking. Try different meats and cheeses like roast beef and provolone or sliced turkey and Swiss cheese. You can use the cast-iron skillet trick whenever you need to improvise a panini press.

1 (12-ounce) loaf French bread, cut in
  half horizontally
¼ cup reduced-fat mayonnaise
4 ounces shredded fresh mozzarella
  cheese, divided (about 1 cup)

2 tablespoons chopped fresh basil
2 plum tomatoes, thinly sliced
2 ounces very thinly sliced prosciutto
Cooking spray

1. Hollow out top and bottom halves of bread, leaving a ½-inch-thick shell; reserve torn bread for another use. Spread 2 tablespoons mayonnaise over cut side of each bread half. Sprinkle ½ cup cheese and basil on bottom half of loaf. Top with tomato slices, prosciutto, and ½ cup cheese. Cover with top half of loaf. Cut filled loaf crosswise into 4 pieces.

2. Heat a grill pan over medium heat. Coat pan with cooking spray. Add sandwiches to pan. Place a cast-iron or other heavy skillet on top of sandwiches; press gently to flatten sandwiches. Cook 3 minutes on each side or until bread is toasted (leave skillet on sandwiches while they cook). Remove from heat, and serve sandwiches immediately.

Serves 4 (serving size: 1 sandwich): Calories 316; Fat 10.6g (sat 4.8g, mono 2.3g, poly 1.9g); Protein 16g; Carb 40g; Fiber 2g; Sugars 5g (est. added sugars: 0g); Chol 31mg; Iron 3mg; Sodium 799mg; Calc 196mg

Seven-Layer Dip,
page 176

LESS-LOADED PARTY STARTERS & MORE

DEVILED EGGS
WITH PICKLED ONIONS

HANDS-ON: 20 MIN. TOTAL: 35 MIN.

We substitute Greek yogurt for some of the mayonnaise for a tangy, creamy, and rich deviled egg.

8 large eggs
¼ cup water
¼ cup cider vinegar
1 tablespoon sugar
¼ cup finely chopped red onion
2 tablespoons plain 2% reduced-fat
  Greek yogurt
2 tablespoons canola mayonnaise

2 teaspoons Dijon mustard
½ teaspoon Sriracha (hot chile sauce)
  or hot pepper sauce
¼ teaspoon freshly ground black
  pepper
⅛ teaspoon kosher salt
2 tablespoons finely chopped chives

1. Add water to a large saucepan to a depth of 1 inch; set a large vegetable steamer in pan. Add eggs to steamer. Bring water to a boil over medium-high heat. Steam eggs, covered, 16 minutes. Remove from heat. Place eggs in a large ice water–filled bowl for 3 minutes.

2. While eggs steam, combine ¼ cup water, vinegar, and sugar in a medium microwave-safe bowl; microwave at HIGH 2 minutes or until boiling. Stir in onion. Let stand at room temperature 15 minutes. Drain. Combine yogurt, mayonnaise, mustard, Sriracha, pepper, and salt in a medium bowl, stirring well to combine.

3. Peel eggs; discard shells. Slice eggs in half lengthwise. Add 6 yolks to yogurt mixture, reserving remaining yolks for another use. Mash with a fork until very smooth. Stir in 2 tablespoons red onion. Spoon mixture into egg white halves (about 1 tablespoon in each half). Garnish egg halves with remaining red onion and chives.

Serves 8 (serving size: 2 egg halves): Calories 76; Fat 4.8g (sat 1.2g, mono 2g, poly 1.1g); Protein 6g; Carb 2g; Fiber 0g; Sugars 1g (est. added sugars: 0g); Chol 140mg; Iron 1mg; Sodium 157mg; Calc 26mg

PARTY BEAN DIP
WITH BAKED TORTILLA CHIPS

CLASSIC: Calories per serving: 291, Sat Fat: 5.8g, Sodium: 572mg, Sugars: 5g
MAKEOVER: Calories per serving: 135, Sat Fat: 2.3g, Sodium: 393mg, Sugars: 2g

HANDS-ON: 15 MIN. TOTAL: 60 MIN.

Making your own tortilla chips helps manage fat levels. Organic refried beans may have at least half the sodium of conventional ones but can have a drier texture. We add a little lime juice to smooth out the beans and enhance the flavor. Using organic salsa also helps keep sodium in check. This bean dip comes together quickly for parties or as an appetizer course.

6 (8-inch) flour tortillas
Cooking spray
1/2 teaspoon paprika
2 teaspoons fresh lime juice
1/2 teaspoon ground cumin
1 (16-ounce) can organic refried beans
1 cup organic bottled salsa
2/3 cup frozen whole-kernel corn, thawed
1/4 cup chopped green onions
2 tablespoons chopped black olives
3 ounces preshredded 4-cheese Mexican-blend cheese (about 3/4 cup)
6 ounces light sour cream (about 3/4 cup)
2 tablespoons chopped fresh cilantro

1. Preheat oven to 350°.

2. Cut each tortilla into 8 wedges; arrange in single layers on 2 baking sheets. Lightly coat wedges with cooking spray; sprinkle with paprika. Bake at 350° for 15 minutes or until lightly browned and crisp. Cool.

3. Combine juice, cumin, and beans in a medium bowl, stirring until well combined. Spread mixture into an 11 x 7–inch glass or ceramic baking dish coated with cooking spray. Spread salsa over beans. Combine corn, onions, and olives; spoon corn mixture over salsa. Sprinkle cheese over corn mixture. Bake at 350° for 20 minutes or until bubbly. Let stand 10 minutes. Top with sour cream; sprinkle with cilantro. Serve with tortilla chips.

Serves 12 (serving size: 1/2 cup dip and 4 tortilla chips): Calories 135; Fat 3.8g (sat 2.3g, mono 0.1g, poly 0.1g); Protein 6g; Carb 21g; Fiber 4g; Sugars 2g (est. added sugars: 0g); Chol 11mg; Iron 0.9mg; Sodium 393mg; Calc 123mg

CHICKEN AND MUSHROOM
EMPANADAS

CLASSIC: Calories per serving: 496, Sat Fat: 13.2g, Sodium: 841mg, Sugars: 3g
MAKEOVER: Calories per serving: 309, Sat Fat: 4g, Sodium: 455mg, Sugars: 4g

HANDS-ON: 25 MIN. TOTAL: 1 HR. 45 MIN.

Food doesn't get much tastier than a deep-fried pocket of flaky dough filled with meaty, cheesy goodness. That's the joy of an empanada, a messy delicacy that's best with a dipping sauce and a mountain of napkins. The downside is that what seems like a snack-sized food can contain 500 calories and tons of salt and fat.

8 ounces all-purpose flour (about 1¾ cups)
1¼ teaspoons salt, divided
½ teaspoon baking powder
⅓ cup plus 1 teaspoon extra-virgin olive oil, divided
5 tablespoons very cold water
1 pound tomatillos, husks removed
6 garlic cloves, peeled and divided
2 jalapeño peppers, stemmed
Cooking spray
1 tablespoon fresh lime juice
½ teaspoon freshly ground black pepper, divided

½ teaspoon sugar
1 cup chopped onion
8 ounces ground chicken
4 ounces chopped mushrooms
1.5 ounces shredded cave-aged Gruyère cheese (about 6 tablespoons)
1 ounce shredded Monterey Jack cheese (about ¼ cup)
1 large egg, lightly beaten
1 teaspoon water

1. Preheat oven to 450°.

2. Weigh or lightly spoon flour into dry measuring cups; level with a knife. Combine flour, ¾ teaspoon salt, and baking powder in a food processor; pulse to combine. Combine ⅓ cup oil and 5 tablespoons water. With processor on, slowly add oil mixture through food chute; process until dough is crumbly. Turn dough out onto a lightly floured surface. Knead 1 minute; add additional flour, if necessary, to prevent dough from sticking. Gently press dough into a 5-inch disk; wrap in plastic wrap, and chill at least 30 minutes.

3. Arrange tomatillos, 4 garlic cloves, and jalapeños in a single layer on a baking sheet coated with cooking spray; lightly coat vegetables with cooking spray. Bake at 450° for 25 minutes or until charred. Combine tomatillo mixture, juice, ¼ teaspoon salt, ¼ teaspoon black pepper, and sugar in a blender; pulse until finely chopped, scraping sides.

4. Reduce oven temperature to 400°.

5. Heat a large nonstick skillet over medium heat. Add 1 teaspoon oil to pan; swirl to coat. Add onion; sauté 5 minutes or until tender. Chop 2 garlic cloves. Add garlic to pan; sauté 1 minute. Add chicken and mushrooms; cook 6 minutes or until chicken is browned, stirring to crumble. Cool slightly. Add ½ cup tomatillo sauce, ¼ teaspoon salt, ¼ teaspoon black pepper, and cheeses, stirring well to combine.

6. Combine egg and 1 teaspoon water in a small bowl, stirring well with a whisk. Remove dough from refrigerator; let stand 5 minutes. Divide dough into 8 equal portions, shaping each into a ball. Roll each dough portion into a 6-inch circle on a lightly floured surface. Working with 1 portion at a time (cover remaining dough to keep from drying), spoon 3 tablespoons chicken mixture into center of each circle. Moisten edges of dough with egg mixture; fold dough over filling. Press edges together with a fork to seal. Brush remaining egg mixture over empanadas. Place empanadas on a parchment-lined baking sheet coated with cooking spray. Bake at 400° for 24 minutes or until lightly browned. Serve immediately with tomatillo sauce.

Serves 8 (serving size: 1 empanada and 1 tablespoon sauce): Calories 309; Fat 16.3g (sat 4g, mono 9.2g, poly 2.1g); Protein 12g; Carb 29g; Fiber 3g; Sugars 4g (est. added sugars: 0g); Chol 57mg; Iron 2mg; Sodium 455mg; Calc 121mg

PICKLED "FRIED" GREEN TOMATOES WITH
BUTTERMILK-HERB DIPPING SAUCE

CLASSIC: Calories per serving: 574, Sat Fat: 5.4g, Sodium: 717mg, Sugars: 7g
MAKEOVER: Calories per serving: 154, Sat Fat: 0.9g, Sodium: 215mg, Sugars: 4g

HANDS-ON: 37 MIN. TOTAL: 40 MIN.

Coating the tomatoes with cooking spray helps the breading mixture adhere and allows you to use less oil in the pan for crisping.

1 cup water
1 cup cider vinegar
2 tablespoons sugar
3/4 teaspoon kosher salt, divided
16 (1/4-inch-thick) slices green tomato
7 tablespoons nonfat buttermilk, divided
2 tablespoons finely chopped fresh basil
3 tablespoons canola mayonnaise
1 teaspoon finely chopped fresh thyme
2 teaspoons cider vinegar

1 garlic clove, minced
1/2 teaspoon freshly ground black pepper, divided
3/4 cup panko (Japanese breadcrumbs)
1/3 cup masa harina
1 large egg
1 large egg white
1.1 ounces all-purpose flour (1/4 cup)
3 tablespoons extra-virgin olive oil, divided

1. Combine 1 cup water, 1 cup vinegar, sugar, and 1/2 teaspoon salt in a medium saucepan; bring to a boil. Add tomatoes; cook 2 minutes. Remove from heat; let stand 15 minutes, stirring occasionally. Drain tomatoes; pat dry.

2. Combine 5 tablespoons buttermilk and next 5 ingredients (through garlic), stirring with a whisk. Stir in 1/4 teaspoon pepper.

3. Heat a large skillet over medium heat. Add panko to pan; cook 2 minutes or until toasted, stirring frequently. Remove from heat; stir in masa harina, 1/4 teaspoon salt, and 1/4 teaspoon pepper. Place panko mixture in a shallow dish. Combine 2 tablespoons buttermilk, egg, and egg white, stirring with a whisk. Place flour in another shallow dish. Dredge tomato slices in flour; dip in egg mixture, and dredge in panko mixture, turning to coat.

4. Heat a large nonstick skillet over medium-high heat. Add 1 tablespoon oil to pan; swirl to coat. Add half of tomatoes; cook 4 minutes. Coat tops of tomatoes with cooking spray. Turn; add 1 1/2 teaspoons oil to pan. Cook 4 minutes or until golden. Repeat procedure with 1 1/2 tablespoons oil, tomatoes, and cooking spray. Serve with sauce.

Serves 8 (serving size: 2 tomato slices and about 1 tablespoon sauce): Calories 154; Fat 7.7g (sat 0.9g, mono 4.8g, poly 1.2g); Protein 4g; Carb 16g; Fiber 1g; Sugars 4g (est. added sugars: 2g); Chol 23mg; Iron 1mg; Sodium 215mg; Calc 41mg

CHEESY SAUSAGE BALLS

CLASSIC: Calories per serving: 122, Sat Fat: 3.6g, Sodium: 265mg, Sugars: 0g
MAKEOVER: Calories per serving: 85, Sat Fat: 2.1g, Sodium: 175mg, Sugars: 0g

HANDS-ON: 10 MIN. TOTAL: 30 MIN.

To make ahead, cover and refrigerate unbaked balls up to 24 hours; or place in a heavy-duty zip-top plastic bag and freeze unbaked balls up to one month. Bake frozen balls at 375° for 22 to 25 minutes or until done.

1 pound reduced-fat pork sausage
4 ounces reduced-fat sharp cheddar
  cheese, shredded (about 1 cup)
1 cup cooked quinoa, chilled

1 tablespoon cornstarch
¼ teaspoon black pepper
Cooking spray

1. Preheat oven to 375°.

2. Combine first 5 ingredients in a bowl. Shape mixture into 40 (1½-inch) balls. Place balls on a foil-lined baking sheet coated with cooking spray. Bake at 375° for 18 minutes or until lightly browned and done.

Serves 20 (serving size: 2 sausage balls): Calories 85; Fat 5.3g (sat 2.1g, mono 2.1g, poly 0.5g); Protein 6g; Carb 3g; Fiber 0g; Sugars 0g (est. added sugars: 0g); Chol 17mg; Iron 1mg; Sodium 175mg; Calc 53mg

STUFFED MUSHROOMS

CLASSIC: Calories per serving: 178, Sat Fat: 3.9g, Sodium: 315mg, Sugars: 2g
MAKEOVER: Calories per serving: 69, Sat Fat: 0.5g, Sodium: 132mg, Sugars: 1g

HANDS-ON: 20 MIN. TOTAL: 42 MIN.

These delightful party bites are a shift from the normally sausage-laden party fare of legend. Whole-grain rice mix adds richness and a meaty texture to the filling.

24 whole button mushrooms (about 16 ounces)
1 (8.5-ounce) pouch microwaveable precooked seven whole-grains mix
1 teaspoon canola oil
½ cup packed baby spinach leaves, finely chopped
¼ cup finely chopped Vidalia or other sweet onion
¼ cup finely chopped red bell pepper
¼ teaspoon kosher salt
¼ teaspoon freshly ground black pepper
2 tablespoons crumbled feta cheese
1 large egg, lightly beaten
Cooking spray
½ cup panko (Japanese breadcrumbs)

1. Preheat oven to 350°.

2. Clean mushrooms, and remove stems. Finely chop mushroom stems; set aside mushroom caps.

3. Microwave whole-grains mix according to package directions; place in a medium bowl.

4. Heat oil in a large nonstick skillet over medium-high heat. Add chopped mushroom stems, spinach, and next 4 ingredients (through black pepper); sauté 8 minutes or until liquid evaporates. Add spinach mixture to whole-grains mix, and stir in cheese. Cool 5 minutes. Stir in egg.

5. Coat mushroom caps with cooking spray; place on a baking sheet coated with cooking spray. Spoon about 1 heaping tablespoon whole-grains mixture into each mushroom cap; top with panko, and lightly coat with cooking spray. Bake at 350° for 22 to 25 minutes or until panko is golden and filling is warm. Serve immediately.

Serves 12 (serving size: 2 stuffed mushrooms): Calories 69; Fat 1.8g (sat 0.5g, mono 0.5g, poly 0.2g); Protein 3g; Carb 11g; Fiber 1g; Sugars 1g (est. added sugars: 0g); Chol 17mg; Iron 1mg; Sodium 132mg; Calc 22mg

ROASTED
RED PEPPER DIP

CLASSIC: Calories per serving: 280, Sat Fat: 3.7g, Sodium: 57mg, Sugars: 2g
MAKEOVER: Calories per serving: 96, Sat Fat: 1.1g, Sodium: 129mg, Sugars: 1g

HANDS-ON: 10 MIN. TOTAL: 10 MIN.

Upping the pepper quantity cuts calories–160 of them. Whole-grain bread thickens and bulks the dip with less fat-filled cheese. Serve with sliced rainbow carrots.

1 cup roasted red bell peppers
2 tablespoons toasted almonds
2 tablespoons grated Parmesan
  cheese
1 ounce whole-grain bread

1 tablespoon olive oil
1 tablespoon sherry vinegar
1 tablespoon water
¼ teaspoon smoked paprika
1 garlic clove

1. Place all ingredients in a food processor; process until smooth.

Serves 4 (serving size: ¼ cup): Calories 96; Fat 6.3g (sat 1.1g, mono 4g, poly 1g); Protein 3g; Carb 7g; Fiber 2g; Sugars 1g
(est. added sugars: 0g); Chol 2mg; Iron 1mg; Sodium 129mg; Calc 68mg

SEVEN-LAYER DIP

HANDS-ON: 45 MIN. TOTAL: 45 MIN.

Loaded with fresh veggies and reduced-fat cheeses, this festive dip will make you the most popular person at the party.

1/4 cup water
3/4 teaspoon salt, divided
1 (16-ounce) can reduced-sodium black beans, rinsed and drained
1/2 cup chopped fresh cilantro, divided
1/4 cup finely chopped red onion
1/4 cup fresh lime juice, divided
1 tablespoon olive oil
1/2 teaspoon freshly ground black pepper, divided
4 plum tomatoes, chopped
2 ripe peeled avocados, halved

2 cups fresh corn kernels
1 cup light sour cream
2 teaspoons chili powder
1 teaspoon ground cumin
1.3 ounces shredded reduced-fat Monterey Jack cheese with jalapeño peppers (about 1/3 cup)
1.3 ounces shredded reduced-fat sharp cheddar cheese (about 1/3 cup)
1/4 cup finely sliced jalapeño pepper
1/4 cup thinly sliced green onions

1. Combine 1/4 cup water, 1/8 teaspoon salt, and beans in a medium saucepan over medium-low heat. Cook 7 minutes, stirring frequently and mashing beans with a wooden spoon until almost smooth. Spread bean mixture in a 2-quart baking dish; cool 5 minutes.

2. Combine 1/4 cup cilantro, onion, 2 tablespoons lime juice, oil, 1/4 teaspoon black pepper, 1/8 teaspoon salt, and tomato; sprinkle over bean mixture.

3. Combine 1/4 cup cilantro, 2 tablespoons lime juice, 1/2 teaspoon salt, 1/8 teaspoon black pepper, and avocado in a bowl; mash with a fork to desired consistency. Spread avocado mixture over tomato mixture; sprinkle with corn.

4. Combine sour cream, chili powder, and cumin; spread over corn. Sprinkle with cheeses, jalapeño pepper, and green onions. Serve immediately, or cover and chill.

Serves 18 (serving size: about 1/3 cup): Calories 106; Fat 6.7g (sat 2.2g, mono 2.8g, poly 0.6g); Protein 4g; Carb 10g; Fiber 3g; Sugars 3g (est. added sugars: 0g); Chol 10mg; Iron 1mg; Sodium 193mg; Calc 52mg

HARD CIDER FONDUE

CLASSIC: Calories per serving: 369, Sat Fat: 15.8g, Sodium: 245mg, Sugars: 1g
MAKEOVER: Calories per serving: 75, Sat Fat: 2.2g, Sodium: 214mg, Sugars: 1g

HANDS-ON: 15 MIN. TOTAL: 50 MIN.

Typically, fondue is a nutritional liability–just a bowl of melted cheese eaten with calorie-dense foods. Here we've supplemented some of the cheese with millet cream, a mild yet creamy base that will not break or seize like a traditional fondue can. Serve this fondue with crudités, whole-grain bread, and fruit.

MILLET CREAM:
2 cups water

½ cup uncooked millet

1 cup 2% reduced-fat milk

HARD CIDER–SWISS FONDUE:
1 (12-ounce) bottle hard cider

1 teaspoon salt

3 ounces shredded Gruyère cheese
   (about ¾ cup)

3 ounces shredded reduced-fat sharp
   white cheddar cheese (about ¾ cup)

1. To prepare millet cream, bring 2 cups water and millet to a boil in a medium saucepan; cover, reduce heat, and simmer 30 minutes. Remove from heat; let stand 5 minutes. Pour mixture into a blender; add milk. Remove center piece of blender lid (to allow steam to escape); secure blender lid on blender. Place a clean towel over opening in blender lid (to avoid splatters). Blend until smooth (about 3 minutes).

2. To prepare fondue, bring hard cider to a boil in a medium saucepan. Cook until reduced to ¾ cup (about 10 minutes). Add 1⅓ cups millet cream and salt, stirring with a whisk. Reserve remaining millet cream for another use. Reduce heat to low; add cheeses, stirring until cheeses melt. Serve immediately.

Serves 14 (serving size: ¼ cup): Calories 75; Fat 3.6g (sat 2.2g, mono 0.7g, poly 0.2g); Protein 4g; Carb 4g; Fiber 0g; Sugars 1g (est. added sugars: 0g); Chol 12mg; Iron 0mg; Sodium 214mg; Calc 116mg

MEDITERRANEAN CHEESE BALL

CLASSIC: Calories per serving: 149, Sat Fat: 5.8g, Sodium: 189mg, Sugars: 1g
MAKEOVER: Calories per serving: 58, Sat Fat: 2.1g, Sodium: 186mg, Sugars: 1g

HANDS-ON: 12 MIN. TOTAL: 42 MIN.

This cheese ball uses canned beans instead of a calorie-laden, creamy cheese as a binder for a delicious and colorful appetizer. Further cut calories and fat by serving with vegetable crudités instead of crackers or chips. Plenty of vegetables and herbs keep the flavor fresh and intense, so a little goes a long way.

8 ounces feta cheese, patted dry and crumbled (about 2 cups)

1 cup rinsed and drained canned chickpeas

2 ounces 1/3-less-fat cream cheese (about 1/4 cup)

1/2 cup finely chopped red bell pepper

1 1/2 teaspoons grated lemon rind, divided

2 tablespoons chopped fresh oregano

1 tablespoon chopped fresh parsley

1/4 teaspoon freshly ground black pepper

6 pitted kalamata olives, chopped

1 cup whole-wheat panko, toasted

Assorted fresh vegetables and crackers

1. Combine first 3 ingredients in a food processor; pulse 5 to 6 times or until mixture is blended but not completely smooth. Transfer cheese mixture to a medium bowl; fold in bell pepper, 1 teaspoon rind, and next 4 ingredients (through olives). Form cheese mixture into a ball, using a rubber spatula.

2. Combine toasted panko and 1/2 teaspoon rind on a large plate. Gently roll cheese ball in panko, coating well. Discard remaining panko. Chill 30 minutes. Serve with assorted fresh vegetables and crackers.

Serves 20 (serving size: 2 tablespoons): Calories 58; Fat 3.5g (sat 2.1g, mono 0.7g, poly 0.2g); Protein 3g; Carb 4g; Fiber 1g; Sugars 1g (est. added sugars: 0g); Chol 12mg; Iron 0mg; Sodium 186mg; Calc 67mg

GRILLED VEGETABLE
GUACAMOLE

CLASSIC: Calories per serving: 284, Sat Fat: 3.6g, Sodium: 604mg, Sugars: 3g
MAKEOVER: Calories per serving: 80, Sat Fat: 0.8g, Sodium: 165mg, Sugars: 2g

HANDS-ON: 20 MIN. TOTAL: 30 MIN.

Although avocados are loaded with potassium and healthful monounsaturated fats, the calories can add up quickly when dipping. Stretching out the avocado with grilled vegetables is an excellent way to push the calories further.

2 medium-sized red, orange, yellow, or green bell peppers
1 large red onion, cut into ¼-inch-thick slices
1 large jalapeño pepper
1 tablespoon canola oil
1 teaspoon kosher salt, divided
Cooking spray
¼ cup chopped fresh cilantro
3 tablespoons fresh lime juice
2 ripe avocados, pitted and cut into chunks
2 plum tomatoes, diced
Baked tortilla chips (optional)

1. Preheat grill to medium-high heat.

2. Cut bell peppers in quarters; discard seeds and membranes. Place pepper quarters, onion slices, and jalapeño pepper on a large jelly-roll pan; drizzle with oil, and sprinkle with ¼ teaspoon salt. Place bell pepper quarters, onion slices, and jalapeño pepper on grill rack coated with cooking spray. Grill 8 to 10 minutes or until bell pepper quarters and onion slices are crisp-tender and jalapeño pepper is blistered, turning after 4 minutes. Remove vegetables from grill; cool slightly.

3. Coarsely chop bell pepper quarters and onion slices; place in a medium bowl. Cut jalapeño pepper in half; discard seeds. Finely chop jalapeño pepper; add to bowl. Stir in cilantro, lime juice, avocado, and ¾ teaspoon salt; stir gently, mashing avocado to desired consistency. Fold in diced tomato, and serve with baked tortilla chips, if desired.

Serves 12 (serving size: ¼ cup guacamole): Calories 80; Fat 6.2g (sat 0.8g, mono 4g, poly 0.1g); Protein 1g; Carb 6g; Fiber 3g; Sugars 2g (est. added sugars: 0g); Chol 0mg; Iron 0mg; Sodium 165mg; Calc 10mg

CARNE ASADA PIZZA

CLASSIC: Calories per serving: 736, Sat Fat: 17.9g, Sodium: 1070mg, Sugars: 10g
MAKEOVER: Calories per serving: 419, Sat Fat: 4.8g, Sodium: 685mg, Sugars: 4g

HANDS-ON: 40 MIN. TOTAL: 1 HR. 15 MIN.

This beefy pie delivers all the zingy flavors of a street taco: tangy lime, fragrant cilantro, and smoky chiles.

12 ounces refrigerated fresh pizza dough
2 small poblano peppers
8 ounces flank steak, trimmed
½ teaspoon ground cumin
½ teaspoon chipotle chile powder
⅛ teaspoon salt
Cooking spray
1 small red onion, cut into ½-inch-thick rings
½ cup lower-sodium marinara sauce
1 tablespoon adobo sauce from 1 can chipotle chiles in adobo sauce

1 tablespoon cornmeal
1 ounce part-skim mozzarella cheese, shredded (about ¼ cup)
1 ounce cheddar cheese, shredded (about ¼ cup)
1 ounce queso fresco, crumbled (about ¼ cup)
1 cup chopped seeded tomato
2 tablespoons fresh lime juice
2 tablespoons minced red onion
Cilantro sprigs (optional)

1. Remove dough from refrigerator. Let stand at room temperature, covered, 30 minutes.

2. Preheat broiler. Arrange poblanos on a foil-lined baking sheet. Broil 8 minutes or until charred on all sides, turning occasionally. Wrap peppers in foil; close tightly. Let stand 15 minutes. Peel and seed peppers; discard skin, membrane, and seeds. Cut into ¼-inch-thick strips. Place a pizza stone or heavy baking sheet in oven. Preheat oven to 500° (keep pizza stone or baking sheet in oven as it preheats).

3. Sprinkle steak with cumin, chipotle powder, and salt. Heat a grill pan over high heat. Coat pan with cooking spray. Add steak to pan; cook 4 minutes on each side or until well marked. Let stand 10 minutes. Thinly slice steak across the grain.

4. Add onion rings to pan; grill 4 minutes on each side or until well marked. Place in a bowl; cover with plastic wrap. Combine marinara and adobo sauce. Roll dough into a 15 x 9–inch rectangle on a lightly floured surface. Pierce dough liberally with a fork. Sprinkle cornmeal on pizza stone. Place dough on hot stone; bake at 500° for 5 minutes. Remove stone from oven. Spread sauce mixture over dough, leaving a ½-inch border; top with mozzarella and cheddar. Arrange poblano and onion slices over pizza; top with steak. Sprinkle with queso fresco. Return stone to oven; bake pizza 9 minutes or until crust is done.

5. Combine tomato, juice, and minced red onion; sprinkle tomato mixture over pizza. Top with cilantro sprigs, if desired.

Serves 4 (serving size: 2 slices): Calories 419; Fat 10.2g (sat 4.8g, mono 3.7g, poly 1g); Protein 26g; Carb 54g; Fiber 9g; Sugars 4g (est. added sugars: 0g); Chol 49mg; Iron 3mg; Sodium 685mg; Calc 153mg

PIZZA SUPREME

CLASSIC: Calories per serving: 746, Sat Fat: 18g, Sodium: 1789mg, Sugars: 10g
MAKEOVER: Calories per serving: 344, Sat Fat: 4.1g, Sodium: 640mg, Sugars: 3g

HANDS-ON: 15 MIN. TOTAL: 30 MIN.

Purchase fresh pizza dough from your supermarket's bakery section. Or you may be able to swing by your favorite pizza parlor and pick some up. Turkey sausage adds meaty flavor with less fat and fewer calories. Fresh mozzarella cheese adds melty goodness with less sodium than preshredded.

1 pound refrigerated fresh pizza dough
Cooking spray
2 teaspoons olive oil
1 (4-ounce) link turkey Italian sausage
1 cup sliced mushrooms
1 cup thinly sliced red bell pepper
1 cup thinly sliced orange bell pepper

1 cup thinly sliced onion
¼ teaspoon crushed red pepper
3 garlic cloves, thinly sliced
¾ cup lower-sodium marinara sauce
5 ounces fresh mozzarella cheese,
  thinly sliced

1. Preheat oven to 500°.

2. Roll dough into a 14-inch circle on a lightly floured surface. Place dough on a 14-inch pizza pan or baking sheet coated with cooking spray.

3. Heat olive oil in a large nonstick skillet over medium-high heat. Remove casing from sausage link. Add sausage to pan; cook 2 minutes, stirring to crumble. Add mushrooms, bell peppers, onion, crushed red pepper, and garlic; sauté 4 minutes, stirring occasionally.

4. Spread sauce over dough, leaving a 1-inch border. Arrange cheese over sauce. Arrange turkey mixture over cheese. Bake at 500° for 15 minutes or until crust and cheese are browned.

Serves 6 (serving size: 2 wedges): Calories 344; Fat 11.3g (sat 4.1g, mono 3.9g, poly 1.8g); Protein 14g; Carb 53g; Fiber 2g; Sugars 3g (est. added sugars: 0g); Chol 31mg; Iron 3mg; Sodium 640mg; Calc 132mg

PEPPERONI
DEEP-DISH PIZZA

CLASSIC: Calories per serving: 693, Sat Fat: 18.8g, Sodium: 1339mg, Sugars: 6g
MAKEOVER: Calories per serving: 404, Sat Fat: 5.9g, Sodium: 607mg, Sugars: 3g

HANDS-ON: 20 MIN. TOTAL: 26 HR.

A homemade dough and pizza sauce keep sodium in check.

1 cup warm water (100° to 110°), divided
12 ounces bread flour (about 2 ½ cups)
1 package dry yeast (about 2 ¼ teaspoons)
4 teaspoons olive oil
½ teaspoon kosher salt
Cooking spray

5 ounces part-skim mozzarella cheese (about 1 ¼ cups), shredded and divided
1 ½ cups Basic Pizza Sauce
2 ounces pepperoni slices
2 tablespoons grated Parmigiano-Reggiano cheese

1. Pour ¾ cup warm water in the bowl of a stand mixer with dough hook attached. Weigh or lightly spoon flour into dry measuring cups; level with a knife. Add flour to ¾ cup water; beat until combined. Cover and let stand 20 minutes. Combine ¼ cup water and yeast in a small bowl; let stand 5 minutes or until bubbly. Add yeast mixture, oil, and salt to flour mixture; beat 5 minutes or until a soft dough forms. Place dough in a large bowl coated with cooking spray; cover surface of dough with plastic wrap lightly coated with cooking spray. Refrigerate 24 hours.

2. Remove dough from refrigerator. Let stand, covered, 1 hour or until dough comes to room temperature. Punch dough down. Roll dough into a 14 x 11–inch rectangle on a lightly floured surface. Press dough into bottom and partially up sides of a 13 x 9–inch metal baking pan coated with cooking spray. Cover dough loosely with plastic wrap.

3. Place a baking sheet in oven on bottom rack. Preheat oven to 450° (leave pan in oven as it preheats).

4. Arrange ¾ cup mozzarella over dough; top with Basic Pizza Sauce, pepperoni slices, Parmigiano-Reggiano, and ½ cup mozzarella. Place pan on baking sheet in oven; bake at 450° for 25 minutes or until crust is golden. Cut pizza into 6 rectangles.

Serves 6 (serving size: 1 rectangle): Calories 404; Fat 16.3g (sat 5.9g, mono 7.8g, poly 1.5g); Protein 17g; Carb 47g; Fiber 3g; Sugars 3g (est. added sugars: 0g); Chol 26mg; Iron 4mg; Sodium 607mg; Calc 244mg

BASIC PIZZA SAUCE:

HANDS-ON: 3 MIN. TOTAL: 35 MIN.

2 tablespoons extra-virgin olive oil
5 garlic cloves, minced
1 (28-ounce) can San Marzano
  tomatoes, undrained

½ teaspoon kosher salt
½ teaspoon dried oregano

1. Heat oil in a medium saucepan over medium heat. Add garlic to pan; cook 1 minute, stirring frequently. Remove tomatoes from can using a slotted spoon, reserving juices. Crush tomatoes. Stir tomatoes, juices, salt, and oregano into garlic mixture; bring to a boil. Reduce heat, and simmer 30 minutes, stirring occasionally.

THREE-CHEESE WHITE PIZZA
WITH FRESH ARUGULA

HANDS-ON: 20 MIN. TOTAL: 40 MIN.

Try this trick to get ultrathin fresh mozzarella slices: Pat mozzarella ball dry, and place in the freezer for about 30 minutes. You'll be able to cut paper-thin slices, which allow for more creamy, cheesy coverage.

12 ounces refrigerated fresh pizza dough
2 teaspoons extra-virgin olive oil
6 garlic cloves, crushed
2/3 cup fat-free ricotta cheese
2 tablespoons canola mayonnaise
2 teaspoons chopped fresh thyme
1/4 teaspoon freshly ground black pepper

1.5 ounces Parmigiano-Reggiano cheese, finely shredded (about 1/3 cup)
3 ounces fresh mozzarella cheese, very thinly sliced
1 teaspoon fresh lemon juice
1 teaspoon balsamic vinegar
1 1/2 cups baby arugula

1. Remove dough from refrigerator. Let stand at room temperature, covered, 20 minutes.

2. Place a pizza stone or heavy baking sheet in oven on middle rack. Preheat oven to 500°. Preheat pizza stone for 30 minutes before baking dough.

3. Heat a small skillet over medium heat. Add oil to pan; swirl to coat. Add garlic; cook 2 minutes or until garlic is lightly browned. Remove garlic with a slotted spoon. Finely chop garlic. Reserve oil.

4. Place chopped garlic, ricotta, mayonnaise, thyme, pepper, and Parmigiano-Reggiano cheese in a medium bowl. Beat with a mixer at medium-high speed until almost smooth (about 2 minutes).

5. Roll dough into a 14-inch circle on a lightly floured surface; pierce surface of dough liberally with a fork. Carefully remove pizza stone from oven. Arrange dough on pizza stone. Bake at 500° for 5 minutes. Spread ricotta mixture over crust, leaving a 1/2-inch border. Arrange mozzarella over ricotta mixture. Bake at 500° for 10 minutes or until crust and cheese are browned.

6. Combine reserved oil, juice, and vinegar in a medium bowl. Add arugula; toss to coat. Top pizza with arugula mixture. Cut pizza into 4 large pieces.

Serves 4 (serving size: 1 piece): Calories 402; Fat 13.3g (sat 5.2g, mono 4.6g, poly 1.5g); Protein 19g; Carb 46g; Fiber 6g; Sugars 2g (est. added sugars: 0g); Chol 31mg; Iron 1mg; Sodium 688mg; Calc 321mg

PIZZA MARGHERITA

CLASSIC: Calories per serving: 508, Sat Fat: 10.2g, Sodium: 1063mg, Sugars: 2g
MAKEOVER: Calories per serving: 360, Sat Fat: 4.9g, Sodium: 424mg, Sugars: 2g

HANDS-ON: 28 MIN. TOTAL: 26 HR. 20 MIN.

Because this classic Neapolitan-style pizza is so simple, it depends on quality ingredients like fresh basil and mozzarella. Making a homemade pizza sauce drastically reduces the sodium.

1 cup warm water (100° to 110°), divided
10 ounces bread flour (about 2 cups
    plus 2 tablespoons)
1 package dry yeast (about
    2 1/4 teaspoons)
4 teaspoons olive oil
3/4 teaspoon kosher salt, divided

Cooking spray
1 tablespoon yellow cornmeal
3/4 cup Basic Pizza Sauce
    (see page 187)
5 ounces thinly sliced fresh mozzarella
    cheese (about 1 1/4 cups)
1/3 cup small fresh basil leaves

1. Pour 3/4 cup warm water in the bowl of a stand mixer with dough hook attached. Weigh or lightly spoon flour into dry measuring cups and spoons; level with a knife. Add flour to 3/4 cup water; beat until combined. Cover and let stand 20 minutes. Combine 1/4 cup water and yeast in a small bowl; let stand 5 minutes or until bubbly. Add yeast mixture, oil, and 1/2 teaspoon salt to flour mixture; beat 5 minutes or until a soft dough forms. Place dough in a large bowl coated with cooking spray; cover surface of dough with plastic wrap lightly coated with cooking spray. Refrigerate 24 hours.

2. Remove dough from refrigerator. Let stand, covered, 1 hour or until dough comes to room temperature. Punch dough down. Press dough into a 12-inch circle on a lightly floured baking sheet, without raised sides, sprinkled with cornmeal. Crimp edges to form a 1/2-inch border. Cover dough loosely with plastic wrap.

3. Place a pizza stone in oven on bottom rack. Preheat oven to 550°. Preheat pizza stone for 30 minutes before baking dough.

4. Remove plastic wrap from dough. Sprinkle dough with 1/4 teaspoon salt. Spread Basic Pizza Sauce over dough, leaving a 1/2-inch border. Arrange cheese over pizza. Slide pizza onto preheated pizza stone, using a spatula as a guide. Bake at 550° for 11 minutes or until crust is golden. Cut pizza into 10 wedges; sprinkle with basil leaves.

Serves 5 (serving size: 2 wedges): Calories 360; Fat 13.6g (sat 4.9g, mono 4.4g, poly 1g); Protein 13g; Carb 46g; Fiber 2g; Sugars 2g (est. added sugars: 0g); Chol 23mg; Iron 2mg; Sodium 424mg; Calc 17mg

BBQ CHICKEN AND BLUE CHEESE PIZZA

HANDS-ON: 10 MIN. TOTAL: 20 MIN.

For a kid-friendly pie, substitute fresh mozzarella for the blue cheese.

1 (8-ounce) prebaked thin pizza crust
1/3 cup barbecue sauce
1 1/2 cups shredded skinless, boneless rotisserie chicken breast
1/2 cup vertically sliced red onion
1/2 cup coarsely chopped yellow bell pepper

2 ounces crumbled blue cheese (about 1/2 cup)
2 plum tomatoes, thinly sliced (about 1/4 pound)

1. Preheat oven to 500°.

2. Place pizza crust on a baking sheet. Spread sauce over crust, leaving a 1/2-inch border. Top with chicken and remaining ingredients. Place baking sheet in oven on middle rack. Bake at 500° for 10 minutes or until cheese melts and crust is crisp. Cut into 12 wedges.

Serves 6 (serving size: 2 wedges): Calories 252; Fat 8.5g (sat 3.1g, mono 2.2g, poly 2.7g); Protein 17g; Carb 27g; Fiber 2g; Sugars 5g (est. added sugars: 4g); Chol 38mg; Iron 2mg; Sodium 494mg; Calc 92mg

FRESH TOMATO–FETA PIZZA

HANDS-ON: 35 MIN. TOTAL: 55 MIN.

A pound of pizza dough is less than most pizzerias use, so it will stretch further for a crispier crust. If serving four people, use 12 ounces of dough for the pizza, and cut the rest into strips; brush with olive oil, garlic, and herbs, and bake for breadsticks.

1 pound refrigerated fresh pizza dough
Cooking spray
4 plum tomatoes, sliced
2 1/2 tablespoons olive oil, divided
2 garlic cloves, minced

1 tablespoon yellow cornmeal
3 ounces feta cheese
1/3 cup pitted kalamata olives, halved
1/4 cup basil leaves

1. Place dough in a bowl coated with cooking spray. Let dough stand, covered, 30 minutes or until dough comes to room temperature.

2. Arrange tomato slices on a jelly-roll pan lined with paper towels; top with additional paper towels. Let stand 30 minutes.

3. Place a pizza stone or heavy baking sheet in oven on bottom rack. Preheat oven to 500°. Preheat pizza stone or heavy baking sheet 30 minutes before baking dough.

4. Combine tomatoes, 2 tablespoons oil, and garlic. Sprinkle cornmeal on a lightly floured baking sheet without raised edges. Roll dough into a 14-inch circle on prepared baking sheet. Pierce dough liberally with a fork. Arrange tomato mixture over dough. Crumble cheese; sprinkle over pizza. Slide pizza onto preheated pizza stone or heavy baking sheet, using a spatula as a guide. Bake at 500° for 19 minutes or until crust is golden and cheese is lightly browned. Remove from oven; top with olives and basil. Brush edges of crust with 1 1/2 teaspoons oil. Cut pizza into 6 wedges.

Serves 6 (serving size: 1 wedge): Calories 314; Fat 12g (sat 3.2g, mono 7.1g, poly 1.3g); Protein 10g; Carb 40g; Fiber 6g; Sugars 2g (est. added sugars: 0g); Chol 13mg; Iron 1mg; Sodium 608mg; Calc 82mg

PIÑA COLADAS

CLASSIC: Calories per serving: 424, Sat Fat: 8.8g, Sodium: 23mg, Sugars: 51g
MAKEOVER: Calories per serving: 158, Sat Fat: 1g, Sodium: 57mg, Sugars: 16g

HANDS-ON: 12 MIN. TOTAL: 4 HR. 25 MIN.

Freezing the cubed fresh pineapple adds a velvety texture and keeps the cocktail frozen longer. It gets sweetened with agave nectar, while aged rum adds depth.

2 cups flaked sweetened coconut
1 (12-ounce) can evaporated fat-free
  milk
2 cups cubed pineapple
2 1/2 cups ice cubes

3/4 cup gold rum
1/4 cup pineapple juice
2 tablespoons light agave nectar
8 pineapple wedges

1. Combine 2 cups coconut and evaporated milk in a medium saucepan over medium heat; cook about 7 minutes or until tiny bubbles form around edge (do not boil). Remove from heat. Cover and chill at least 4 hours or up to overnight.

2. Arrange pineapple cubes in a single layer on a baking sheet; freeze at least 1 hour or until firm.

3. Strain coconut mixture through a sieve over a medium bowl, pressing coconut with the back of a spoon to remove as much milk as possible. Discard solids.

4. Combine pineapple, ice cubes, rum, juice, and agave nectar in a blender; process until smooth. Add milk mixture; process until smooth. Serve with pineapple wedges.

Serves 8 (serving size: about 2/3 cup): Calories 158; Fat 1.2g (sat 1g, mono 0.1g, poly 0g); Protein 4g; Carb 19g; Fiber 1g; Sugars 16g (est. added sugars: 4g); Chol 2mg; Iron 0mg; Sodium 57mg; Calc 124mg

CHERRY-PEACH
SANGRIA

CLASSIC: Calories per serving: 220, Sat Fat: 0g, Sodium: 13mg, Sugars: 18g
MAKEOVER: Calories per serving: 155, Sat Fat: 0g, Sodium: 11mg, Sugars: 15g

HANDS-ON: 20 MIN. TOTAL: 8 HR. 20 MIN.

We recommend zesty Spanish albariño, but you can use any other refreshing white wine. Adding club soda and peach slices bulks up this refreshing cocktail.

¼ cup sugar
¼ cup brandy
2 ½ cups pitted Rainier cherries or
   sliced strawberries
1 (750-milliliter) bottle albariño wine,
   chilled

1 cup chilled club soda
1 peach, thinly sliced
3 thyme sprigs
1 purple basil sprig (optional)
1 sweet basil sprig (optional)

1. Combine sugar and brandy in a pitcher; stir until sugar dissolves. Add cherries or strawberries and wine; chill 8 hours or up to overnight. Just before serving, stir in club soda, peach slices, thyme, and basil, if desired.

Serves 8 (serving size: about ⅔ cup): Calories 155; Fat 0.2g (sat 0g, mono 0g, poly 0g); Protein 1g; Carb 18g; Fiber 1g; Sugars 15g (est. added sugars: 6g); Chol 0mg; Iron 1mg; Sodium 11mg; Calc 18mg

PEACH LEMONADE

CLASSIC: Calories per serving: 188, Sat Fat: 0g, Sodium: 1mg, Sugars: 46g
MAKEOVER: Calories per serving: 98, Sat Fat: 0g, Sodium: 0mg, Sugars: 23g

HANDS-ON: 12 MIN. TOTAL: 3 HR. 42 MIN.

The natural sweetness of juicy, ripe peaches means you need less added sugar, and you get the nutritional benefit of fresh fruit.

4 cups water
2 cups coarsely chopped peaches
3/4 cup sugar
1 cup fresh lemon juice (about
  6 lemons)

4 cups ice
1 peach, cut into 8 wedges

1. Combine first 3 ingredients in a medium saucepan over medium-high heat. Bring to a boil; reduce heat, and simmer 3 minutes. Place peach mixture in a blender; let stand 20 minutes. Remove center piece of blender lid (to allow steam to escape); secure blender lid on blender. Place a clean towel over opening in blender lid (to avoid splatters). Blend until smooth. Pour into a large bowl. Refrigerate at least 3 hours.

2. Press peach mixture through a sieve over a bowl, reserving liquid; discard solids. Stir in lemon juice. Place 1/2 cup ice in each of 8 glasses. Pour about 2/3 cup lemonade into each glass; garnish each serving with 1 peach wedge.

Serves 8: Calories 98; Fat 0.1g (sat 0g, mono 0g, poly 0g); Protein 1g; Carb 26g; Fiber 1g; Sugars 23g (est. added sugars: 19g); Chol 0mg; Iron 0mg; Sodium 0mg; Calc 4mg

MARGARITA FIZZ

CLASSIC: Calories per serving: 562, Sat Fat: 0g, Sodium: 1443mg, Sugars: 63g
MAKEOVER: Calories per serving: 164, Sat Fat: 0g, Sodium: 3mg, Sugars: 1g

HANDS-ON: 8 MIN. TOTAL: 8 MIN.

Full of flavor, this beautifully presented beverage is made lighter and effervescent with the addition of lime-flavored sparkling water. All of the flavor, none of the guilt, and very refreshing.

2 cups ice cubes
½ cup fresh lime juice
2 tablespoons kosher salt (optional)
3 ounces premium silver tequila
1 ounce Cointreau (orange-flavored liqueur)

Lime slices
Orange slices
1 cup lime-flavored sparkling water

1. Place ice cubes in a small heavy-duty zip-top plastic bag. Lightly crush ice cubes with a meat mallet or small heavy skillet until you have medium-sized crushed ice. Place ice in freezer.

2. Place lime juice in a bowl. Place salt on a small plate. Dip rims of 2 tall glasses in lime juice; gently roll rims of glasses in salt, if desired. Discard remaining salt.

3. Combine remaining lime juice, tequila, and Cointreau in a cocktail shaker filled with whole ice cubes; shake vigorously.

4. Divide crushed ice, lime slices, and orange slices between prepared glasses. Strain tequila mixture into glasses, and top each with ½ cup sparkling water; stir gently. Serve immediately.

Serves 2 (serving size: about 1 cup): Calories 164; Fat 0g (sat 0g, mono 0g, poly 0g); Protein 0g; Carb 10g; Fiber 0g; Sugars 1g (est. added sugars: 0g); Chol 0mg; Iron 0mg; Sodium 3mg; Calc 9mg

ZUCCHINI-PINEAPPLE
QUICK BREAD

CLASSIC: Calories per serving: 208, Sat Fat: 1.5g, Sodium: 148mg, Sugars: 16g
MAKEOVER: Calories per serving: 167, Sat Fat: 0.5g, Sodium: 151mg, Sugars: 16g

HANDS-ON: 10 MIN. TOTAL: 1 HR. 45 MIN.

This zucchini quick bread has a tropical twist to it–crushed pineapple. Cinnamon and vanilla tie the flavors together and make this a delicious treat for breakfast or a snack.

13.5 ounces sifted all-purpose flour
  (about 3 cups)
1½ teaspoons ground cinnamon
1 teaspoon salt
1 teaspoon baking soda
½ teaspoon baking powder
2 large eggs
2 cups sugar

2 cups grated zucchini (about
  1½ medium zucchini)
⅔ cup canola oil
½ cup egg substitute
2 teaspoons vanilla extract
2 (8-ounce) cans crushed pineapple in
  juice, drained
Baking spray with flour

> **CRAZY TRICK**
> Crushed pineapple adds natural sweetness while zucchini adds bulk for fewer calroies.

1. Preheat oven to 325°.

2. Lightly spoon flour into dry measuring cups, and level with a knife. Combine flour, cinnamon, and next 3 ingredients (through baking powder) in a large bowl, stirring well with a whisk.

3. Beat eggs with a mixer at medium speed until foamy. Add sugar, zucchini, oil, egg substitute, and vanilla, beating until well blended. Add zucchini mixture to flour mixture, stirring just until moist. Fold in pineapple. Spoon batter into 2 (9 x 5–inch) loaf pans coated with baking spray. Bake at 325° for 1 hour or until a wooden pick inserted in center comes out clean. Cool 10 minutes in pans on a wire rack; remove from pans. Cool completely on wire rack.

Serves 14 (serving size: 1 slice): Calories 167; Fat 5.9g (sat 0.5g, mono 3.3g, poly 1.7g); Protein 2g; Carb 27g; Fiber 1g; Sugars 16g (est. added sugars: 14g); Chol 15mg; Iron 1mg; Sodium 151mg; Calc 16mg

PUMPKIN-HONEY BEER
QUICK BREAD

CLASSIC: Calories per serving: 291, Sat Fat: 1.9g, Sodium: 365mg, Sugars: 26g
MAKEOVER: Calories per serving: 194, Sat Fat: 0.6g, Sodium: 287mg, Sugars: 19g

HANDS-ON: 10 MIN. TOTAL: 1 HR. 30 MIN.

Give the second loaf away, or wrap in plastic wrap and freeze for up to two months.

14.6 ounces all-purpose flour (about 3¼ cups)
2 teaspoons salt
2 teaspoons baking soda
1 teaspoon baking powder
1 teaspoon ground cinnamon
1 teaspoon pumpkin pie spice
½ cup water
⅓ cup ground flaxseed

2½ cups sugar
⅔ cup canola oil
⅔ cup honey beer (at room temperature)
½ cup egg substitute
2 large eggs
1 (15-ounce) can pumpkin
Cooking spray

SECRET TO SUCCESS
Ground flaxseed and water add moisture to the batter for a smooth-textured bread.

1. Preheat oven to 350°.

2. Weigh or lightly spoon flour into dry measuring cups; level with a knife. Combine flour, salt, and next 4 ingredients (through pumpkin pie spice) in a medium bowl; stir with a whisk.

3. Combine ½ cup water and flaxseed.

4. Place sugar and next 4 ingredients (through eggs) in a large bowl; beat with a mixer at medium-high speed until well blended. Add flaxseed mixture and pumpkin; beat at low speed just until blended. Add flour mixture; beat just until combined. Divide batter between 2 (9 x 5–inch) loaf pans coated with cooking spray. Bake at 350° for 1 hour and 10 minutes or until a wooden pick inserted in center comes out clean. Cool 10 minutes in pan on a wire rack; remove from pans. Cool completely on wire rack.

Serves 14 (serving size: 1 slice): Calories 194; Fat 6.5g (sat 0.6g, mono 3.4g, poly 2.1g); Protein 3g; Carb 31g; Fiber 1g; Sugars 19g (est. added sugars: 18g); Chol 15mg; Iron 1mg; Sodium 287mg; Calc 27mg

CLASSIC BANANA BREAD

CLASSIC: Calories per serving: 365, Sat Fat: 7.9g, Sodium: 338mg, Sugars: 32g
MAKEOVER: Calories per serving: 191, Sat Fat: 1.5g, Sodium: 165mg, Sugars: 17g

HANDS-ON: 10 MIN. TOTAL: 3 HR. 25 MIN.

Sautéing the bananas in butter and brown sugar until lightly caramelized deepens the banana flavor in this bread, while canola oil and buttermilk ensure a moist, tender crumb. Try to scrape all of the caramelized bits from your skillet after cooking the bananas to extract every bit of flavor.

2 tablespoons butter
¼ cup packed brown sugar
3 ripe bananas, sliced
⅔ cup granulated sugar
½ cup low-fat buttermilk
¼ cup canola oil
1 teaspoon vanilla extract

2 large eggs, lightly beaten
9 ounces all-purpose flour (about
  2 cups)
¾ teaspoon baking soda
½ teaspoon salt
¼ teaspoon ground cinnamon
Cooking spray

1. Preheat oven to 350°.

2. Melt butter in a large skillet over medium-high heat. Add brown sugar and banana; cook 4 minutes or until banana is lightly caramelized, stirring occasionally. Place banana mixture in a large bowl; cool 10 minutes. Beat banana mixture with a mixer at medium speed until smooth. Add granulated sugar and next 4 ingredients (through eggs); beat until smooth.

3. Weigh or lightly spoon flour into dry measuring cups; level with a knife. Combine flour and next 3 ingredients (through cinnamon), stirring with a whisk; add to banana mixture, and beat at low speed just until combined. Scrape batter into a 9 x 5–inch loaf pan coated with cooking spray.

4. Bake at 350° for 55 minutes or until a wooden pick inserted in center comes out with moist crumbs clinging. Cool 10 minutes in pan on a wire rack. Remove bread from pan, and cool on wire rack.

Serves 16 (serving size: 1 slice): Calories 191; Fat 5.9g (sat 1.5g, mono 2.8g, poly 1.3g); Protein 3g; Carb 32g; Fiber 1g; Sugars 17g (est. added sugars: 8g); Chol 28mg; Iron 1mg; Sodium 165mg; Calc 19mg

BRIOCHE ROLLS

HANDS-ON: 35 MIN. TOTAL: 12 HR. 16 MIN.

Slimming down the trinity of butter, eggs, and sugar doesn't sacrifice flavor and texture thanks to an overnight rise.

1 package dry yeast (about 2 1/4 teaspoons)
1/3 cup warm 1% low-fat milk (100° to 110°)
15.75 ounces all-purpose flour (about 3 1/2 cups)
1/3 cup sugar

1/2 teaspoon salt
4 large eggs, lightly beaten
8 1/2 tablespoons unsalted butter, softened and divided
Cooking spray
1 tablespoon water
1 large egg white

CRAZY TRICK
You don't need a brioche pan for this recipe–a muffin tin works well. Be sure to start the dough a day ahead, as the overnight rise is essential for bakery-like flavor.

1. Dissolve yeast in warm milk in the bowl of a stand mixer fitted with the paddle attachment; let stand 5 minutes. Weigh or lightly spoon flour into dry measuring cups; level with a knife. Add flour, sugar, salt, and lightly beaten eggs to milk mixture; beat at low speed until smooth, scraping sides of bowl with a spatula as needed. Remove paddle attachment; insert dough hook. Beat dough at low speed 5 minutes or until soft and elastic and dough just begins to pull away from sides of bowl. Cut 6 1/2 tablespoons butter into large cubes; add half of butter cubes to dough, beating at medium speed to blend. Add remaining half of butter cubes to dough, beating at medium speed until incorporated. Beat dough at medium speed 4 minutes or until smooth and elastic.

2. Place dough in a large bowl coated with cooking spray, turning to coat top. Cover and let rise in a warm place (85°), free from drafts, 1 hour or until doubled in size. (Gently press two fingers into dough. If indentation remains, dough has risen enough.) Punch dough down; form into a ball. Return dough to bowl; cover with plastic wrap. Refrigerate 8 hours or overnight.

3. Uncover dough; let stand 90 minutes or until dough reaches room temperature. Divide dough into 4 equal portions. Working with 1 portion at a time (cover remaining dough to keep from drying), cut dough portion into 6 equal pieces. Roll each piece into a 1 1/2-inch ball. Repeat procedure with remaining 3 dough portions to make 24 rolls total. Place rolls in muffin cups coated with cooking spray. Cover and let rise 45 minutes or until almost doubled in size.

4. Preheat oven to 350°.

5. Combine 1 tablespoon water and egg white; stir with a whisk. Gently brush rolls with egg mixture. Bake at 350° for 14 minutes or until golden. Place pans on wire racks. Place 2 tablespoons butter in a microwave-safe bowl; microwave at HIGH 20 seconds or until butter melts. Brush butter onto rolls.

Serves 24 (serving size: 1 roll): Calories 128; Fat 4.9g (sat 2.8g, mono 1.4g, poly 0.4g); Protein 3g; Carb 17g; Fiber 1g; Sugars 3g (est. added sugars: 3g); Chol 41mg; Iron 1mg; Sodium 94mg; Calc 13mg

CREAM CHEESE DANISH BRAID

CLASSIC: Calories per serving: 415, Sat Fat: 14.3g, Sodium: 237mg, Sugars: 22g
MAKEOVER: Calories per serving: 224, Sat Fat: 4.1g, Sodium: 218mg, Sugars: 12g

HANDS-ON: 52 MIN. TOTAL: 3 HR. 37 MIN.

We trimmed sugar and fat like a pro by using honey instead of sugar, light sour cream, less butter, and a light powdered sugar glaze.

SPONGE:
6 tablespoons warm 1% low-fat milk (120° to 130°)
2 tablespoons all-purpose flour
1 teaspoon granulated sugar
1 package quick-rise yeast (about 2 1/4 teaspoons)

DOUGH:
7.9 ounces all-purpose flour, divided (about 1 3/4 cups)
2.25 ounces whole-wheat pastry flour (about 1/2 cup)
1/4 cup granulated sugar
1/4 cup light sour cream
3 tablespoons butter, softened
1 teaspoon vanilla extract
3/4 teaspoon salt
1 large egg
Cooking spray

FILLING:
4 ounces 1/3-less-fat cream cheese
1/3 cup part-skim ricotta cheese
2 tablespoons honey
2 teaspoons fresh lemon juice
Dash of salt

REMAINING INGREDIENTS:
1 teaspoon water
1 large egg
1/3 cup powdered sugar
2 teaspoons 1% low-fat milk
2 tablespoons sliced almonds, toasted

> **SECRET TO SUCCESS**
> The Danish can be made the night before, through step 4. Cover, refrigerate overnight, and bring braid to room temperature before proceeding with step 5.

1. To prepare sponge, combine first 4 ingredients in a medium bowl, stirring well with a whisk. Cover loosely with plastic wrap; let stand 15 minutes.

2. To prepare dough, weigh or lightly spoon 6.75 ounces (about 1 1/2 cups) all-purpose flour and pastry flour into dry measuring cups; level with a knife. Combine 1/4 cup granulated sugar, sour cream, butter, vanilla, 3/4 teaspoon salt, 1 egg, and sponge in a large bowl; beat with a mixer at medium speed 1 minute or until well combined. Add flours; beat at low speed 3 minutes or until a soft dough forms. Turn dough out onto a lightly floured surface. Knead until smooth and elastic (about 4 minutes), adding 1.15 ounces all-purpose flour, 1 tablespoon at a time, to prevent dough from sticking. Place dough in a large bowl coated with cooking spray. Cover and let rise in a warm place (85°), free from drafts, 1 hour and 15 minutes or until doubled in size. (Gently press two fingers into dough. If indentation remains, dough has risen enough.)

3. To prepare filling, combine cream cheese and next 4 ingredients (through dash of salt) in a medium bowl; beat with a mixer at medium speed until smooth.

4. Punch dough down; roll dough into a 12 x 15–inch rectangle on lightly floured parchment paper. Spread cream cheese mixture down center of dough, leaving about a 5-inch border on each side and a 1-inch border at top and bottom of rectangle. Make 5-inch cuts about 1 inch apart on both sides of dough to meet filling using a sharp knife or kitchen shears. Remove 4 outer corner strips of dough from rectangle; discard. Fold top and bottom 1-inch portions of dough over filling. Fold strips over filling, alternating strips diagonally over filling. Press ends to seal. Transfer braid and parchment paper to a baking sheet. Cover and let rise 45 minutes.

5. Preheat oven to 375°. Combine 1 teaspoon water and 1 egg; stir with a whisk. Brush braid with egg mixture. Bake at 375° for 20 minutes or until golden. Cool on a wire rack 10 minutes.

6. Combine powdered sugar and 2 teaspoons milk in a bowl, stirring until smooth. Drizzle glaze over braid; sprinkle with nuts.

Serves 12 (serving size: 1 slice): Calories 224; Fat 7.9g (sat 4.1g, mono 2.3g, poly 0.6g); Protein 6g; Carb 32g; Fiber 2g; Sugars 12g (est. added sugars: 10g); Chol 50mg; Iron 2mg; Sodium 218mg; Calc 63mg

WHOLE-GRAIN BRAN MUFFINS

CLASSIC: Calories per serving: 339, Sat Fat: 5.7g, Sodium: 456mg, Sugars: 32g
MAKEOVER: Calories per serving: 168, Sat Fat: 1.7g, Sodium: 183mg, Sugars: 10g

HANDS-ON: 25 MIN. TOTAL: 1 HR. 25 MIN.

Bring the bran muffin back into balanced territory with 100% whole grains and no refined sugar–but still keep it moist and packed with flavor.

4 1/4 ounces wheat bran (about
  1 3/4 cups)
1 cup whole pitted dates (about 6
  ounces)
3/4 cup fresh orange juice
1 cup nonfat buttermilk
1/2 cup mashed ripe banana (about 1
  medium)
2 tablespoons butter, melted
2 tablespoons canola oil

1 teaspoon vanilla extract
4.5 ounces whole-grain pastry flour
  (about 1 cup)
1 1/2 teaspoons baking powder
1/2 teaspoon baking soda
1/2 teaspoon ground cinnamon
1/4 teaspoon salt
2 large eggs, lightly beaten
Cooking spray

1. Preheat oven to 350°.

2. Spread bran on a baking sheet. Bake at 350° for 8 to 10 minutes or until lightly browned, stirring once.

3. Combine dates and juice in a medium saucepan over medium heat; bring to a boil. Cover, reduce heat, and simmer 20 minutes. Remove from heat; uncover and let stand 5 minutes. Place date mixture in a food processor or blender; process until smooth. Add buttermilk and next 4 ingredients (through vanilla); process until smooth.

4. Weigh or lightly spoon flour into a dry measuring cup; level with a knife. Combine flour, bran, baking powder, and next 3 ingredients (through salt) in a medium bowl, stirring with a whisk. Add date mixture to bran mixture, stirring just until moist. Add eggs, stirring just until combined. Place 12 muffin cup liners in muffin cups; coat liners with cooking spray. Spoon batter into muffin cups. Bake at 350° for 28 minutes or until a wooden pick inserted in center comes out clean. Remove muffins from pan; cool on a wire rack.

Serves 12 (serving size: 1 muffin): Calories 168; Fat 5.4g (sat 1.7g, mono 2.3g, poly 0.9g); Protein 4g; Carb 29g; Fiber 7g; Sugars 10g (est. added sugars: 0g); Chol 36mg; Iron 2mg; Sodium 183mg; Calc 89mg

BLUEBERRY–SOUR CREAM
MUFFINS

CLASSIC: Calories per serving: 274, Sat Fat: 7.8g, Sodium: 247mg, Sugars: 20g
MAKEOVER: Calories per serving: 248, Sat Fat: 4g, Sodium: 258mg, Sugars: 16g

HANDS-ON: 15 MIN. TOTAL: 38 MIN., PLUS COOLING TIME

Heart-healthy canola oil, whole-wheat flour, and reduced-fat sour cream provide plenty of moisture and richness, and with a crumbly, sweet streusel topping, you'll never miss the fat and calories of the original.

Cooking spray
1/3 cup old-fashioned rolled oats
1/4 cup packed brown sugar
1 tablespoon white whole-wheat flour
1/8 teaspoon ground cinnamon
3 1/2 tablespoons unsalted butter, melted and divided
9 ounces white whole-wheat flour (about 2 cups)

2 teaspoons baking powder
1/2 teaspoon salt
1/4 teaspoon baking soda
1 cup reduced-fat sour cream
1/2 cup granulated sugar
1/4 cup canola oil
1 teaspoon vanilla extract
1 large egg
1 1/2 cups fresh blueberries

1. Preheat oven to 425°. Place 12 muffin cup liners in muffin cups. Lightly coat liners with cooking spray.

2. To prepare topping, place oats, brown sugar, 1 tablespoon flour, and cinnamon in a bowl, stirring with a whisk. Drizzle 1 tablespoon melted butter over top; toss with a fork until combined.

3. To prepare muffins, weigh or lightly spoon 9 ounces (about 2 cups) flour into dry measuring cups; level with a knife. Combine flour, baking powder, salt, and baking soda in a bowl, stirring with a whisk.

4. Place 2 tablespoons melted butter, sour cream, granulated sugar, oil, vanilla, and egg in a bowl; stir well with a whisk to completely combine. Add sour cream mixture to flour mixture; stir just until combined. Gently stir in blueberries. Divide batter among prepared muffin cups. Sprinkle with topping. Bake at 425° for 5 minutes. Reduce oven temperature to 375°; bake an additional 13 minutes or until a wooden pick inserted in center comes out clean. Cool muffins in pan 5 minutes. Remove from pan; cool completely on a wire rack.

Serves 12 (serving size: 1 muffin): Calories 248; Fat 10.8g (sat 4g, mono 4g, poly 1.6g); Protein 5g; Carb 32g; Fiber 3g; Sugars 16g (est. added sugars 13g); Chol 24mg; Iron 1mg; Sodium 258mg; Calc 68mg

20-MINUTE FLUFFY BUTTERMILK
DROP BISCUITS

HANDS-ON: 7 MIN. TOTAL: 20 MIN.

Stir melted butter into cold, nonfat buttermilk and let everything get lumpy as the butter solidifies. Those little pockets of butter disperse evenly throughout the batter, allowing us to use half the amount of the original. White whole-wheat flour adds nutty, whole-grain goodness, and a touch of canola oil keeps the biscuits nice and tender.

5.6 ounces all-purpose flour (about 1¼ cups)
3.6 ounces white whole-wheat flour (about ¾ cup)
2 teaspoons baking powder
1 teaspoon sugar
¾ teaspoon salt
½ teaspoon baking soda
¼ cup unsalted butter
1¼ cups very cold nonfat buttermilk
1 tablespoon canola oil

1. Preheat oven to 450°.

2. Weigh or lightly spoon flours into dry measuring cups; level with a knife. Combine flours, baking powder, sugar, salt, and baking soda in a large bowl, stirring with a whisk to combine.

3. Place butter in a microwave-safe bowl. Microwave at HIGH 1 minute or until completely melted. Add cold buttermilk, stirring until butter forms small clumps. Add oil, stirring to combine.

4. Add buttermilk mixture to flour mixture; stir with a rubber spatula just until incorporated (do not overmix) and batter pulls away from sides of bowl (batter will be very wet).

5. Drop batter in mounds of 2 heaping tablespoonfuls onto a baking sheet lined with parchment paper. Bake at 450° for 11 minutes or until golden. Cool 3 minutes; serve warm.

Serves 12 (serving size: 1 biscuit): Calories 133; Fat 5.4g (sat 2.6g, mono 1.8g, poly 0.6g); Protein 4g; Carb 18g; Fiber 1g; Sugars 0g (est. added sugars: 0g); Chol 10mg; Iron 1mg; Sodium 305mg; Calc 82mg

HOT CROSS BUNS

CLASSIC: Calories per serving: 268, Sat Fat: 4.8g, Sodium: 277mg, Sugars: 20g
MAKEOVER: Calories per serving: 179, Sat Fat: 1.4g, Sodium: 111mg, Sugars: 12g

HANDS-ON: 40 MIN. TOTAL: 3 HR. 15 MIN.

Whole-grain pastry flour adds nutty goodness but keeps a light crumb.

½ cup golden raisins
½ cup dried currants
¼ cup warm orange juice (120° to 130°)
19 ounces all-purpose flour, divided
4.5 ounces whole-grain pastry flour
1 teaspoon salt
1 teaspoon grated lemon rind
1 teaspoon grated orange rind
½ teaspoon ground cinnamon
¼ teaspoon grated whole nutmeg
1 package quick-rise yeast (about 2 ¼ teaspoons)
1 cup warm fat-free milk (120° to 130°)
¼ cup honey
¼ cup unsalted butter, melted
2 large eggs, lightly beaten
Cooking spray
1 tablespoon water
1 large egg white
1 cup powdered sugar
1 tablespoon 2% reduced-fat milk
1 teaspoon fresh lemon juice

1. To prepare rolls, combine first 3 ingredients in a small bowl; let stand 10 minutes. Drain fruit in a colander over a bowl, reserving fruit and juice.

2. Weigh or lightly spoon 18.5 ounces (about 4 cups plus 2 tablespoons) all-purpose flour and pastry flour into dry measuring cups; level with a knife. Combine flours, salt, and next 5 ingredients (through yeast) in the bowl of a stand mixer with dough hook attached; beat until combined. Combine reserved orange juice, fat-free milk, honey, butter, and 2 eggs in a bowl, stirring with a whisk. With mixer on, slowly add milk mixture to flour mixture; beat at medium-low speed 7 minutes. Turn dough out onto a lightly floured surface. Add reserved fruit. Knead 2 minutes or until smooth and elastic; add enough of 2 tablespoons all-purpose flour to prevent dough from sticking. Place dough in a large bowl coated with cooking spray, turning to coat top. Cover and let rise in a warm place (85°), free from drafts, 1 hour or until doubled in size. Punch dough down; cover and let rest 5 minutes. Divide into 24 equal portions; roll each portion into a ball. Place rolls in muffin cups coated with cooking spray. Cover and let rise 1 hour or until almost doubled in size.

3. Preheat oven to 350°. Combine 1 tablespoon water and egg white; stir with a whisk. Gently brush rolls with egg white mixture. Bake at 350° for 20 minutes or until golden, rotating pans once during baking. Remove from pans; cool 10 minutes on a wire rack.

4. In a bowl, whisk 1 cup powdered sugar, 1 tablespoon milk, and lemon juice. Microwave at HIGH 20 seconds. Pipe a cross on top of warm bun.

Serves 24 (serving size: 1 bun): Calories 179; Fat 2.8g (sat 1.4g, mono 0.7g, poly 0.2g); Protein 5g; Carb 35g; Fiber 2g; Sugars 12g (est. added sugars: 8g); Chol 23mg; Iron 1mg; Sodium 111mg; Calc 29mg

ORANGE ROLLS

CLASSIC: Calories per serving: 345, Sat Fat: 4.5g, Sodium: 232mg, Sugars: 39g
MAKEOVER: Calories per serving: 178, Sat Fat: 3.2g, Sodium: 146mg, Sugars: 16g

HANDS-ON: 30 MIN. TOTAL: 3 HR.

The biggest change occurred when we slashed the butter content in the dough to ¼ cup, but we kept enough to maintain the original's tender, pillowy texture. We kept most of the butter originally in the glaze because it imparts rich flavor at first bite.

DOUGH:

1 package dry yeast (about 2 ¼ teaspoons)
½ cup warm water (100° to 110°)
1 cup sugar, divided
½ cup reduced-fat sour cream
2 tablespoons butter, softened

1 teaspoon salt
1 large egg, lightly beaten
3 ½ cups all-purpose flour, divided
Cooking spray
2 tablespoons butter, melted
2 tablespoons grated orange rind

GLAZE:

¾ cup sugar
¼ cup butter

2 tablespoons fresh orange juice
½ cup reduced-fat sour cream

1. To prepare dough, dissolve yeast in ½ cup warm water in a large bowl; let stand 5 minutes. Add ¼ cup sugar, ½ cup sour cream, 2 tablespoons softened butter, salt, and egg; beat with a mixer at medium speed until smooth. Lightly spoon flour into dry measuring cups; level with a knife. Add 2 cups flour to yeast mixture; beat until smooth. Add 1 cup flour to yeast mixture, stirring until a soft dough forms. Turn dough out onto a floured surface. Knead until smooth and elastic (about 10 minutes), adding enough of remaining flour, 1 tablespoon at a time, to prevent dough from sticking to hands (dough will feel sticky).

2. Place dough in a large bowl coated with cooking spray, turning to coat top. Cover and let rise in a warm place (85°), free from drafts, 1 hour and 15 minutes or until doubled in size. (Gently press two fingers into dough. If indentation remains, dough has risen enough.)

3. Punch dough down; cover and let rest 5 minutes. Divide dough in half. Working with 1 portion at a time (cover remaining dough to prevent drying), roll each portion of dough into a 12-inch circle on a floured surface. Brush surface of each circle with 1 tablespoon melted butter. Combine ¾ cup sugar and rind. Sprinkle half of sugar mixture over each circle. Cut each circle into 12 wedges. Roll up each wedge tightly, beginning at wide end. Place rolls, point sides down, in a 13 x 9–inch baking pan coated with cooking spray. Cover and let rise 25 minutes or until doubled in size.

4. Preheat oven to 350°.

5. Uncover dough. Bake at 350° for 25 minutes or until golden brown.

6. While rolls bake, prepare glaze. Combine ³⁄₄ cup sugar, ¹⁄₄ cup butter, and orange juice in a small saucepan; bring to a boil over medium-high heat. Cook 3 minutes or until sugar dissolves, stirring occasionally. Remove from heat; cool slightly. Stir in ¹⁄₂ cup sour cream. Drizzle glaze over warm rolls; let stand 20 minutes before serving.

Serves 24 (serving size: 1 roll): Calories 178; Fat 5.6g (sat 3.2g, mono 1.3g, poly 0.3g); Protein 3g; Carb 30g; Fiber 1g; Sugars 16g (est. added sugars: 15g); Chol 24mg; Iron 1mg; Sodium 146mg; Calc 23mg

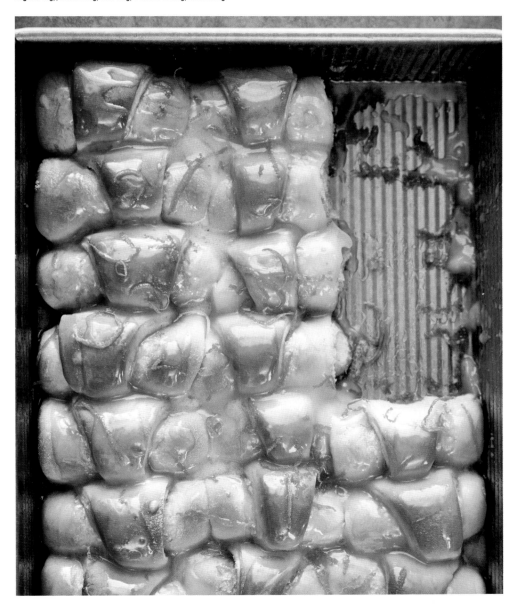

PECAN STICKY ROLLS

HANDS-ON: 30 MIN. TOTAL: 2 HR. 16 MIN.

Egg substitute adds to the rich, yeasty flavor without adding fat.

DOUGH:

3/4 cup warm fat-free milk (100° to 110°)
1/4 cup granulated sugar
1/2 teaspoon salt
1 package dry yeast (about 2 1/4 teaspoons)
1/4 cup warm water (100° to 110°)

1/2 cup egg substitute
3 tablespoons butter, melted and cooled
18 ounces all-purpose flour (about 4 cups), divided
Cooking spray

SAUCE:

3/4 cup packed dark brown sugar
3 tablespoons butter, melted

2 tablespoons hot water
1/3 cup finely chopped pecans, toasted

FILLING:

2/3 cup granulated sugar
1 tablespoon ground cinnamon

1 1/2 tablespoons butter, melted

1. To prepare dough, combine first 3 ingredients in a large bowl.

2. Dissolve yeast in 1/4 cup warm water in a small bowl; let stand 5 minutes. Stir yeast mixture into milk mixture. Add egg substitute and 3 tablespoons melted butter; stir until well combined.

3. Weigh or lightly spoon flour into dry measuring cups; level with a knife. Add 16.8 ounces (about 3 3/4 cups) flour to yeast mixture; stir until smooth. Turn dough out onto a lightly floured surface. Knead until smooth and elastic (about 8 minutes), adding enough of remaining flour, 1 tablespoon at a time, to prevent dough from sticking to hands (dough will feel slightly soft and tacky).

4. Place dough in a large bowl coated with cooking spray, turning to coat top. Cover and let rise in a warm place (85°), free from drafts, 45 minutes. Punch dough down, and turn over in bowl; lightly coat with cooking spray. Cover and let rise another 45 minutes. Punch dough down; cover and let rest 5 minutes.

5. To prepare sauce, combine brown sugar, 3 tablespoons butter, and 2 tablespoons hot water in a small bowl; stir with a whisk until smooth. Scrape sugar mixture into a 13 x 9–inch baking pan coated with cooking spray, spreading over bottom of pan with a spatula. Sprinkle sugar mixture with pecans, and set aside.

6. To prepare filling, combine 2/3 cup granulated sugar and cinnamon in a small bowl. Turn dough out onto a lightly floured surface; pat dough into a 16 x 12–inch rectangle. Brush dough with 1 1/2 tablespoons

melted butter. Sprinkle sugar mixture over dough, leaving a ½-inch border. Beginning with a long side, roll up dough, jelly-roll fashion; pinch seam to seal (do not seal ends of roll). Cut roll into 15 slices (approximately 1 inch wide). Arrange slices, cut sides up, in prepared pan. Lightly coat rolls with cooking spray; cover and let rise in a warm place (85°), free from drafts, 30 minutes or until doubled in size.

7. Preheat oven to 350°.

8. Uncover rolls, and bake at 350° for 20 minutes or until lightly browned. Let stand 1 minute; carefully invert onto serving platter.

Serves 15 (serving size: 1 roll): Calories 275; Fat 7.6g (sat 3.8g, mono 2.6g, poly 0.8g); Protein 5g; Carb 47g; Fiber 1g; Sugars 24g (est. added sugars: 23g); Chol 15mg; Iron 2mg; Sodium 146mg; Calc 37mg

CHERRY-ALMOND-RICOTTA
DROP SCONES

HANDS-ON: 36 MIN. TOTAL: 51 MIN.

These crumbly, cakelike biscuits are best enjoyed the day they are made. Plumping dried fruit in juice adds more vivid flavor. Fresh fruit would add too much moisture and dilute the buttery batter.

½ cup dried tart cherries
¼ cup fresh orange juice
1 cup part-skim ricotta cheese
¼ cup packed brown sugar, divided
1 teaspoon grated orange rind
1 teaspoon vanilla extract
⅓ cup plus 1 tablespoon nonfat buttermilk, divided
2 tablespoons canola oil

4.5 ounces whole-grain pastry flour (about 1 cup)
3.4 ounces all-purpose flour (about ¾ cup)
1 tablespoon baking powder
½ teaspoon salt
4 tablespoons cold unsalted butter, diced
⅓ cup sliced almonds, toasted
1 large egg, lightly beaten

CRAZY TRICK
Replace the heavy cream with part-skim ricotta to save a ton of calories and saturated fat.

1. Preheat oven to 425°.

2. Combine cherries and juice in a small microwave-safe bowl. Microwave at HIGH 1 minute; let stand 5 minutes. Drain; discard liquid. Finely chop cherries.

3. Combine ricotta cheese, 1 tablespoon sugar, rind, and vanilla in a medium bowl. Reserve ½ cup of ricotta mixture. Add ⅓ cup buttermilk and canola oil to remaining ricotta mixture, stirring until smooth.

4. Weigh or lightly spoon flours into dry measuring cups; level with a knife. Combine flours, 3 tablespoons sugar, baking powder, and salt in a large bowl; cut in butter with a pastry blender or 2 knives until mixture resembles coarse meal. Add cherries and almonds; toss. Add buttermilk mixture; stir just until combined.

5. Drop dough by ¼-cupfuls 3 inches apart onto a baking sheet lined with parchment paper. Combine egg and 1 tablespoon buttermilk, stirring with a whisk. Gently brush top and sides of dough with egg mixture. Bake at 425° for 15 to 16 minutes or until golden. Remove from pan; cool slightly on a wire rack.

6. Beat reserved ricotta mixture with a mixer at medium speed 3 minutes or until fluffy. Serve with warm scones.

Serves 10 (serving size: 1 scone and about 2 teaspoons ricotta mixture): Calories 261; Fat 11.7g (sat 4.6g, mono 4.7g, poly 1.5g); Protein 7g; Carb 32g; Fiber 3g; Sugars 10g (est. added sugars: 5g); Chol 39mg; Iron 2mg; Sodium 287mg; Calc 187mg

CINNAMON-PECAN SWEET POTATO ROLLS
WITH CREAM CHEESE GLAZE

CLASSIC: Calories per serving: 497, Sat Fat: 10.3g, Sodium: 298mg, Sugars: 38g
MAKEOVER: Calories per serving: 269, Sat Fat: 3.1g, Sodium: 137mg, Sugars: 23g

HANDS-ON: 28 MIN. TOTAL: 2 HR. 51 MIN.

These sweet, nutty rolls are just as satisfying as their traditional counterparts. The addition of mashed sweet potato to the filling mimics the gooey goodness usually created by copious amounts of butter and brown sugar.

ROLLS:

1 cup warm 1% low-fat milk (100° to 110°)
6 tablespoons granulated sugar, divided
1 package dry yeast (about 2 1/4 teaspoons)
5 tablespoons melted butter, divided
1 large egg, lightly beaten
15.75 ounces all-purpose flour (about 3 1/2 cups)
1/2 teaspoon salt
Cooking spray
3/4 cup mashed cooked peeled sweet potato
2/3 cup packed dark brown sugar
1/4 cup finely chopped pecans, toasted
1 tablespoon ground cinnamon

GLAZE:

1 cup powdered sugar
2 tablespoons 1/3-less-fat cream cheese, softened
1 tablespoon 1% low-fat milk
1/2 teaspoon vanilla extract

1. To prepare rolls, combine 1 cup milk, 1 tablespoon granulated sugar, and yeast in the bowl of a stand mixer, stirring with a whisk. Let stand 10 minutes. Stir in 5 tablespoons granulated sugar, 3 tablespoons melted butter, and egg. Weigh or lightly spoon flour into dry measuring cups; level with a knife. Add flour and salt to yeast mixture. Beat at low speed using dough hook just until combined. Increase speed to medium-low, and beat 5 minutes (dough will be soft and sticky). Scrape dough into a large bowl coated with cooking spray; coat top of dough with cooking spray. Cover and let rise in a warm place (85°), free from drafts, 1 hour or until doubled in size. (Gently press two fingers into dough. If indentation remains, dough has risen enough.)

2. Punch dough down; turn dough out onto a lightly floured surface. Roll dough into a 15 x 11–inch rectangle. Spread sweet potato in a thin layer over dough, spreading all the way to edges. Combine 2 tablespoons melted butter, brown sugar, pecans, and cinnamon in a bowl; sprinkle mixture over sweet potato. Beginning with a long side, gently roll up dough, jelly-roll fashion; pinch seam to seal (do not seal ends of roll). Cut roll into 15 (1-inch) slices using a sharp knife. Place slices, cut sides up, in a 13 x 9–inch metal baking pan coated with cooking spray. Cover and let rise in a warm place (85°), free from drafts, 45 minutes or until doubled in size.

3. Preheat oven to 350°.

4. Uncover dough. Bake at 350° for 28 minutes or until lightly browned. Cool slightly.

5. To prepare glaze, combine powdered sugar, cream cheese, milk, and vanilla, stirring vigorously with a whisk until smooth. Spread glaze over warm rolls.

Serves 15 (serving size: 1 roll): Calories 269; Fat 6.4g (sat 3.1g, mono 2.1g, poly 0.8g); Protein 5g; Carb 49g; Fiber 2g; Sugars 23g (est. added sugars: 21g); Chol 25mg; Iron 2mg; Sodium 137mg; Calc 37mg

GLAZED YEAST DOUGHNUTS

CLASSIC: Calories per serving: 398, Sat Fat: 6.6g, Sodium: 293mg, Sugars: 26g
MAKEOVER: Calories per serving: 232, Sat Fat: 3.3g, Sodium: 183mg, Sugars: 19g

HANDS-ON: 25 MIN. TOTAL: 1 HR. 45 MIN.

Reduced-fat milk and quick-rising yeast help the texture to be light and fluffy. Baking instead of deep-frying cuts the fat by half.

DOUGHNUTS:
1 cup warm 2% reduced-fat milk (100° to 110°)
¼ cup granulated sugar, divided
1 package quick-rise yeast (about 2¼ teaspoons)
5½ tablespoons butter, melted and divided

1 large egg, lightly beaten
13.5 ounces all-purpose flour (about 3 cups)
¾ teaspoon salt
Cooking spray

GLAZE:
1½ cups powdered sugar
¼ cup 2% reduced-fat milk
¼ teaspoon vanilla extract

SECRET TO SUCCESS
Insulated baking sheets prevent overbrowned bottoms; if you don't have them, bake the doughnuts in the upper third of your oven.

1. To prepare doughnuts, combine 1 cup warm milk, 1 tablespoon granulated sugar, and yeast in the bowl of a stand mixer, stirring with a whisk. Let stand 5 minutes. Stir in 3 tablespoons granulated sugar, ¼ cup melted butter, and egg. Weigh or lightly spoon flour into dry measuring cups; level with a knife. Add flour and salt to yeast mixture. Beat at low speed using dough hook attachment just until combined. Increase speed to medium-low; beat 5 minutes or until dough is smooth and slightly elastic (dough will be soft and sticky). Scrape dough into a large bowl coated with cooking spray; coat top of dough with cooking spray. Cover and let rise in a warm place (85°), free from drafts, 30 to 40 minutes or until doubled in size. (Gently press two fingers into dough. If indentation remains, dough has risen enough.)

2. Punch dough down; turn out onto a lightly floured surface. Sprinkle dough with flour, and fold gently several times. Roll dough to ½-inch thickness; cut with a 3½-inch doughnut cutter. Place doughnuts on 2 large baking sheets lined with parchment paper. Brush with 1½ tablespoons melted butter. Cover loosely with plastic wrap, and let rise in a warm place (85°), free from drafts, 30 to 40 minutes or until doubled in size.

3. Preheat oven to 400°. Uncover dough. Bake at 400° for 10 to 12 minutes or until golden brown.

4. To prepare glaze, combine powdered sugar, ¼ cup milk, and vanilla, stirring with a whisk until smooth. Dip hot doughnuts into glaze, letting excess drip off. Place doughnuts on a wire rack; let stand 5 minutes or until glaze sets. Serve warm.

Serves 14 (serving size: 1 doughnut): Calories 232; Fat 5.6g (sat 3.3g, mono 1.5g, poly 0.4g); Protein 4g; Carb 42g; Fiber 1g; Sugars 19g (est. added sugars: 18g); Chol 27mg; Iron 1mg; Sodium 183mg; Calc 34mg

Easy, Cheesy Potato
Gratin, page 253

SUCCULENT SIDE DISHES

HEIRLOOM TOMATO PIE
WITH CORNMEAL CRUST

CLASSIC: Calories per serving: 523, Sat Fat: 39.9g, Sodium: 1000mg, Sugars: 4g
MAKEOVER: Calories per serving: 205, Sat Fat: 2.1g, Sodium: 242mg, Sugars: 3g

HANDS-ON: 17 MIN. TOTAL: 2 HR. 17 MIN.

Instead of a traditional piecrust containing 1/2 cup butter or shortening (or some combination of the two), we've opted for a rustic crust made of white whole-wheat flour and cornmeal. Heart-healthy olive oil in the crust leaves plenty of room for the cheesy topping.

4.5 ounces whole-wheat pastry flour
  (about 1 cup)
1/2 cup stone-ground yellow cornmeal
3/4 teaspoon freshly ground black
  pepper, divided
1/2 teaspoon salt, divided
1/3 cup extra-virgin olive oil
1/4 cup water
Cooking spray
2 pounds heirloom tomatoes, seeded
  and thinly sliced
2 teaspoons olive oil
1 1/2 cups chopped onion
3 tablespoons chopped fresh basil
1.3 ounces shredded reduced-fat sharp
  white cheddar cheese (about 1/3 cup)
1/3 cup canola mayonnaise
3 tablespoons grated Parmigiano-
  Reggiano cheese
1 1/2 tablespoons minced fresh chives

1. Preheat oven to 400°.

2. Weigh or lightly spoon flour into a dry measuring cup; level with a knife. Combine flour, cornmeal, 1/4 teaspoon pepper, and 1/4 teaspoon salt in a medium bowl. Combine 1/3 cup extra-virgin oil and 1/4 cup water; drizzle over flour mixture. Stir with a fork until dough forms. Press dough into bottom and up sides of a 9-inch pie plate coated with cooking spray. Bake at 400° for 15 minutes or until edges are lightly browned. Cool 30 minutes on a wire rack. Reduce oven temperature to 350°.

3. While crust cools, place tomato slices in a single layer on a baking sheet lined with 2 layers of paper towels; sprinkle with 1/4 teaspoon pepper and 1/4 teaspoon salt. Let stand 15 minutes.

4. Heat 2 teaspoons olive oil in a medium nonstick skillet over medium-high heat. Add onion to pan; sauté 5 minutes or until tender. Remove from heat; cool slightly.

5. Layer tomato, onion, and basil in prepared crust. Combine cheddar, 1/4 teaspoon pepper, mayonnaise, and remaining ingredients in a bowl; spread over center of piecrust, leaving a 1-inch border. Bake at 350° for 40 minutes or until golden brown. Cool 30 minutes on a wire rack before serving.

Serves 10 (serving size: 1 slice): Calories 205; Fat 12g (sat 2.1g, mono 7.8g, poly 1.7g); Protein 5g; Carb 19g; Fiber 4g; Sugars 3g (est. added sugars: 0g); Chol 4mg; Iron 1mg; Sodium 242mg; Calc 71mg

PESTO POTATO SALAD

HANDS-ON: 20 MIN. TOTAL: 32 MIN.

We start with a pot of cold water, then add a tablespoon of vinegar to help the potatoes hold their shape. Instead of a heavy mayonnaise sauce, we use fresh pesto and yogurt to add creaminess. Toss together the arugula mixture just before serving.

1 1/2 pounds fingerling potatoes, cut into 3/4-inch slices

2 tablespoons white wine vinegar, divided

1 cup fresh basil leaves

1/2 cup chopped fresh parsley

1.5 ounces shaved Parmigiano-Reggiano cheese, divided (about 1/3 cup

2 tablespoons 2% reduced-fat Greek yogurt

1 1/2 tablespoons olive oil mayonnaise

1 tablespoon roasted, salted sunflower seed kernels

1 tablespoon water

2 1/2 teaspoons fresh lemon juice, divided

3/8 teaspoon kosher salt

1 garlic clove, crushed

1 tablespoon olive oil

2 cups baby arugula

1 cup cherry tomatoes, halved

2 tablespoons fresh dill

1. Place potatoes in a saucepan; cover with cold water to 2 inches above potatoes. Add 1 tablespoon vinegar. Bring to a boil; reduce heat, and simmer 10 minutes or until tender. Drain; let stand 10 minutes.

2. Combine basil, parsley, 1 ounce cheese, yogurt, mayonnaise, sunflower seeds, 1 tablespoon vinegar, 1 tablespoon water, 1 1/2 teaspoons juice, salt, and garlic in the bowl of a food processor. Pulse 8 to 10 times or until smooth. Place potatoes in a medium bowl. Add pesto; toss to coat.

3. Combine 1 teaspoon lemon juice and oil in a medium bowl, stirring with a whisk. Add arugula, tomatoes, and 0.5 ounce cheese; toss to coat. Place about 1/2 cup salad on each of 6 plates. Top each salad with 1/2 cup potato mixture. Sprinkle with dill.

Serves 6: Calories 163; Fat 6.4g (sat 1.7g, mono 2.9g, poly 1.1g); Protein 6g; Carb 21g; Fiber 3g; Sugars 3g (est. added sugars: 0g); Chol 7mg; Iron 2mg; Sodium 286mg; Calc 122mg

ZESTY BROCCOLI CASSEROLE

CLASSIC: Calories per serving: 329, Sat Fat: 11.9g, Sodium: 524mg, Sugars: 5g
MAKEOVER: Calories per serving: 141, Sat Fat: 2.6g, Sodium: 484mg, Sugars: 5g

HANDS-ON: 15 MIN. TOTAL: 40 MIN.

Regular breadcrumbs can be used in place of the panko in this casserole. If the broccoli florets are very large, cut them into bite-sized pieces.

3 (10-ounce) packages frozen broccoli florets, thawed
Cooking spray
1 1/2 cups fat-free milk
2 1/2 tablespoons all-purpose flour
1/2 teaspoon salt
1/4 teaspoon freshly ground black pepper
3 ounces shredded sharp cheddar cheese (about 3/4 cup)
4 ounces fat-free cream cheese, softened (about 1/2 cup)
1 cup fat-free mayonnaise
3/4 cup chopped onion (about 1/2 medium)
1 (8-ounce) can water chestnuts, rinsed, drained, and sliced
3/4 cup panko (Japanese breadcrumbs)
2 teaspoons butter, melted

CRAZY TRICK
To mimic the "tang" of Miracle Whip, we used fat-free mayonnaise instead.

1. Preheat oven to 375°.

2. Arrange broccoli in an even layer in an 11 x 7–inch glass or ceramic baking dish coated with cooking spray; set aside.

3. Combine milk, flour, salt, and pepper in a large saucepan over medium-high heat; bring to a boil. Cook 1 minute or until thick, stirring constantly. Remove from heat. Add cheeses; stir until smooth. Stir in mayonnaise, onion, and water chestnuts. Spoon cheese mixture over broccoli.

4. Place panko in a small bowl. Drizzle with butter; toss. Sprinkle breadcrumb mixture over cheese mixture. Lightly coat breadcrumb layer with cooking spray. Bake at 375° for 25 minutes or until mixture begins to bubble and breadcrumbs brown.

Serves 10 (serving size: about 3/4 cup): Calories 141; Fat 4.9g (sat 2.6g, mono 1.3g, poly 0.7g); Protein 9g; Carb 18g; Fiber 4g; Sugars 5g (est. added sugars: 1g); Chol 15mg; Iron 1mg; Sodium 484mg; Calc 173mg

CREAMY WILD RICE,
MUSHROOM, AND LEEK CASSEROLE

CLASSIC: Calories per serving: 318, Sat Fat: 10g, Sodium: 583mg, Sugars: 4g
MAKEOVER: Calories per serving: 207, Sat Fat: 2.9g, Sodium: 244mg, Sugars: 4g

HANDS-ON: 20 MIN. TOTAL: 1 HR. 18 MIN.

Creamy without the cream! This decadent rice and mushroom casserole gets its luxurious sauce from a mixture of brown rice cream and low-fat cream cheese.

1 cup uncooked wild rice
2 cups water
½ cup uncooked instant brown rice
½ cup 2% reduced-fat milk
1½ cups thinly sliced leek (about 1 large)
2 (8-ounce) packages sliced cremini mushrooms
Cooking spray
½ teaspoon kosher salt
¼ teaspoon freshly ground black pepper
4 ounces ⅓-less-fat cream cheese (about ½ cup)
1 ounce shredded fresh Parmesan cheese (about ¼ cup)
½ cup sliced almonds

1. Cook wild rice according to package directions, omitting salt and fat. Place wild rice in a large bowl; set aside, and keep warm.

2. While wild rice cooks, bring 2 cups water and brown rice to a boil in a medium saucepan. Cover, reduce heat, and simmer 30 minutes. Remove from heat, and let stand 5 minutes. Transfer brown rice to a blender, and add milk. Remove center piece of blender lid (to allow steam to escape); secure blender lid on blender. Place a clean towel over opening in blender lid (to avoid splatters). Blend until smooth (about 3 minutes); set aside.

3. Preheat oven to 350°.

4. Heat a large nonstick skillet over medium-high heat. Coat leek and mushrooms with cooking spray. Add leek, mushrooms, salt, and pepper to pan; sauté 8 to 9 minutes or until mushrooms are lightly browned. Remove pan from heat, and add cream cheese, stirring just until cheese melts. Gently fold mushroom mixture into wild rice. Add brown rice mixture and Parmesan cheese; stir gently. Spoon mixture into an 8 x 8–inch glass or ceramic baking dish coated with cooking spray; sprinkle with almonds. Bake at 350° for 20 minutes or until edges are bubbly and almonds are toasted.

Serves 8 (serving size: ¾ cup): Calories 207; Fat 7.9g (sat 2.9g, mono 3g, poly 1g); Protein 10g; Carb 27g; Fiber 3g; Sugars 4g (est. added sugars: 0g); Chol 14mg; Iron 1mg; Sodium 244mg; Calc 119mg

GREEN BEANS AMANDINE

CLASSIC: Calories per serving: 254, Sat Fat: 7g, Sodium: 755mg, Sugars: 4g
MAKEOVER: Calories per serving: 100, Sat Fat: 2.1g, Sodium: 178mg, Sugars: 3g

HANDS-ON: 15 MIN. TOTAL: 15 MIN.

Toasting almonds in butter lends a deep, nutty flavor. Sherry vinegar and Dijon mustard emulsify with the nut-butter mixture to form a rich sauce that delicately coats the green beans.

1 pound haricots verts (French green beans)
1 tablespoon unsalted butter
2 tablespoons sliced almonds
2 teaspoons sherry vinegar
$\frac{1}{2}$ teaspoon grated lemon rind
$\frac{1}{2}$ teaspoon Dijon mustard
$\frac{1}{4}$ teaspoon kosher salt
1 teaspoon almond oil or olive oil

1. Cook haricots verts in boiling water 3 minutes or until crisp-tender. Drain and plunge haricots verts into ice water; drain.

2. Melt butter in a large nonstick skillet over medium heat. Add almonds to pan; cook 1 to 2 minutes or until golden brown, stirring frequently.

3. Combine vinegar and next 3 ingredients (through salt) in a medium bowl, stirring with a whisk. Stir almonds into vinegar mixture; gradually stir in almond oil.

4. Heat skillet over medium-high heat. Add haricots verts to pan. Cook 2 minutes or until thoroughly heated, stirring occasionally. Add haricots verts to vinaigrette; toss gently, and serve immediately.

Serves 4 (serving size: $\frac{1}{4}$ of haricots verts): Calories 100; Fat 6.4g (sat 2.1g, mono 2.8g, poly 1g); Protein 3g; Carb 8g; Fiber 3g; Sugars 3g (est. added sugars: 0g); Chol 8mg; Iron 1mg; Sodium 178mg; Calc 53mg

BROCCOLI
WITH WHITE CHEDDAR SAUCE

CLASSIC: Calories per serving: 141, Sat Fat: 5.7g, Sodium: 587mg, Sugars: 4g
MAKEOVER: Calories per serving: 70, Sat Fat: 1.9g, Sodium: 172mg, Sugars: 2g

HANDS-ON: 14 MIN. TOTAL: 14 MIN.

Broccoli with cheese sauce is a classic combination, and it can be deceptively high in sodium and saturated fat. This technique of tossing cheese with cornstarch and cooking with evaporated fat-free milk creates a silky smooth sauce that's definitely a crowd-pleaser.

6 cups broccoli florets
4 ounces reduced-fat shredded sharp white cheddar cheese (about 1 cup)
1 ounce shredded Gruyère cheese (about ¼ cup)
4 teaspoons all-purpose flour
¼ teaspoon salt
¼ teaspoon dry mustard
¼ teaspoon freshly ground black pepper
1 cup evaporated fat-free milk

1. Add water to a large saucepan to a depth of 1 inch; bring to a simmer over medium-high heat. Place broccoli in a steamer basket, and place steamer basket in pan. Cover and cook 5 to 6 minutes or until broccoli is tender.

2. While broccoli steams, combine cheddar cheese and next 5 ingredients (through pepper) in a medium saucepan. Stir in evaporated milk; bring to a simmer over medium-low heat, stirring constantly with a whisk (about 8 minutes). Simmer 1 minute or until thick and smooth, stirring constantly. Serve cheese sauce with broccoli.

Serves 12 (serving size: ½ cup broccoli and 5 teaspoons cheese sauce): Calories 70; Fat 3g (sat 1.9g, mono 0.3g, poly 0.1g); Protein 6g; Carb 5g; Fiber 1g; Sugars 2g (est. added sugars: 0g); Chol 10mg; Iron 0mg; Sodium 172mg; Calc 170mg

SQUASH CASSEROLE

CLASSIC: Calories per serving: 481, Sat Fat: 12g, Sodium: 802mg, Sugars: 8g
MAKEOVER: Calories per serving: 127, Sat Fat: 2.2g, Sodium: 231mg, Sugars: 4g

HANDS-ON: 25 MIN. TOTAL: 60 MIN.

Whole-wheat panko stars as both a binder and a crunchy topping for this remake of a cheesy, home-style squash casserole. Canola mayonnaise, reduced-fat sour cream, and fat-free milk provide the base for the custard, and fresh herbs liven up the flavors in this traditional favorite.

1 tablespoon canola oil
1 1/2 cups chopped onion
3/4 cup chopped red bell pepper
2 garlic cloves, minced
8 cups sliced yellow squash (about 2 pounds)
1/3 cup canola mayonnaise
1/3 cup reduced-fat sour cream
1/3 cup fat-free milk
2 tablespoons chopped fresh basil
1/2 teaspoon freshly ground black pepper
1/4 teaspoon salt
1 large egg, lightly beaten
1 cup whole-wheat panko (Japanese breadcrumbs), divided
2 ounces shredded reduced-fat sharp cheddar cheese (about 1/2 cup), divided
2 ounces shredded Parmigiano-Reggiano cheese (about 1/2 cup), divided
Cooking spray
1 tablespoon chopped fresh parsley

1. Preheat oven to 350°.

2. Heat oil in a large nonstick skillet over medium-high heat. Add onion and bell pepper to pan; sauté 4 minutes or until almost tender. Add garlic; sauté 1 minute. Stir in squash; cook 3 to 5 minutes or just until squash begins to soften, stirring frequently. Cover and cook 5 minutes or until squash is tender, stirring once. Remove from heat; cool slightly.

3. Combine mayonnaise and next 6 ingredients (through egg) in a large bowl, stirring with a whisk. Stir in 1/2 cup panko, 1/4 cup cheddar cheese, 1/4 cup Parmigiano-Reggiano cheese, and squash mixture. Spoon mixture into an 11 x 7–inch glass or ceramic baking dish coated with cooking spray.

4. Combine 1/2 cup panko, 1/4 cup cheddar cheese, 1/4 cup Parmigiano-Reggiano, and parsley; sprinkle over squash mixture. Bake at 350° for 35 minutes or until mixture is set and topping is golden brown.

Serves 12 (serving size: about 1/2 cup): Calories 127; Fat 6.7g (sat 2.2g, mono 2.6g, poly 1.2g); Protein 6g; Carb 11g; Fiber 2g; Sugars 4g (est. added sugars: 0g); Chol 26mg; Iron 1mg; Sodium 231mg; Calc 135mg

BAKED BEANS

CLASSIC: Calories per serving: 474, Sat Fat: 3.3g, Sodium: 1595mg, Sugars: 40g
MAKEOVER: Calories per serving: 214, Sat Fat: 0.8g, Sodium: 269mg, Sugars: 8g

HANDS-ON: 20 MIN. TOTAL: 20 MIN.

Make these beans for special occasions and festive backyard barbecues. Substituting turkey for the usual pork and beef lightens them up, and you'll never miss the flavor. A crispy topping makes them extra special.

4 ounces lean mild turkey breakfast sausage
4 ounces smoked turkey sausage, diced
1 cup finely chopped onion
4 garlic cloves, chopped
½ cup fat-free, lower-sodium chicken broth
1 tablespoon chopped fresh thyme
¼ cup packed brown sugar
1 tablespoon dry mustard
½ teaspoon Spanish smoked paprika
¼ teaspoon crushed red pepper
3 (15-ounce) cans lower-sodium Great Northern beans, rinsed and drained
1 (8-ounce) can unsalted tomato sauce
1 cup panko (Japanese breadcrumbs)
Cooking spray

1. Cook sausages in a 10-inch cast-iron skillet over medium heat 5 minutes or until browned, stirring to crumble breakfast sausage. Add onion and garlic; cook 4 minutes, stirring frequently. Add broth and thyme, scraping pan to loosen browned bits. Stir in brown sugar and next 5 ingredients (through tomato sauce). Bring to a simmer; reduce heat, and simmer 5 minutes or until slightly thick, stirring occasionally. Remove from heat.

2. Preheat broiler.

3. Sprinkle bean mixture with panko; coat with cooking spray. Broil 1 minute or until panko is golden brown.

Serves 10 (serving size: about ⅔ cup): Calories 214; Fat 4.7g (sat 0.8g, mono 1g, poly 0.8g); Protein 10g; Carb 33g; Fiber 9g; Sugars 8g (est. added sugars: 5g); Chol 26mg; Iron 2mg; Sodium 269mg; Calc 87mg

CRANBERRY-ALMOND
BROCCOLI SALAD

CLASSIC: Calories per serving: 373, Sat Fat: 6.1g, Sodium: 345mg, Sugars: 6g
MAKEOVER: Calories per serving: 104, Sat Fat: 0.8g, Sodium: 224mg, Sugars: 5g

HANDS-ON: 10 MIN. TOTAL: 1 HR. 15 MIN.

Broccoli salad is usually drowning in a creamy, often very sweet dressing and studded with 1/2 pound of crumbled bacon. Most versions of this salad are more about the creamy dressing and bacon than they are about the broccoli. Ours uses a combination of canola mayonnaise and Greek yogurt to keep the calories in check. We've opted for center-cut bacon (a bit less of it) and swapped the usual raisins for unsweetened dried cranberries to pack a subtle punch of tart. The best part of this salad? The longer it sits, the better it gets.

1/4 cup finely chopped red onion
1/3 cup canola mayonnaise
3 tablespoons 2% reduced-fat Greek yogurt
1 tablespoon cider vinegar
1 tablespoon honey
1/4 teaspoon salt
1/4 teaspoon freshly ground black pepper

4 cups coarsely chopped broccoli florets (about 1 bunch)
1/3 cup slivered almonds, toasted
1/3 cup reduced-sugar dried cranberries
4 center-cut bacon slices, cooked and crumbled

1. Soak red onion in cold water 5 minutes; drain.

2. Combine mayonnaise and next 5 ingredients (through pepper), stirring well with a whisk. Stir in red onion, broccoli, and remaining ingredients. Cover and chill 1 hour before serving.

Serves 8 (serving size: about 1/2 cup): Calories 104; Fat 5.9g (sat 0.8g, mono 3g, poly 1.5g); Protein 4g; Carb 11g; Fiber 3g; Sugars 5g (est. added sugars 4g); Chol 4mg; Iron 1mg; Sodium 224mg; Calc 34mg

LEMONY ROASTED CAULIFLOWER
WITH BREADCRUMBS

CLASSIC: Calories per serving: 361, Sat Fat: 2.4g, Sodium: 117mg, Sugars: 4g
MAKEOVER: Calories per serving: 114, Sat Fat: 0.4g, Sodium: 169mg, Sugars: 3g

HANDS-ON: 8 MIN. TOTAL: 31 MIN.

Nutty flavors enhanced by oven roasting make the cauliflower taste decadent and earthy, while the fresh addition of lemon keeps the flavors bright. Crunchy panko breadcrumbs add a textural element that puts this dish over the top.

2 tablespoons canola oil
1 teaspoon grated lemon rind
1 tablespoon fresh lemon juice
¼ teaspoon salt
¼ teaspoon freshly ground black
  pepper
1 large head cauliflower, cut into florets
½ cup panko (Japanese breadcrumbs)
Cooking spray
1 tablespoon thyme leaves

1. Preheat oven to 425°.

2. Combine first 5 ingredients in a large bowl; add cauliflower, tossing gently to coat. Spread cauliflower in a single layer on a jelly-roll pan; reserve any remaining oil mixture in bowl. Bake at 425° for 25 minutes or until tender and lightly browned, stirring after 15 minutes.

3. While cauliflower bakes, place panko in a small bowl. Coat panko heavily with cooking spray, tossing gently. Heat a medium nonstick skillet over medium-high heat. Add panko to pan; cook 2 minutes or until toasted, stirring frequently.

4. Return cauliflower to remaining oil mixture in bowl. Add toasted panko and thyme; toss gently to coat. Serve immediately.

Serves 6 (serving size: ½ cup): Calories 114; Fat 5.4g (sat 0.4g, mono 3g, poly 1.3g); Protein 4g; Carb 14g; Fiber 3g; Sugars 3g (est. added sugars: 0g); Chol 0mg; Iron 1mg; Sodium 169mg; Calc 33mg

CREAMY PASTA SALAD

CLASSIC: Calories per serving: 506, Sat Fat: 5g, Sodium: 822mg, Sugars: 4g
MAKEOVER: Calories per serving: 161, Sat Fat: 0.6g, Sodium: 278mg, Sugars: 3g

HANDS-ON: 10 MIN. TOTAL: 1 HR. 15 MIN.

This all-American cookout favorite is often very heavy on the mayonnaise and even sugar. Here, we've opted for canola mayonnaise and a bit of light sour cream. There's just a hint of sugar to balance the dressing, and the addition of capers adds the perfect hit of briny flavor.

8 ounces uncooked orecchiette ("little ears" pasta; about 2 1/2 cups)
1/2 cup canola mayonnaise
1/4 cup light sour cream
1 1/2 tablespoons red wine vinegar
1 teaspoon sugar
1 1/2 teaspoons Dijon mustard
1/4 teaspoon salt
1/4 teaspoon freshly ground black pepper
1/2 cup thinly sliced celery
1/2 cup finely chopped red bell pepper
1/3 cup finely chopped shallots
2 tablespoons chopped fresh parsley
2 tablespoons drained capers, chopped

1. Cook pasta according to package directions, omitting salt and fat. Drain and rinse with cold water; drain.

2. Combine mayonnaise and next 6 ingredients (through black pepper), stirring with a whisk. Stir in cooked pasta, celery, and remaining ingredients. Cover and chill at least 1 hour or until ready to serve.

Serves 8 (serving size: about 1/2 cup): Calories 161; Fat 5.2g (sat 0.6g, mono 2.3g, poly 1.4g); Protein 4g; Carb 24g; Fiber 2g; Sugars 3g (est. added sugars: 1g); Chol 4mg; Iron 1mg; Sodium 278mg; Calc 19mg

STOVETOP CREAMED
SPINACH

CLASSIC: Calories per serving: 234, Sat Fat: 9.8g, Sodium: 768mg, Sugars: 5g
MAKEOVER: Calories per serving: 108, Sat Fat: 9g, Sodium: 240mg, Sugars: 3g

HANDS-ON: 20 MIN. TOTAL: 20 MIN.

Instead of heavy cream, this comforting side dish uses unsweetened cashew milk, which comes in at a mere 25 calories per cup.

2 (5-ounce) packages fresh baby
  spinach
2 (5-ounce) packages fresh baby kale
2 teaspoons canola oil
2 shallots, chopped
1¼ cups unsweetened cashew milk
3 tablespoons all-purpose flour

2 tablespoons grated fresh
  Parmigiano-Reggiano cheese
⅛ teaspoon salt
⅛ teaspoon freshly ground black
  pepper
¼ cup panko (Japanese breadcrumbs)
2 teaspoons chopped fresh parsley

1. Add water to a large saucepan to a depth of 1 inch. Bring to a simmer over medium-high heat. Add 1 package spinach; cook 1 minute or until spinach wilts. Repeat procedure 3 times with remaining spinach and kale. Drain well.

2. Wipe pan dry with a paper towel. Heat oil in pan over medium heat. Add shallots; sauté 2 minutes or until tender. Combine milk and flour, stirring with a whisk. Gradually add milk mixture to pan, stirring constantly with a whisk. Bring to a simmer, stirring constantly; simmer 2 to 3 minutes or until thick, stirring constantly with a whisk. Remove pan from heat; add cheese, salt, and pepper, stirring with a whisk until cheese melts. Stir in spinach and kale. Cover and keep warm.

3. Heat a small nonstick skillet over medium-high heat. Add panko to pan; cook 2 to 3 minutes or until toasted, stirring frequently. Stir in parsley. Divide spinach mixture evenly among 6 plates; sprinkle with panko mixture.

Serves 6 (serving size: ½ cup spinach mixture and about 2 teaspoons panko mixture): Calories 108; Fat 14.5g (sat 9g, mono 4g, poly 0.6g); Protein 6g; Carb 20g; Fiber 7g; Sugars 3g (est. added sugars: 0g); Chol 48mg; Iron 5mg; Sodium 240mg; Calc 152mg

CORN PUDDING

CLASSIC: Calories per serving: 494, Sat Fat: 22.6g, Sodium: 774mg, Sugars: 13g
MAKEOVER: Calories per serving: 164, Sat Fat: 0.8g, Sodium: 266mg, Sugars: 8g

HANDS-ON: 15 MIN. TOTAL: 65 MIN.

Soufflé-like in texture with both sweet and savory elements, this side dish is a welcome addition to any holiday table.

2 (10-ounce) packages frozen whole-kernel corn, thawed
¼ cup chopped fresh chives
1 tablespoon millet flour
2 tablespoons grapeseed oil
1 tablespoon honey
Dash of grated whole nutmeg
1 (12-ounce) can evaporated low-fat milk
2 large eggs, lightly beaten
½ vanilla bean
¾ teaspoon salt
2 large egg whites
Cooking spray

SECRET TO SUCCESS
Swap heavy cream for evaporated milk and beaten egg whites, which provide a light and fluffy texture that's still creamy in flavor.

1. Preheat oven to 350°.

2. Place 1 package corn in a food processor; pulse 10 times or until chopped. Set aside.

3. Combine chives and next 6 ingredients (through whole eggs) in a large bowl, stirring with a whisk. Scrape seeds from vanilla bean into milk mixture; discard bean. Stir in whole-kernel corn, chopped corn, and salt.

4. Beat egg whites with a mixer at high speed until stiff peaks form (do not overbeat). Gently fold egg whites into corn mixture. Pour into an 11 x 7–inch glass or ceramic baking dish coated with cooking spray.

5. Bake at 350° for 45 minutes or until set. Let stand 5 minutes before serving.

Serves 8 (serving size: about ¾ cup): Calories 164; Fat 6g (sat 0.8g, mono 1.2g, poly 2.9g); Protein 8g; Carb 22g; Fiber 2g; Sugars 8g (est. added sugars: 2g); Chol 54mg; Iron 1mg; Sodium 266mg; Calc 131mg

ROOT VEGETABLE
HASH AND BACON

CLASSIC: Calories per serving: 330, Sat Fat: 6.6g, Sodium: 758mg, Sugars: 3g
MAKEOVER: Calories per serving: 122, Sat Fat: 1.7g, Sodium: 245mg, Sugars: 9g

HANDS-ON: 37 MIN. TOTAL: 37 MIN.

Hash is usually a great way to use up last night's leftover roast, but it doesn't have to be overloaded with meat. Use a combination of colorful vegetables to make a hearty side dish that's lower in fat and calories.

2 bacon slices
1½ teaspoons olive oil
1 cup (½-inch) cubed peeled turnips
1 cup (½-inch) cubed peeled golden beets
1 cup chopped Vidalia or other sweet onion
¾ cup (½-inch-thick) slices carrot
¾ cup (½-inch-thick) slices parsnip
½ cup chopped bottled roasted red bell peppers

2 teaspoons finely chopped fresh rosemary
1½ teaspoons finely chopped fresh thyme
½ teaspoon freshly ground black pepper
⅛ teaspoon salt
3 garlic cloves, minced
1½ teaspoons white balsamic vinegar

1. Cook bacon in a large nonstick skillet over medium heat 6 minutes or until crisp. Remove bacon from pan, reserving 1 tablespoon drippings in pan. Crumble bacon; set aside.

2. Add oil to drippings in pan; return to medium heat. Add turnip and next 4 ingredients (through parsnip); sauté 7 minutes or until vegetables are tender. Flatten vegetables against bottom of pan using a spatula; cook, without stirring, 2 minutes or until vegetables begin to brown. Stir gently; cook, without stirring, 2 minutes.

3. Stir in roasted red bell peppers and next 5 ingredients (through garlic); cook 8 minutes or until vegetables are tender and browned, stirring occasionally. Stir in vinegar, scraping pan to loosen browned bits. Stir in bacon; serve immediately.

Serves 6 (serving size: about ⅓ cup): Calories 122; Fat 5.8g (sat 1.7g, mono 2.8g, poly 0.7g); Protein 3g; Carb 16g; Fiber 3g; Sugars 9g (est. added sugars: 0g); Chol 7mg; Iron 1mg; Sodium 245mg; Calc 42mg

BUTTERMILK-PARMESAN
MASHED POTATOES

HANDS-ON: 10 MIN. TOTAL: 20 MIN.

Be sure to purchase a crumbly wedge of Parmigiano-Reggiano for this super quick potato side dish. Buttermilk adds tanginess without as much fat as heavy cream.

2 pounds baking potatoes
$2/3$ cup fat-free milk
3 tablespoons butter
$1/2$ cup buttermilk
$1 1/2$ ounces fresh Parmigiano-Reggiano cheese, grated (about $1/3$ cup)

$1/2$ teaspoon salt
$1/4$ teaspoon freshly ground black pepper

1. Pierce each potato several times with a fork. Microwave at HIGH 16 minutes or until tender, turning after 8 minutes. Let stand 2 minutes. Cut each potato in half lengthwise; scoop out flesh with a large spoon, and transfer to a bowl.

2. Combine fat-free milk and butter in a microwave-safe bowl; microwave at HIGH 2 minutes or until butter melts. Add milk mixture to potatoes; mash with a potato masher to desired consistency. Stir in buttermilk and remaining ingredients.

Serves 6 (serving size: $3/4$ cup): Calories 240; Fat 7.9g (sat 4.9g, mono 1.9g, poly 0.3g); Protein 8g; Carb 35g; Fiber 4g; Sugars 4g (est. added sugars: 0g); Chol 22mg; Iron 2mg; Sodium 366mg; Calc 117mg

SWEET POTATO CASSEROLE

HANDS-ON: 10 MIN. TOTAL: 1 HR. 10 MIN.

Evaporated milk is a secret ingredient that adds richness and texture. It's naturally low-fat and adds natural sweetness so you won't have to use as much sugar.

POTATOES:

2 pounds sweet potatoes, peeled and chopped
3/4 cup granulated sugar
1/4 cup evaporated low-fat milk
3 tablespoons butter, melted

1/2 teaspoon salt
1 teaspoon vanilla extract
2 large eggs
Cooking spray

TOPPING:

1.5 ounces all-purpose flour (about 1/3 cup)
2/3 cup packed brown sugar

1/8 teaspoon salt
2 tablespoons butter, melted
1/2 cup chopped pecans

1. Preheat oven to 350°.

2. To prepare potatoes, place potatoes in a Dutch oven; cover with water. Bring to a boil. Reduce heat, and simmer 20 minutes or until tender; drain. Cool 5 minutes.

3. Place potatoes in a large bowl; add granulated sugar, evaporated milk, 3 tablespoons melted butter, 1/2 teaspoon salt, and vanilla. Beat with a mixer at medium speed until smooth. Add eggs; beat well. Pour potato mixture into a 13 x 9–inch baking pan coated with cooking spray.

4. To prepare topping, weigh or lightly spoon flour into a dry measuring cup; level with a knife. Combine flour, brown sugar, and 1/8 teaspoon salt; stir with a whisk. Stir in 2 tablespoons melted butter. Sprinkle flour mixture over potato mixture; arrange pecans over top. Bake at 350° for 25 minutes or just until golden.

5. Preheat broiler (remove casserole from oven).

6. Broil casserole 45 seconds or until topping is bubbly. Let stand 10 minutes before serving.

Serves 12 (serving size: about 2/3 cup): Calories 258; Fat 9.2g (sat 3.6g, mono 3.6g, poly 1.5g); Protein 3g; Carb 42g; Fiber 3g; Sugars 30g (est. added sugars: 25g); Chol 43mg; Iron 1mg; Sodium 199mg; Calc 54mg

EASY, CHEESY
POTATO GRATIN

CLASSIC: Calories per serving: 363, Sat Fat: 14.9g, Sodium: 389mg, Sugars: 5g
MAKEOVER: Calories per serving: 159, Sat Fat: 2.8g, Sodium: 226mg, Sugars: 3g

HANDS-ON: 15 MIN. TOTAL: 45 MIN.

Refrigerated presliced potatoes slash tons of prep and cook time. The combo of Gruyère and Parm-Regg cheeses is delicious, but you can use all one type if you prefer.

2 (20-ounce) bags home-style potato slices
Cooking spray
1½ tablespoons butter
1 tablespoon chopped fresh thyme
4 garlic cloves, minced
6 tablespoons all-purpose flour
3 cups 2% reduced-fat milk, divided

½ teaspoon salt
¼ teaspoon freshly ground black pepper
1.5 ounces aged Gruyère cheese, shredded (about ⅓ cup)
1 ounce Parmigiano-Reggiano cheese, grated (about ¼ cup)
1 tablespoon chopped fresh chives

1. Preheat oven to 400°.

2. Arrange potatoes in a broiler-safe 11 x 7–inch glass or ceramic baking dish coated with cooking spray. Cover with plastic wrap; vent. Microwave at HIGH 10 minutes; uncover carefully.

3. Melt butter in a medium saucepan over medium heat; swirl to coat. Add thyme and garlic; sauté 3 minutes. Sprinkle with flour; stir in ⅓ cup milk. Cook 1 minute, stirring constantly with a whisk. Stir in 2⅔ cups milk. Bring mixture to a simmer; cook 4 minutes or until slightly thick, stirring frequently. Remove from heat. Stir in salt, pepper, and Gruyère. Pour sauce over potato mixture; sprinkle with Parmigiano-Reggiano. Bake at 400° for 20 minutes or until potatoes are tender when pierced with a knife.

4. Turn broiler on (leave dish in oven). Broil gratin 2 minutes or until browned. Sprinkle with chives.

Serves 12 (serving size: about ⅔ cup): Calories 159; Fat 4.5g (sat 2.8g, mono 1.3g, poly 0.2g); Protein 6g; Carb 24g; Fiber 2g; Sugars 3g (est. added sugars: 0g); Chol 15mg; Iron 1mg; Sodium 226mg; Calc 138mg

CREAMY, CHEESY, DOUBLE-POTATO
HASH BROWN CASSEROLE

CLASSIC: Calories per serving: 480, Sat Fat: 19g, Sodium: 872mg, Sugars: 3g
MAKEOVER: Calories per serving: 125, Sat Fat: 2.8g, Sodium: 192mg, Sugars: 3g

HANDS-ON: 30 MIN. TOTAL: 45 MIN.

Meaty, pan-seared center-cut bacon and earthy mushrooms deliver full savory satisfaction to every bite, allowing us to cut salt in half. Reduced-fat kettle chips add savory crunch on top.

1 cup unsalted chicken stock
2 cups chopped onion, divided
2 (8-ounce) packages presliced white mushrooms, divided
6 garlic cloves
½ cup light sour cream
1 teaspoon freshly ground black pepper
½ teaspoon kosher salt
4 ounces reduced-fat sharp cheddar cheese, shredded and divided (about 1 cup)

3 center-cut bacon slices
1 (30-ounce) package frozen shredded hash brown potatoes, thawed
1 tablespoon olive oil, divided
2 large eggs, lightly beaten
2 ounces 40%-less-fat original kettle-style potato chips, crushed
3 tablespoons chopped fresh flat-leaf parsley

CRAZY TRICK
Simmer and puree fresh mushrooms and garlic with light sour cream to create a silky sauce, replacing canned mushroom soup, full-fat sour cream, and butter.

1. Preheat oven to 400°.

2. Combine stock, 1 cup onion, half of mushrooms, and garlic in a saucepan; bring to a boil. Cover, reduce heat, and simmer 10 minutes or until mushrooms are tender. Place mixture in a blender. Remove center piece of blender lid (to allow steam to escape); secure blender lid on blender. Place a clean towel over opening in blender lid (to avoid splatters); blend until smooth. Stir in sour cream, pepper, salt, and 2 ounces cheese; blend until smooth.

3. Cook bacon in a large cast-iron skillet over medium heat until crisp. Remove bacon from pan; crumble. Add half of potatoes to drippings in pan; cover and cook 4 minutes on each side or until browned. Remove potatoes from pan. Repeat procedure with remaining potatoes and 2 teaspoons oil. Remove from pan.

4. Add 1 teaspoon oil to pan; swirl to coat. Add 1 cup onion and remaining half of mushrooms to pan; cook 6 minutes or until tender, stirring occasionally. Return potatoes to pan; add eggs, stirring well to combine. Pour sour cream mixture over potato mixture. Sprinkle with bacon, 2 ounces cheese, chips, and parsley. Bake at 400° for 10 minutes or until cheese melts. Turn broiler on (do not remove pan from oven); broil 1½ minutes or until lightly browned.

Serves 8 (serving size: 1 wedge): Calories 125; Fat 4.5g (sat 2.8g, mono 1.3g, poly 0.2g); Protein 5g; Carb 16g; Fiber 1g; Sugars 3g (est. added sugars: 0g); Chol 15mg; Iron 1mg; Sodium 192mg; Calc 139mg

TWICE-BAKED POTATOES

CLASSIC: Calories per serving: 400, Sat Fat: 10.4g, Sodium: 603mg, Sugars: 5g
MAKEOVER: Calories per serving: 237, Sat Fat: 4g, Sodium: 341mg, Sugars: 2g

HANDS-ON: 1 HR. 15 MIN. TOTAL: 1 HR. 45 MIN.

Baking the potatoes on a layer of salt yields a crispier exterior and an even fluffier interior without added fat, extra calories, or excess sodium-absorption. Roasted garlic adds a bit of sweetness next to the slightly bitter greens.

1 whole garlic head
2 cups kosher salt
1 tablespoon thyme leaves
4 (12-ounce) baking potatoes
4 ounces diced pancetta
8 ounces curly kale, coarsely chopped
1 tablespoon white balsamic vinegar
$\frac{1}{2}$ cup fat-free, lower-sodium chicken broth

1$\frac{1}{2}$ teaspoons unsalted butter
$\frac{1}{2}$ cup plain 2% reduced-fat Greek yogurt
$\frac{1}{2}$ teaspoon freshly ground white pepper
2 ounces goat cheese, crumbled (about $\frac{1}{2}$ cup)
Cooking spray

1. Preheat oven to 450°.

2. Remove and discard papery outer skin of garlic head. Cut top off garlic head; discard top. Combine salt and thyme in a 13 x 9–inch glass or ceramic baking dish. Pierce potatoes with a fork; arrange potatoes and garlic in salt mixture. Cover with foil; bake at 450° for 1 hour or until potatoes are tender. Let potatoes and garlic cool 10 minutes (do not discard salt mixture).

3. While potatoes bake, cook pancetta in a large nonstick skillet over medium-low heat 8 minutes or until crisp. Remove pancetta from pan; drain. Add kale to drippings in pan, and increase heat to medium; cover and cook 3 minutes. Stir in vinegar; cook 1 minute or until kale is tender, stirring frequently. Set aside.

4. Squeeze roasted garlic cloves into a small saucepan; discard garlic skins. Add broth and butter to saucepan; bring to a simmer over medium heat, stirring with a whisk. Cook 2 minutes or until butter melts, stirring occasionally. Puree garlic mixture with an immersion blender until smooth.

5. Cut each potato in half lengthwise; scoop out pulp, leaving a $\frac{1}{4}$-inch-thick shell. Place potato pulp in a large bowl; mash with a potato masher until smooth. Fold in garlic mixture, yogurt, and pepper. Gently fold in kale, pancetta, and goat cheese.

6. Increase oven temperature to 500°.

7. Coat potato shells with cooking spray. Scoop potato mixture into shells; arrange stuffed shells in salt mixture in baking dish. Bake at 500° for 15 to 20 minutes or until skins are crispy and filling is golden brown. Discard salt mixture or reserve for another use; serve potatoes warm.

Serves 8 (serving size: 1 stuffed potato shell): Calories 237; Fat 7.4g (sat 4g, mono 0.6g, poly 0.2g); Protein 9g; Carb 34g; Fiber 3g; Sugars 2g (est. added sugars: 0g); Chol 16mg; Iron 2mg; Sodium 341mg; Calc 87mg

OVEN "FRIED"
SWEET POTATO WEDGES

CLASSIC: Calories per serving: 476, Sat Fat: 3.3g, Sodium: 614mg, Sugars: 10g
MAKEOVER: Calories per serving: 152, Sat Fat: 0.8g, Sodium: 182mg, Sugars: 5g

HANDS-ON: 10 MIN. TOTAL: 55 MIN.

Sweet potato fries are such a treat in restaurants. Now you can enjoy a healthier version at home, without the messy frying. Make sure to leave space between each wedge on the baking sheet for optimal browning and crisping.

3 small sweet potatoes (about
  2 pounds)
Cooking spray
2 tablespoons cornstarch
3 tablespoons olive oil
2 teaspoons salt-free garlic and herb
  seasoning blend
1 teaspoon dry mustard
½ teaspoon kosher salt
¼ teaspoon freshly ground black
  pepper
1 tablespoon chopped fresh thyme

1. Preheat oven to 450°.

2. Cut each potato lengthwise into 8 wedges. Coat a baking sheet with cooking spray.

3. Combine cornstarch and next 5 ingredients (through pepper) in a medium bowl, stirring well with a whisk. Add potato wedges to bowl; toss gently to coat. Arrange potato wedges on prepared baking sheet; reserve any remaining oil mixture in bowl. Bake at 450° for 30 minutes. Turn potato wedges over; bake an additional 15 minutes. Return potato wedges to remaining oil mixture in bowl; sprinkle with thyme. Toss gently to coat; serve immediately.

Serves 8 (serving size: 3 wedges): Calories 152; Fat 5.4g (sat 0.8g, mono 3.8g, poly 0.8g); Protein 2g; Carb 25g; Fiber 4g; Sugars 5g (est. added sugars: 0g); Chol 0mg; Iron 1mg; Sodium 182mg; Calc 36mg

Cheesecake,
page 269

DREAMY DESSERTS

FRESH STRAWBERRY SHORTCAKES WITH YOGURT CREAM

HANDS-ON: 20 MIN. TOTAL: 33 MIN.

If you have a minute to spare, swap out the vanilla extract for a vanilla bean. Split the bean lengthwise, scrape half of the seeds into the shortcake recipe, and whip the remaining half into the yogurt cream. It will add an extra level of flavor-packed intensity to the recipe.

5.6 ounces all-purpose flour (about 1 ¼ cups)
3.6 ounces whole-wheat flour (about ¾ cup)
¼ cup packed brown sugar
2 teaspoons baking powder
¾ teaspoon salt
½ teaspoon baking soda
¼ cup unsalted butter
1¼ cups very cold nonfat buttermilk
2 tablespoons canola oil
1 teaspoon vanilla extract
1½ pounds strawberries
¼ cup sugar, divided
1 teaspoon fresh lemon juice
½ cup plain 2% reduced-fat Greek yogurt
⅓ cup heavy whipping cream

1. Preheat oven to 450°.

2. Weigh or lightly spoon flours into dry measuring cups; level with a knife. Combine flours, brown sugar, baking powder, salt, and baking soda in a large bowl, stirring with a whisk to combine.

3. Place butter in a medium microwave-safe bowl. Microwave at HIGH 1 minute or until melted. Add cold buttermilk, stirring until butter forms small lumps. Add oil and vanilla, stirring to combine.

4. Add buttermilk mixture to flour mixture, stirring just until incorporated (do not overmix) and batter pulls away from sides of bowl (batter will be very wet).

5. Drop batter into 12 mounds (about 2 heaping tablespoonfuls each) onto a baking sheet lined with parchment paper. Bake at 450° for 12 minutes or until golden.

6. While biscuits bake, slice strawberries. Combine strawberries, 2 tablespoons sugar, and lemon juice; toss to coat. Set aside.

7. Place yogurt, cream, and 2 tablespoons sugar in a bowl; beat with a mixer at medium speed until soft peaks form. Split biscuits; fill with berry mixture and cream.

Serves 12 (serving size: 1 biscuit, about ⅓ cup strawberries, and about 1½ tablespoons cream mixture): Calories 224; Fat 9.3g (sat 4.3g, mono 3.2g, poly 1.1g); Protein 5g; Carb 32g; Fiber 2g; Sugars 12g (est. added sugars: 9g); Chol 20mg; Iron 1mg; Sodium 313mg; Calc 106mg

CHOCOLATE MOLTEN LAVA CAKES

CLASSIC: Calories per serving: 631, Sat Fat: 23g, Sodium: 46mg, Sugars: 48g
MAKEOVER: Calories per serving: 249, Sat Fat: 5.1g, Sodium: 135mg, Sugars: 24g

HANDS-ON: 20 MIN. TOTAL: 2 HR.

Whole-wheat pastry flour lightens up the batter and creates a crisp outer crust, a lovely contrast to the melty center.

3 tablespoons unsalted butter
2 tablespoons canola oil
3 ounces high-quality dark or
   bittersweet chocolate (60% to 70%
   cacao), chopped
3 ounces whole-wheat pastry flour
   (about ⅔ cup)
½ cup unsweetened cocoa

1½ teaspoons baking powder
¼ teaspoon kosher salt
½ cup granulated sugar
½ cup packed brown sugar
½ teaspoon vanilla extract
3 large eggs
Baking spray with flour
Powdered sugar (optional)

CRAZY TRICK
Create the molten action with just a bit of melted chocolate slipped inside each cake.

1. Combine butter, oil, and chocolate in the top of a double boiler. Cook over simmering water until chocolate almost fully melts, stirring gently with a spatula. Remove top of double boiler; stir until chocolate fully melts.

2. Weigh or lightly spoon flour into a dry measuring cup; level with a knife. Combine flour, cocoa, baking powder, and salt in a bowl; stir well with a whisk.

3. Place granulated sugar, brown sugar, vanilla, and eggs in a large bowl; beat with a mixer at medium speed until light and fluffy (about 2 minutes). Set aside 2½ tablespoons chocolate mixture. Gradually pour remaining chocolate mixture in a thin stream over egg mixture, beating at medium speed. Gently fold flour mixture into egg mixture. Divide batter among 10 (5-ounce) ramekins coated with baking spray. Working with 1 ramekin at a time, spoon ¾ teaspoon reserved chocolate mixture into center, pushing teaspoon toward center of batter. Repeat with remaining ramekins and chocolate mixture. Arrange ramekins on a jelly-roll pan. Cover and refrigerate 1 hour.

4. Preheat oven to 400°.

5. Let ramekins stand at room temperature 15 minutes. Uncover and bake at 400° for 13 minutes or until cakes are puffy and slightly crusty on top (centers will not be set). Place a dessert plate on top of ramekin. Using a dry kitchen towel to steady ramekin, invert each cake onto plate. Sprinkle with powdered sugar, if desired. Serve immediately.

Serves 10 (serving size: 1 cake): Calories 249; Fat 11.8g (sat 5.1g, mono 4.4g, poly 1.3g); Protein 4g; Carb 35g; Fiber 3g; Sugars 24g (est. added sugars: 21g); Chol 65mg; Iron 2mg; Sodium 135mg; Calc 71mg

CHOCOLATE CUPCAKES

HANDS-ON: 60 MIN. TOTAL: 2 HR. 33 MIN.

Cocoa and bittersweet chocolate provide an extra punch of flavor.

CUPCAKES:

7 ounces cake flour (about 1 3/4 cups)
1/2 teaspoon salt
1/2 teaspoon baking soda
1/2 teaspoon baking powder
1/2 cup unsweetened cocoa
1 1/2 cups sugar
1/2 cup butter, softened
2 large egg yolks

1/2 teaspoon vanilla extract
1 cup whole buttermilk
2 ounces unsweetened baking
  chocolate
3 large egg whites
1/4 teaspoon cream of tartar
Baking spray with flour

FROSTING:

1 1/3 cups sugar
1/3 cup water
1/2 vanilla bean
3 large egg whites

1/4 teaspoon cream of tartar
1/8 teaspoon salt
1/4 cup unsweetened cocoa
1 ounce bittersweet chocolate

1. Preheat oven to 350°. To prepare cupcakes, combine flour, salt, baking soda, and baking powder; stir with a whisk. Stir in 1/2 cup cocoa. Place sugar and butter in a large bowl; beat with a mixer at high speed until well blended. Add egg yolks, beating well after each addition. Stir in vanilla extract. Reduce mixer speed to low. Add flour mixture and buttermilk alternately to butter mixture, beginning and ending with flour mixture; beat just until combined. Melt unsweetened chocolate; stir into batter. Using clean, dry beaters, beat egg whites and cream of tartar at high speed until stiff peaks form. Fold one-third of egg whites into batter. Gently fold in remaining egg whites. Line 24 muffin cups with cupcake liners; coat with baking spray. Spoon batter into cups. Bake at 350° for 23 minutes or until a wooden pick inserted in centers comes out with moist crumbs clinging. Cool in pans 10 minutes. Remove from pans; cool completely on wire racks.

2. To prepare frosting, place sugar, water, and vanilla bean in a saucepan; bring to a boil. Cook, without stirring, 3 minutes or until a candy thermometer registers 250°; discard vanilla bean. Combine egg whites, cream of tartar, and salt in a large bowl; using clean, dry beaters, beat with a mixer at high speed until foamy. Pour hot sugar syrup in a thin stream over egg whites, beating at high speed until stiff peaks form. Reduce mixer speed to low; beat until mixture cools (12 minutes). Fold in 1/4 cup cocoa. Top cupcakes with frosting. Shave bittersweet chocolate over frosted cupcakes.

Serves 24 (serving size: 1 cupcake): Calories 185; Fat 6.6g (sat 3.8g, mono 1.2g, poly 0.3g); Protein 3g; Carb 31g; Fiber 1g; Sugars 24g (est. added sugars: 23g); Chol 27mg; Iron 1mg; Sodium 158mg; Calc 11mg

MISSISSIPPI MUD PIE

CLASSIC: Calories per serving: 815, Sat Fat: 20.8g, Sodium: 480mg, Sugars: 77g
MAKEOVER: Calories per serving: 277, Sat Fat: 5.5g, Sodium: 162mg, Sugars: 24g

HANDS-ON: 21 MIN. TOTAL: 1 HR. 31 MIN.

Don't be tempted to use Dutch process cocoa powder in the crust or the texture will be tough.

CRUST:

4.5 ounces all-purpose flour (about 1 cup)
2 tablespoons sugar
2 tablespoons unsweetened cocoa
1/4 teaspoon salt
2 1/2 tablespoons vegetable shortening
2 tablespoons chilled butter, cut into
   small pieces
1/4 cup ice water
Cooking spray

FILLING:

3 tablespoons butter
1 ounce semisweet chocolate chips
1 teaspoon vanilla extract
4 large egg whites
1 cup sugar
3.4 ounces all-purpose flour (about
   3/4 cup)
1/3 cup Dutch process cocoa
1/2 teaspoon baking powder
Dash of salt

1. To prepare crust, weigh or lightly spoon 4.5 ounces (about 1 cup) flour into a dry measuring cup; level with a knife. Combine 4.5 ounces flour, 2 tablespoons sugar, 2 tablespoons unsweetened cocoa, and 1/4 teaspoon salt in a food processor; pulse 2 times or until blended. Add shortening and chilled butter; pulse 6 times or until mixture resembles coarse meal. With processor on, slowly pour 1/4 cup ice water through food chute, processing just until blended (do not allow dough to form a ball); remove from bowl. Gently press mixture into a 4-inch circle; wrap in plastic wrap. Chill 30 minutes.

2. Preheat oven to 350°. Unwrap and place chilled dough on plastic wrap. Lightly sprinkle dough with flour; roll to a 10-inch circle. Fit dough, plastic wrap side up, into a 9-inch pie plate coated with cooking spray. Remove remaining plastic wrap. Fold edges under, and flute.

3. To prepare filling, place 3 tablespoons butter and chocolate chips in a microwave-safe bowl. Microwave at HIGH 30 seconds or until butter and chocolate melt, stirring well to combine. Place vanilla and egg whites in a bowl; beat with a mixer at medium speed until foamy. Gradually add 1 cup sugar; beat until soft peaks form (about 2 minutes). Gently fold melted chocolate mixture into egg white mixture.

4. Combine flour, cocoa, baking powder, and dash of salt in a small bowl, stirring with a whisk. Fold flour mixture into egg white mixture. Pour mixture into prepared crust. Bake at 350° for 40 minutes or until a wooden pick inserted in center comes out clean. Cool on a wire rack.

Serves 10 (serving size: 1 slice): Calories 277; Fat 10.2g (sat 5.5g, mono 2.5g, poly 1.2g); Protein 5g; Carb 44g; Fiber 2g; Sugars 24g (est. added sugars: 23g); Chol 15mg; Iron 2mg; Sodium 162mg; Calc 24mg

NEW CLASSIC
RED VELVET CAKE

CLASSIC: Calories per serving: 880, Sat Fat: 19.7g, Sodium: 457mg, Sugars: 67g
MAKEOVER: Calories per serving: 284, Sat Fat: 3.7g, Sodium: 199mg, Sugars: 33g

HANDS-ON: 48 MIN. TOTAL: 2 HR. 7 MIN.

Vegetables in a cake? Absolutely, thanks to the neutral flavor of beets.

CAKE:
1 (10-ounce) beet, peeled and cut into
  8 wedges
$^3/_4$ cup nonfat buttermilk
$1^1/_2$ teaspoons vanilla extract
8 ounces cake flour (about 2 cups)
3 tablespoons unsweetened cocoa
$1^1/_4$ teaspoons baking powder

$^1/_2$ teaspoon salt
$1^1/_2$ cups granulated sugar
$^1/_4$ cup butter, softened
$^1/_4$ cup canola oil
2 large eggs
1 large egg white
Baking spray with flour

FILLING:
4 ounces $^1/_3$-less-fat cream cheese,
  softened (about $^1/_2$ cup)
2 tablespoons heavy whipping cream
2 tablespoons 2% reduced-fat Greek
  yogurt

$^1/_2$ teaspoon vanilla extract
Dash of salt
$^1/_2$ cup powdered sugar

MERINGUE FROSTING:
$^2/_3$ cup granulated sugar
4 large egg whites

$^1/_4$ teaspoon cream of tartar
Dash of salt

SNEAK ATTACK
Cooking the vibrant-red, naturally sweet beets with nonfat buttermilk and vanilla, and then pureeing the mixture into a luscious cream, adds an ultramoist, velvety texture to the cake.

1. Preheat oven to 350°.

2. To prepare cake, place beet in a small saucepan; cover with water. Bring to a boil. Cook 10 minutes or until tender. Drain and cool slightly.

3. Place beet in a food processor; process until very finely chopped. Remove 1 cup beet from processor; reserve remaining beet for another use. Combine 1 cup beet, buttermilk, and $1^1/_2$ teaspoons vanilla in food processor. Process until very smooth.

4. Weigh or lightly spoon flour into dry measuring cups; level with a knife. Combine flour, cocoa, baking powder, and $^1/_2$ teaspoon salt in a bowl, stirring well with a whisk.

5. Place $1^1/_2$ cups granulated sugar, butter, and oil in a large bowl; beat with a mixer at medium speed until fluffy (about 5 minutes). Add eggs and 1 egg white, 1 at a time, beating until incorporated. Add flour mixture and beet mixture alternately to butter mixture, beginning and ending with flour mixture. Divide batter among 3 (8-inch) round metal cake pans coated with baking spray. Bake at 350° for

23 to 24 minutes or until a wooden pick inserted in center comes out clean. Cool 15 minutes in pans on a wire rack. Remove cake from pans; cool completely on wire rack.

6. To prepare filling, place cream cheese, cream, yogurt, 1/2 teaspoon vanilla, and dash of salt in a medium bowl; beat with a mixer at high speed until smooth. Add powdered sugar; beat at low speed 1 minute or until well combined (do not overbeat).

7. To prepare meringue frosting, combine 2/3 cup granulated sugar, 4 egg whites, cream of tartar, and dash of salt in the top of a double boiler. Cook over simmering water 2 to 3 minutes or until a candy thermometer registers 160°, stirring constantly with a whisk. Remove from heat. Beat egg mixture with a mixer at medium speed until soft peaks form; beat at high speed until stiff peaks form (do not overbeat).

8. Place 1 cake layer on a plate; spread half of filling over top. Top with another cake layer; spread remaining filling over top. Top with remaining cake layer; spread meringue frosting over top and sides of cake.

Serves 16 (serving size: 1 slice): Calories 284; Fat 9.6g (sat 3.7g, mono 3.9g, poly 1.4g); Protein 5g; Carb 46g; Fiber 1g; Sugars 33g (est. added sugars: 27g); Chol 39mg; Iron 1mg; Sodium 199mg; Calc 55mg

CARAMELIZED PINEAPPLE
UPSIDE-DOWN CAKE

CLASSIC: Calories per serving: 700, Sat Fat: 10g, Sodium: 493mg, Sugars: 101g
MAKEOVER: Calories per serving: 292, Sat Fat: 4.4g, Sodium: 177mg, Sugars: 29g

HANDS-ON: 15 MIN. TOTAL: 1 HR. 15 MIN.

Caramelizing fresh pineapple in its own juices drastically lowers the calories and sugar. The rum will ignite when you tilt the pan; this burns off the alcohol.

1/2 cup packed brown sugar
1/4 cup unsalted butter, divided
1 vanilla bean, split lengthwise
6 (1/2-inch-thick) slices fresh pineapple
1/4 cup dark rum
Cooking spray
5 ounces gluten-free multipurpose flour (about 1 cup)

1/4 cup almond flour
1/2 teaspoon baking powder
1/2 teaspoon kosher salt
1/4 teaspoon baking soda
1/2 cup light sour cream
2 tablespoons canola oil
2/3 cup granulated sugar
2 large eggs

1. Preheat oven to 350°.

2. Combine brown sugar, 2 tablespoons butter, and vanilla bean in a large skillet over medium heat; cook 6 minutes or until butter melts and sugar dissolves, stirring frequently. Add pineapple in a single layer. Carefully pour rum over pineapple; tilt pan to ignite. Simmer 5 minutes on each side or until slightly tender and caramelized. Remove vanilla bean.

3. Coat a 9-inch cake pan with cooking spray. Arrange pineapple in a single layer in bottom of pan; pour sugar mixture over pineapple, tilting pan to coat bottom.

4. Weigh or lightly spoon multipurpose flour into a dry measuring cup; level with a knife. Combine multipurpose flour, almond flour, baking powder, salt, and baking soda; stir with a whisk. Place 2 tablespoons butter in a microwave-safe dish; microwave at HIGH 35 seconds. Place melted butter, sour cream, and oil in a bowl, stirring well with a whisk.

5. Place granulated sugar and eggs in a large bowl; beat with a mixer at high speed 5 minutes or until fluffy. Reduce speed to medium. Add flour mixture and sour cream mixture alternately to egg mixture, beginning and ending with flour mixture. Spoon batter over pineapple, spreading evenly. Bake at 350° for 38 minutes or until a wooden pick inserted in center comes out clean. Cool in pan 15 minutes on a wire rack. Loosen cake from edges of pan with a knife; invert onto a plate.

Serves 10 (serving size: 1 wedge): Calories 292; Fat 11.2g (sat 4.4g, mono 3.7g, poly 1.2g); Protein 4g; Carb 44g; Fiber 1g; Sugars 29g (est. added sugars: 24g); Chol 54mg; Iron 1mg; Sodium 177mg; Calc 87mg

CHEESECAKE

CLASSIC: Calories per serving: 680, Sat Fat: 28g, Sodium: 640mg, Sugars: 58g
MAKEOVER: Calories per serving: 152, Sat Fat: 2.1g, Sodium: 257mg, Sugars: 10g

HANDS-ON: 30 MIN. TOTAL: 5 HR. 32 MIN.

This cheesecake is shockingly lighter, thanks to whole-grain cereal and fat-free Greek yogurt. Serve with fresh fruit and granola or a fruit compote.

Cooking spray
2 cups gluten-free whole-grain flake
 cereal with brown sugar
2 tablespoons butter, melted
2 cups 1% low-fat cottage cheese
½ cup plain fat-free Greek yogurt

6 tablespoons sugar
3 tablespoons all-purpose flour
1 teaspoon grated lemon rind
1 teaspoon vanilla extract
2 large eggs, lightly beaten

1. Preheat oven to 350°.

2. Coat a 7-inch springform pan with cooking spray.

3. Place cereal in a food processor; pulse until finely crushed. Add butter; pulse just until combined. Press mixture into bottom of prepared pan. Bake at 350° for 5 minutes. Clean food processor; wipe dry.

4. Combine cottage cheese and yogurt in food processor; process until smooth. Add sugar and next 4 ingredients (through eggs); pulse until combined. Pour mixture into prepared crust. Bake at 350° for 55 to 60 minutes or until center barely moves when pan is touched. Remove cheesecake from oven; cool to room temperature. Cover and chill at least 4 hours. Cut into 8 slices.

Serves 8 (serving size: 1 slice): Calories 152; Fat 4g (sat 2.1g, mono 1.1g, poly 0.4g); Protein 9g; Carb 20g; Fiber 1g; Sugars 10g (est. added sugars: 8g); Chol 45mg; Iron 1mg; Sodium 257mg; Calc 45mg

CARROT CAKE

CLASSIC: Calories per serving: 1460, Sat Fat: 28g, Sodium: 972mg, Sugars: 111g
MAKEOVER: Calories per serving: 284, Sat Fat: 4.9g, Sodium: 172mg, Sugars: 35g

HANDS-ON: 15 MIN. TOTAL: 1 HR. 53 MIN.

Creamy butter and smooth buttermilk create a perfectly moist, tender texture while earthy brown sugar brings out the warm cinnamon spices. Real-deal cream cheese, fromage blanc, and butter maximize frosting flavor with a light sprinkle of toasted pecans to make it a special, vastly lighter treat.

CAKE:

10.1 ounces all-purpose flour (about 2 1/4 cups)

2 teaspoons baking powder

1 1/2 teaspoons ground cinnamon

1/4 teaspoon salt

2 cups grated carrot

1 cup granulated sugar

1/2 cup packed brown sugar

6 tablespoons butter, softened

3 large eggs

1 teaspoon vanilla extract

1/2 cup low-fat buttermilk

Cooking spray

FROSTING:

6 ounces cream cheese, softened (about 3/4 cup)

1 ounce fromage blanc

2 tablespoons butter, softened

1/2 teaspoon vanilla extract

1/8 teaspoon salt

3 cups powdered sugar

1/4 cup chopped pecans, toasted

1. Preheat oven to 350°.

2. To prepare cake, weigh or lightly spoon flour into dry measuring cups; level with a knife. Combine flour, 2 teaspoons baking powder, cinnamon, and 1/4 teaspoon salt in a medium bowl, stirring with a whisk. Add carrot, tossing to combine.

3. Place granulated sugar, brown sugar, and 6 tablespoons butter in a large bowl. Beat with a mixer at medium speed until combined. Add eggs, 1 at a time, beating well after each addition. Stir in 1 teaspoon vanilla. Add flour mixture and buttermilk alternately to sugar mixture, beginning and ending with flour mixture. Spread batter into a 13 x 9–inch metal baking pan coated with cooking spray. Bake at 350° for 28 minutes or until a wooden pick inserted in center comes out clean. Cool completely on a wire rack.

4. To prepare frosting, place cream cheese and next 4 ingredients (through 1/8 teaspoon salt) in a medium bowl. Beat with a mixer at medium speed until fluffy. Gradually add powdered sugar, beating at medium speed until combined (do not overbeat). Spread frosting over top of cake. Sprinkle with pecans.

Serves 20 (serving size: 1 piece): Calories 284; Fat 9.7g (sat 4.9g, mono 2.8g, poly 0.8g); Protein 4g; Carb 47g; Fiber 1g; Sugars 35g (est. added sugars: 33g); Chol 49mg; Iron 1mg; Sodium 172mg; Calc 68mg

POUND CAKE
WITH BROWNED BUTTER GLAZE

HANDS-ON: 25 MIN. TOTAL: 1 HR. 50 MIN.

Heart-healthy canola oil helps lighten this classic dessert. An ingenious technique of soaking a vanilla bean in the oil adds deep, rich flavor.

CAKE:

6 tablespoons canola oil
1 vanilla bean, split lengthwise
1 3/4 cups sugar
1/2 cup unsalted butter, softened
2 large eggs

12 ounces cake flour (about 3 cups)
2 teaspoons baking powder
1/2 teaspoon salt
1 cup nonfat buttermilk
Baking spray with flour

GLAZE:

1 tablespoon unsalted butter
1/4 cup sugar

2 tablespoons 2% reduced-fat milk
1/2 teaspoon vanilla extract

1. Preheat oven to 350°.

2. To prepare cake, combine oil and vanilla bean in a small skillet over medium-high heat, and bring to a simmer. Remove from heat. Let stand 10 minutes or until mixture cools to room temperature. Scrape seeds from bean, and stir into oil; discard bean.

3. Combine oil mixture, 1 3/4 cups sugar, and 1/2 cup butter in a large bowl; beat with a mixer at medium speed until well blended (about 5 minutes). Add eggs, 1 at a time, beating well after each addition. Weigh or lightly spoon flour into dry measuring cups; level with a knife. Combine flour, baking powder, and salt, stirring well with a whisk. Add flour mixture and buttermilk alternately to sugar mixture, beginning and ending with flour mixture.

4. Spoon batter into a 10-inch tube pan coated with baking spray, and spread evenly. Bake at 350° for 1 hour or until a wooden pick inserted in center comes out clean. Cool in pan 10 minutes on a wire rack, and remove from pan.

5. To prepare glaze, melt 1 tablespoon butter in a small skillet over medium heat; cook 2 minutes or until lightly browned. Remove from heat. Add 1/4 cup sugar, reduced-fat milk, and vanilla extract, stirring until smooth. Drizzle glaze over warm cake.

Serves 16 (serving size: 1 piece): Calories 294; Fat 12.6g (sat 4.7g, mono 5.3g, poly 1.9g); Protein 3g; Carb 43g; Fiber 0g; Sugars 26g (est. added sugars: 25g); Chol 44mg; Iron 2mg; Sodium 149mg; Calc 60mg

KEY LIME PIE

CLASSIC: Calories per serving: 466, Sat Fat: 12.3g, Sodium: 186mg, Sugars: 46g
MAKEOVER: Calories per serving: 280, Sat Fat: 3.6g, Sodium: 147mg, Sugars: 36g

HANDS-ON: 25 MIN. TOTAL: 3 HR. 4 MIN.

This pie boasts 75% less fat than the original and makes this Key lime treat a dessert you can enjoy all year long, thanks to white chocolate and fat-free condensed milk.

CRUST:
1 cup graham cracker crumbs
1 ounce premium white chocolate, grated or finely chopped
1 tablespoon brown sugar
1/8 teaspoon salt

2 tablespoons butter, melted and cooled
1 tablespoon canola oil
Cooking spray

FILLING:
1/2 cup plain 2% reduced-fat Greek yogurt
1/2 cup fresh Key lime juice or fresh lime juice
1/2 teaspoon grated lime rind

3 large egg yolks
1 (14-ounce) can fat-free sweetened condensed milk
3/4 cup frozen fat-free whipped topping, thawed

CRAZY TRICK
Finding a replacement for the tons of butter usually found in a graham cracker crust was a challenge. We discovered that a little white chocolate binds the crumbs as it melts and then hardens when cooled.

1. Preheat oven to 350°.

2. To prepare crust, combine crumbs, chocolate, sugar, and salt in a bowl, stirring well to combine. Add butter and oil; toss with a fork until moist. Press crumb mixture into bottom and up sides of a 9-inch pie plate coated with cooking spray. Bake at 350° for 8 to 10 minutes or until beginning to brown; cool completely on a wire rack.

3. To prepare filling, place yogurt and next 4 ingredients (through milk) in a bowl; beat with a mixer at medium speed 2 minutes. Pour mixture into prepared crust. Bake at 350° for 14 minutes or until set. Cool completely on a wire rack. Cover loosely, and chill at least 2 hours. Serve with whipped topping.

Serves 8 (serving size: 1 pie slice and 1 1/2 tablespoons whipped topping): Calories 280; Fat 8.9g (sat 3.6g, mono 3.4g, poly 1.3g); Protein 7g; Carb 43g; Fiber 0g; Sugars 36g (est. added sugars: 27g); Chol 84mg; Iron 1mg; Sodium 147mg; Calc 144mg

APPLE CAKE

HANDS-ON: 18 MIN. TOTAL: 1 HR. 23 MIN.

Whole-wheat pastry flour in place of all-purpose triples the fiber per slice to a hearty 4 grams. For a chunkier cake texture, use chopped apples.

CAKE:

2/3 cup packed brown sugar

2/3 cup nonfat buttermilk

1/3 cup canola oil

1 teaspoon vanilla extract

2 large eggs

7.5 ounces whole-wheat pastry flour (about 1 2/3 cups)

1 teaspoon baking powder

1/2 teaspoon baking soda

1/2 teaspoon ground cinnamon

1/2 teaspoon kosher salt

1/8 teaspoon ground ginger

2 cups shredded peeled apple (about 2 large; such as Gala or Honeycrisp)

Baking spray with flour

STREUSEL:

3 tablespoons quick-cooking oats

2 tablespoons chopped walnuts

1 tablespoon brown sugar

1 1/2 tablespoons frozen unsalted butter, grated

Dash of kosher salt

YOGURT CREAM:

1/2 cup plain 2% reduced-fat Greek yogurt

3 tablespoons heavy whipping cream

1 tablespoon brown sugar

1. Preheat oven to 350°.

2. To prepare cake, place first 5 ingredients in a large bowl; beat with a mixer at medium speed 30 seconds or until well combined. Weigh or lightly spoon flour into dry measuring cups; level with a knife. Combine flour and next 5 ingredients (through ginger) in a medium bowl, stirring well with a whisk. Add flour mixture to sugar mixture; beat at low speed just until combined. Stir in apple by hand. Spread batter into a 9-inch springform pan coated with baking spray.

3. To prepare streusel, combine oats and next 4 ingredients (through dash of salt) in a small bowl; toss to combine. Sprinkle over batter. Bake at 350° for 45 minutes or until a wooden pick inserted in center comes out with moist crumbs clinging. Cool in pan 10 minutes on a wire rack; remove sides of pan.

4. To prepare cream, place yogurt, whipping cream, and 1 tablespoon sugar in a bowl; beat with a mixer at medium speed until soft peaks form. Serve with warm cake.

Serves 10 (serving size: 1 cake wedge and about 1 tablespoon cream): Calories 299; Fat 13.5g (sat 3.3g, mono 6.2g, poly 3.2g); Protein 6g; Carb 40g; Fiber 4g; Sugars 20g (est. added sugars: 17g); Chol 49mg; Iron 1mg; Sodium 252mg; Calc 94mg

COCONUT CREAM PIE

CLASSIC: Calories per serving: 478, Sat Fat: 16g, Sodium: 278mg, Sugars: 17g
MAKEOVER: Calories per serving: 266, Sat Fat: 5.7g, Sodium: 189mg, Sugars: 23g

HANDS-ON: 10 MIN. TOTAL: 4 HR. 10 MIN.

Reducing the butter and using low-fat milk shaved more than 200 calories and 10 grams saturated fat without losing the creamy, light texture.

½ (14.1-ounce) package refrigerated
  pie dough
Cooking spray
2 cups 1% low-fat milk
1 cup half-and-half
1½ cups flaked sweetened coconut
1 vanilla bean, split lengthwise
⅔ cup sugar
⅓ cup cornstarch
¼ teaspoon salt

4 large egg yolks
2 tablespoons butter
3 large egg whites, at room
  temperature
½ teaspoon cream of tartar
½ cup sugar
¼ cup water
¼ cup flaked sweetened coconut,
  toasted

1. Preheat oven to 425°.

2. Fit dough into a 9-inch pie plate coated with cooking spray. Fold edges under; flute. Line dough with foil; arrange pie weights or dried beans on foil. Bake at 425° for 10 minutes; remove weights and foil, and bake an additional 10 minutes or until golden. Cool completely on a wire rack.

3. Combine milk and half-and-half in a medium saucepan over medium heat. Add 1½ cups coconut. Scrape seeds from vanilla bean; stir seeds and pod into milk mixture. Bring milk mixture to a simmer; immediately remove from heat. Cover and let stand 15 minutes. Strain through a cheesecloth-lined sieve into a bowl. Gather edges of cheesecloth; squeeze over bowl to release moisture. Discard solids.

4. Combine ⅔ cup sugar, cornstarch, salt, and egg yolks in a large bowl, stirring with a whisk. Gradually add milk mixture to egg yolk mixture, stirring constantly. Return milk mixture to pan; bring to a boil, stirring constantly with a whisk. Remove from heat. Add butter; stir with a whisk until smooth. Place pan in a large ice-filled bowl for 6 minutes, stirring to cool. Pour into prepared crust. Cover and chill at least 1 hour.

5. Place 3 egg whites and cream of tartar in a large bowl; beat with a mixer at high speed until soft peaks form. Combine ½ cup sugar and ¼ cup water in a saucepan; bring to a boil. Cook, without stirring, until candy thermometer registers 250°. Pour hot sugar syrup in a thin stream over egg whites, beating at high speed until thick. Spread meringue over pie. Cover and refrigerate at least 2 hours. Top with toasted coconut before serving.

Serves 12 (serving size: 1 wedge): Calories 266; Fat 11.5g (sat 5.7g, mono 1.3g, poly 0.3g); Protein 4g; Carb 36g; Fiber 0g; Sugars 23g (est. added sugars: 21g); Chol 79mg; Iron 0mg; Sodium 189mg; Calc 79mg

BROWNED BUTTER
PECAN PIE

CLASSIC: Calories per serving: 588, Sat Fat: 11.5g, Sodium: 347mg, Sugars: 38g
MAKEOVER: Calories per serving: 304, Sat Fat: 5.3g, Sodium: 206mg, Sugars: 18g

HANDS-ON: 15 MIN. TOTAL: 3 HR. 35 MIN.

We browned the butter and toasted the pecan halves to enhance the nutty flavor and enriched a refrigerated piecrust by adding finely chopped nuts.

½ (14.1-ounce) package refrigerated
  pie dough
Cooking spray
3 tablespoons finely chopped pecans
3 tablespoons butter
⅔ cup light-colored corn syrup

½ cup packed brown sugar
1 teaspoon vanilla extract
⅛ teaspoon salt
2 large eggs, lightly beaten
2 large egg whites, lightly beaten
¾ cup pecan halves, lightly toasted

1. Preheat oven to 425°.

2. Unroll dough; fit into a 9-inch tart pan coated with cooking spray. Press dough into bottom and sides of pan. Sprinkle with chopped pecans, pressing pecans gently into bottom of dough. Line bottom of dough with foil; arrange pie weights or dried beans on foil. Bake at 425° for 15 minutes. Remove pie weights and foil; bake an additional 5 minutes or until crust is set and edges are beginning to brown. Cool 30 minutes on a wire rack. Reduce oven temperature to 350°.

3. Melt butter in a small skillet over medium heat; cook 2 to 3 minutes or until browned, stirring occasionally. Transfer browned butter to a medium bowl. Stir in corn syrup and next 3 ingredients (through salt). Add eggs and egg whites; stir with a whisk until blended.

4. Arrange pecan halves in bottom of prepared crust; gently pour filling over pecan halves. Bake at 350° for 30 minutes or until golden brown and filling is just set. Cool 2 hours on a wire rack before slicing.

Serves 10 (serving size: 1 slice): Calories 304; Fat 16.5g (sat 5.3g, mono 5.1g, poly 2.4g); Protein 4g; Carb 39g; Fiber 1g; Sugars 18g (est. added sugars: 17g); Chol 49mg; Iron 1mg; Sodium 206mg; Calc 26mg

RICH CHOCOLATE MOUSSE

CLASSIC: Calories per serving: 669, Sat Fat: 31g, Sodium: 389mg, Sugars: 49g
MAKEOVER: Calories per serving: 223, Sat Fat: 5.4g, Sodium: 39mg, Sugars: 28g

HANDS-ON: 30 MIN. TOTAL: 8 HR. 30 MIN.

In this makeover, a splash of coconut milk adds the perfect amount of richness to silken tofu. Dates lend natural sweetness with notes of caramel and honey, while whipped egg whites give volume in place of heavy cream. Don't give in to temptation too soon–the mousse needs to chill at least 8 hours to properly set. Serve chilled with fresh berries.

¼ cup coconut milk, whisked to
  combine cream and water
8 pitted dates, finely chopped,
  or ½ cup date paste
1 tablespoon unsweetened cocoa
3 ounces premium bittersweet
  chocolate, chopped

½ teaspoon vanilla extract
8 ounces soft silken tofu
¼ cup reduced-fat sour cream
3 pasteurized egg whites

1. Combine coconut milk and dates in a small saucepan over medium-high heat; bring to a boil. Reduce heat and simmer 2 minutes. Remove dates from milk; set aside. Add cocoa to pan; simmer 1 minute, stirring with a whisk to combine. Add chocolate; reduce heat to medium-low, and stir until chocolate melts. Stir in vanilla.

2. Place tofu, sour cream, and dates in a blender; process until very smooth, scraping sides as needed.

3. Add chocolate mixture to tofu mixture; blend until smooth. Transfer to a bowl.

4. In a medium bowl, beat egg whites with a mixer at high speed 2 minutes or until stiff peaks form. Fold into chocolate mixture. Place about ½ cup chocolate mixture in each of 6 ramekins or dishes; refrigerate until set, about 8 hours or overnight.

Serves 6 (serving size: 1 ramekin): Calories 223; Fat 8.8g (sat 5.4g, mono 2.2g, poly 0.8g); Protein 6g; Carb 34g; Fiber 4g; Sugars 28g (est. added sugars: 5g); Chol 3mg; Iron 2mg; Sodium 39mg; Calc 60mg

VANILLA BEAN
CRÈME BRÛLÉE

CLASSIC: Calories per serving: 605, Sat Fat: 29.6g, Sodium: 67mg, Sugars: 30g
MAKEOVER: Calories per serving: 188, Sat Fat: 3.7g, Sodium: 111mg, Sugars: 24g

HANDS-ON: 18 MIN. TOTAL: 5 HR. 8 MIN.

Often made entirely of heavy cream and egg yolks, classic crème brûlée is hard to beat. This version gets deep, authentic flavor from a vanilla bean and is still creamy and luscious thanks to a combination of whole milk and half-and-half.

1½ cups whole milk
½ cup half-and-half
½ cup granulated sugar, divided
1 teaspoon vanilla bean paste

⅛ teaspoon salt
2 large eggs, lightly beaten
2 large egg yolks, lightly beaten
2 tablespoons superfine sugar

1. Preheat oven to 300°.

2. Combine milk, half-and-half, 6 tablespoons granulated sugar, vanilla bean paste, and salt in a medium, heavy saucepan. Bring to a simmer over medium heat, stirring to dissolve sugar (do not boil). Remove pan from heat.

3. Combine 2 tablespoons granulated sugar, eggs, and egg yolks in a medium bowl, stirring well with a whisk. Gradually add milk mixture to egg mixture, stirring constantly with a whisk. Divide mixture among 6 (4-ounce) ramekins or custard cups. Place ramekins in a 13 x 9–inch metal baking pan; add hot water to pan to a depth of 1 inch.

4. Bake at 300° for 50 minutes or until centers barely move when ramekins are touched. Remove ramekins from pan; cool completely on a wire rack. Cover and chill at least 4 hours or overnight.

5. Preheat broiler. Sift 2 tablespoons superfine sugar over custards. Place ramekins on a baking sheet; broil 1 minute or until sugar melts. Serve immediately.

Serves 6 (serving size: 1 crème brûlée): Calories 188; Fat 7.4g (sat 3.7g, mono 1.8g, poly 0.7g); Protein 6g; Carb 25g; Fiber 0g; Sugars 24g (est. added sugars: 17g); Chol 137mg; Iron 1mg; Sodium 111mg; Calc 107mg

TIRAMISU

CLASSIC: Calories per serving: 577, Sat Fat: 22.7g, Sodium: 288mg, Sugars: 17g
MAKEOVER: Calories per serving: 282, Sat Fat: 4.3g, Sodium: 331mg, Sugars: 13g

HANDS-ON: 45 MIN. TOTAL: 8 HR. 45 MIN.

Blending mascarpone cheese with fat-free cream cheese is the key to this divine tiramisu. The richness and flavor of the mascarpone cheese still shines through but with less saturated fat and fewer calories than traditional recipes. We used gluten-free ladyfingers so that everyone could enjoy this decadent dessert.

1 cup espresso or strong brewed coffee
2 tablespoons Kahlúa (coffee-flavored liquer)
12 ounces fat-free cream cheese (about 1½ cups), softened
4 ounces mascarpone cheese (about ½ cup), softened
1 cup powdered sugar
½ teaspoon vanilla extract
2 cups frozen fat-free whipped topping, thawed
24 gluten-free ladyfingers
½ ounce bittersweet chocolate

1. Place espresso and Kahlúa in a medium bowl, stirring to combine.

2. Place cream cheese and mascarpone cheese in a large bowl; beat with a mixer at medium speed until smooth and creamy. Add powdered sugar, 3 tablespoons espresso mixture, and vanilla; beat with a mixer until blended. Fold in half of whipped topping, stirring just until combined. Repeat with remaining whipped topping.

3. Dip 12 ladyfingers in espresso mixture for 2 to 3 seconds each; place in an 8-inch square glass or ceramic baking dish. Top with half of cheese mixture, spreading over ladyfingers. Top with 12 ladyfingers. Brush top of ladyfingers with remaining espresso mixture. Spread remaining cheese mixture over ladyfingers; cover and refrigerate at least 6 hours. Grate chocolate over top.

Serves 9 (serving size: 1 piece): Calories 282; Fat 8.6g (sat 4.3g, mono 1g, poly 0.4g); Protein 9g; Carb 39g; Fiber 0g; Sugars 13g (est. added sugars: 11g); Chol 82mg; Iron 1mg; Sodium 331mg; Calc 180mg

VANILLA BEAN
ICE CREAM

CLASSIC: Calories per serving: 303, Sat Fat: 13.9g, Sodium: 46mg, Sugars: 18g
MAKEOVER: Calories per serving: 161, Sat Fat: 3.1g, Sodium: 108mg, Sugars: 19g

HANDS-ON: 20 MIN. TOTAL: 3 HR. 50 MIN.

Our version of this classic has 75% less fat but it's still creamy and rich, thanks to one secret ingredient–evaporated low-fat milk.

1 cup half-and-half
½ cup sugar, divided
2 tablespoons light-colored corn syrup
⅛ teaspoon salt

1 (12-ounce) can evaporated low-fat milk
1 vanilla bean, split lengthwise
3 large egg yolks

CRAZY TRICK
With 60% of the water removed, evaporated low-fat milk yields fewer ice crystals and a creamier texture.

1. Combine half-and-half, ¼ cup sugar, corn syrup, salt, and evaporated milk in a medium, heavy saucepan. Scrape seeds from vanilla bean; add seeds and bean to milk mixture. Heat milk mixture to 180° or until tiny bubbles form around edge (do not boil). Remove pan from heat; cover and let stand 10 minutes.

2. Combine ¼ cup sugar and egg yolks in a medium bowl, stirring well with a whisk. Gradually add hot milk mixture to egg mixture, stirring constantly with a whisk. Return milk mixture to pan. Cook over medium heat until a thermometer registers 160°, stirring constantly. Remove from heat.

3. Place pan in a large ice-filled bowl for 20 minutes or until mixture is cool, stirring occasionally. Pour milk mixture through a fine sieve into the freezer can of an ice-cream freezer; discard solids. Freeze according to manufacturer's instructions. Spoon ice cream into a freezer-safe container; cover and freeze 3 hours or until firm.

Serves 8 (serving size: about ½ cup): Calories 161; Fat 5.9g (sat 3.1g, mono 1.9g, poly 0.4g); Protein 5g; Carb 23g; Fiber 0g; Sugars 19g (est. added sugars: 14g); Chol 88mg; Iron 0mg; Sodium 108mg; Calc 161mg

DOUBLE CHOCOLATE
ICE CREAM

CLASSIC: Calories per serving: 317, Sat Fat: 8.9g, Sodium: 47mg, Sugars: 38g
MAKEOVER: Calories per serving: 196, Sat Fat: 5.1g, Sodium: 102mg, Sugars: 19g

HANDS-ON: 26 MIN. TOTAL: 7 HR. 31 MIN.

This ice cream achieves a rich, creamy texture from whole-grain "millet cream" which is overcooked millet blended with reduced-fat milk–rather than heavy cream and egg yolks.

1 1/3 cups water
1/3 cup uncooked millet
1 cup 2% reduced-fat milk, divided
3 ounces high-quality semisweet
  chocolate, finely chopped

1 cup half-and-half
1/2 cup sugar
1/4 cup unsweetened cocoa
1/4 teaspoon salt
1 teaspoon vanilla extract

1. Bring 1 1/3 cups water and millet to a boil in a medium saucepan; cover, reduce heat, and simmer 30 minutes or until liquid is nearly absorbed. Remove from heat; let stand, covered, 5 minutes. Pour cooked millet into a blender; add 2/3 cup milk and chocolate. Remove center piece of blender lid (to allow steam to escape); secure lid on blender. Place a clean towel over opening in blender lid (to avoid splatters). Blend until smooth (about 3 minutes). Pour into a medium bowl.

2. Combine 1/3 cup milk, half-and-half, and next 3 ingredients (through salt) in a medium saucepan. Bring to a simmer over medium heat, stirring occasionally; cook 1 minute, stirring to dissolve sugar. Add to millet mixture in bowl; stir to combine. Stir in vanilla. Place bowl in a large ice water–filled bowl for 15 minutes or until millet mixture comes to room temperature, stirring occasionally. Cover and chill 4 hours.

3. Pour mixture into the freezer can of an ice-cream freezer; freeze according to manufacturer's instructions. Spoon ice cream into a freezer-safe container; cover and freeze 2 hours or until firm.

Serves 8 (serving size: about 1/2 cup): Calories 196; Fat 8.6g (sat 5.1g, mono 0.4g, poly 0.2g); Protein 4g; Carb 29g; Fiber 2g; Sugars 19g (est. added sugars: 16g); Chol 14mg; Iron 1mg; Sodium 102mg; Calc 73mg

CHOCOLATE CHIP CANNOLI

HANDS-ON: 16 MIN. TOTAL: 12 HR. 16 MIN.

Part-skim ricotta cheese and less-fat cream cheese cut the fat and calories significantly. Grated orange rind and vanilla extract boost the flavor, making this a rich and decadent dessert.

$^2/_3$ cup part-skim ricotta cheese
2 tablespoons $^1/_3$-less-fat cream
  cheese
1 teaspoon grated orange rind
$^1/_4$ teaspoon vanilla extract
$^1/_4$ cup powdered sugar

4 (5-inch-long) cannoli shells
1$^1/_2$ tablespoons finely chopped
  roasted pistachios
1 teaspoon finely chopped bittersweet
  chocolate

1. Place ricotta, cream cheese, orange rind, and vanilla in a mini food processor; process until smooth. Add powdered sugar, and pulse until well combined. Place ricotta mixture in a small heavy-duty zip-top plastic bag; seal bag. Snip a $^1/_2$-inch hole in one bottom corner of the bag. Fill cannoli shells evenly with ricotta mixture. Combine pistachios and chocolate in a small bowl. Evenly dip ends of cannoli in pistachio mixture.

Serves 4 (serving size: 1 cannolo): Calories 240; Fat 13g (sat 5.2g, mono 4.4g, poly 2.4g); Protein 8g; Carb 23g; Fiber 0g; Sugars 13g (est. added sugars: 10g); Chol 28mg; Iron 0mg; Sodium 109mg; Calc 122mg

LIGHTER CHANTILLY CREAM

CLASSIC: Calories per serving: 110, Sat Fat: 6.9g, Sodium: 11mg, Sugars: 2g
MAKEOVER: Calories per serving: 35, Sat Fat: 1.7g, Sodium: 8mg, Sugars: 2g

HANDS-ON: 10 MIN. TOTAL: 10 MIN.

We lighten traditional sweetened whipped cream with both plain yogurt and a Swiss meringue; the yogurt gives it a pleasant tang.

½ cup heavy whipping cream
¼ cup plain fat-free yogurt
½ teaspoon vanilla extract

1 large egg white
2 tablespoons sugar

1. Combine cream, yogurt, and vanilla in a large bowl. Beat with a mixer at high speed until medium-stiff peaks form.

2. Add water to a medium saucepan to a depth of 1 inch; bring to a simmer. Combine egg white and sugar in a heatproof bowl; stir with a whisk. Place bowl over simmering water; cook 1 minute or until mixture reaches 160° and sugar dissolves, stirring constantly. Remove from heat. Beat egg mixture with a mixer at medium-high speed until stiff peaks form and mixture is cool to the touch using clean, dry beaters.

3. Carefully fold one-third of egg white mixture into whipped cream mixture; gradually fold in remaining egg white mixture.

Serves 16 (serving size: 2 tablespoons): Calories 35; Fat 2.8g (sat 1.7g, mono 0.8g, poly 0.1g); Protein 1g; Carb 2g; Fiber 0g; Sugars 2g (est. added sugars: 2g); Chol 10mg; Iron 0mg; Sodium 8mg; Calc 10mg

BREAD PUDDING
WITH SALTED CARAMEL SAUCE

CLASSIC: Calories per serving: 843, Sat Fat: 30.2g, Sodium: 328mg, Sugars: 55g
MAKEOVER: Calories per serving: 300, Sat Fat: 2.4g, Sodium: 349mg, Sugars: 34g

HANDS-ON: 25 MIN. TOTAL: 1 HR. 50 MIN.

This succulent bread pudding is perfectly moist and creamy thanks to the evaporated fat-free milk. The layer of bourbon-splashed caramel sauce in the middle is the secret to the velvety-rich interior.

BREAD PUDDING:
5 cups (½-inch) cubed French bread (about 8 ounces)
1 cup evaporated fat-free milk
¾ cup 1% low-fat milk
⅓ cup granulated sugar

2 tablespoons bourbon
1 tablespoon vanilla extract
1 teaspoon ground cinnamon
¼ teaspoon kosher salt
2 large eggs

SAUCE:
¾ cup packed brown sugar
3 tablespoons bourbon
1 tablespoon unsalted butter
6 tablespoons half-and-half, divided

1 teaspoon vanilla extract
⅛ teaspoon kosher salt
Cooking spray

1. Preheat oven to 350°.

2. To prepare bread pudding, arrange bread in a single layer on a baking sheet. Bake at 350° for 8 minutes or until lightly toasted.

3. Combine evaporated milk and next 7 ingredients (through eggs) in a large bowl; stir with a whisk. Add bread cubes. Let stand 20 minutes, occasionally pressing on bread to soak up milk.

4. To prepare sauce, combine brown sugar, 3 tablespoons bourbon, and butter in a small saucepan over medium-high heat; bring to a boil. Simmer 2 minutes or until sugar dissolves, stirring frequently. Stir in 5 tablespoons half-and-half; simmer 10 minutes or until reduced to about 1 cup. Remove pan from heat. Stir in 1 tablespoon half-and-half, 1 teaspoon vanilla, and ⅛ teaspoon salt. Keep warm.

5. Spoon half of bread mixture into a 9 x 5–inch loaf pan coated with cooking spray. Drizzle 3 tablespoons sauce over bread mixture. Spoon remaining half of bread mixture over sauce. Bake at 350° for 45 minutes or until a knife inserted in center comes out clean. Serve warm sauce with bread pudding.

Serves 8 (serving size: 1 slice bread pudding and about 1½ tablespoons sauce): Calories 300; Fat 4.8g (sat 2.4g, mono 1.4g, poly 0.5g); Protein 9g; Carb 51g; Fiber 1g; Sugars 34g (est. added sugars: 28g); Chol 63mg; Iron 2mg; Sodium 349mg; Calc 172mg

ROASTED BANANA PUDDING

CLASSIC: Calories per serving: 819, Sat Fat: 28g, Sodium: 343mg, Sugars: 56g
MAKEOVER: Calories per serving: 295, Sat Fat: 2.1g, Sodium: 165mg, Sugars: 36g

HANDS-ON: 36 MIN. TOTAL: 2 HR. 26 MIN.

Roasting bananas brings out the natural sugars so less is needed in this classic comforting dessert.

5 ripe unpeeled medium bananas
  (about 2 pounds)
2 cups 2% reduced-fat milk
²/₃ cup sugar, divided
2 tablespoons cornstarch
¼ teaspoon salt

2 large eggs
1 tablespoon butter
2 teaspoons vanilla extract
1 (12-ounce) container frozen fat-free
  whipped topping, thawed and divided
45 vanilla wafers, divided

1. Preheat oven to 350°.

2. Place bananas on a jelly-roll pan covered with parchment paper. Bake at 350° for 20 minutes. Remove 3 bananas; cool completely. Peel and cut into ½-inch-thick slices. Bake remaining 2 bananas at 350° for an additional 20 minutes. Carefully peel and place 2 bananas in a small bowl, and mash with a fork until smooth.

3. Combine milk and ⅓ cup sugar in a saucepan over medium-high heat. Bring to a simmer (do not boil).

4. Combine ⅓ cup sugar, cornstarch, salt, and eggs in a medium bowl; stir well with a whisk. Gradually add hot milk mixture to sugar mixture, stirring constantly with a whisk. Return milk mixture to pan. Cook over medium heat until thick and bubbly (about 3 minutes), stirring constantly. Remove from heat. Add mashed bananas, butter, and vanilla, stirring until butter melts. Place pan in a large ice-filled bowl for 15 minutes or until mixture comes to room temperature, stirring occasionally. Fold half of whipped topping into pudding.

5. Spread 1 cup custard over bottom of an 11 x 7–inch glass or ceramic baking dish. Top with 20 vanilla wafers and half of banana slices. Spoon half of remaining custard over banana. Repeat procedure with 20 wafers, banana slices, and custard. Spread half of whipped topping over top. Crush 5 vanilla wafers, and sprinkle over top. Refrigerate 1 hour or until chilled.

Serves 10 (serving size: about ²/₃ cup): Calories 295; Fat 5.6g (sat 2.1g, mono 1.7g, poly 0.2g); Protein 4g; Carb 57g; Fiber 2g; Sugars 36g (est. added sugars: 22g); Chol 46mg; Iron 1mg; Sodium 165mg; Calc 73mg

SEA SALT–CARAMEL
ÉCLAIRS

CLASSIC: Calories per serving: 467, Sat Fat: 17.7g, Sodium: 202mg, Sugars: 33g
MAKEOVER: Calories per serving: 228, Sat Fat: 4.7g, Sodium: 166mg, Sugars: 20g

HANDS-ON: 1 HR. 12 MIN. TOTAL: 2 HR.

We build the dough from whole-wheat pastry flour and keep it fluffy and light with whipped eggs and egg whites. Instead of whipped cream, we make a vanilla bean custard from half-and-half and fat-free milk, a combo that adds richness and body with far less fat than heavy cream.

PASTRY CREAM:

⅓ cup granulated sugar
2 tablespoons cornstarch
¼ teaspoon salt
1 large egg yolk

1 cup fat-free milk
½ cup half-and-half
1 vanilla bean, split lengthwise

PASTRY DOUGH:

3 ounces whole-wheat pastry flour
  (about ⅔ cup)
1.5 ounces all-purpose flour (about
  ⅓ cup)
1 cup water

3 tablespoons butter
2 teaspoons granulated sugar
2 large eggs
2 large egg whites

CARAMEL GLAZE:

½ cup packed brown sugar
¼ cup half-and-half
1 tablespoon butter
2 teaspoons light-colored corn syrup

1 tablespoon bourbon
¼ teaspoon vanilla extract
⅛ teaspoon flake salt, divided

1. To prepare pastry cream, combine first 4 ingredients in a saucepan; stir with a whisk. Stir in milk, ½ cup half-and-half, and vanilla bean. Cook over medium heat until mixture boils, stirring constantly. Reduce heat to low; cook 1 minute or until thick, stirring constantly. Pour into a bowl. Press plastic wrap onto surface; chill.

2. Preheat oven to 425°.

3. To prepare dough, weigh or lightly spoon flours into dry measuring cups; level with a knife. Combine 1 cup water, 3 tablespoons butter, and 2 teaspoons granulated sugar in a saucepan; bring to a boil. Reduce heat to low; add flours. Stir constantly with a wooden spoon until mixture is smooth and begins to pull away from sides of pan. Remove from heat; cool 5 minutes.

4. Place mixture in a large bowl. Beat with a mixer at medium speed 1 minute. Add 2 eggs and 2 egg whites, 1 at a time, beating well after each addition. Scrape sides of bowl; beat 1 minute.

5. Spoon dough into a pastry bag with a ½-inch round tip. Pipe 10 (4½ x 1–inch) logs onto a baking sheet lined with parchment paper. Bake at 425° for 20 minutes.

6. Reduce oven temperature to 350°. Remove pan from oven; place another baking pan underneath to prevent overbrowning. Immediately return to oven, rotating pan. Bake an additional 25 minutes or until éclairs are lightly browned and sound hollow when tapped. Remove from pan, and place on a wire rack; pierce top of each with the tip of a knife (to allow steam to escape). Cool completely.

7. To prepare glaze, combine brown sugar, ¼ cup half-and-half, 1 tablespoon butter, and syrup in a saucepan over medium-high heat; bring to a boil. Simmer 10 minutes or until reduced to ½ cup. Remove from heat. Stir in bourbon, vanilla extract, and half of flake salt. Cool 10 minutes.

8. Using a serrated knife, cut éclairs in half lengthwise. Discard vanilla bean from pastry cream. Fill bottom of each éclair with 2 tablespoons pastry cream. Spread 2 teaspoons glaze over top of each pastry (if glaze is too cool, microwave at HIGH 15 seconds or until spreadable). Replace tops, glaze side up; sprinkle with remaining flake salt. Cover and refrigerate until ready to serve.

Serves 10 (serving size: 1 éclair): Calories 228; Fat 8.3g (sat 4.7g, mono 2.4g, poly 0.5g); Protein 5g; Carb 33g; Fiber 1g; Sugars 20g (est. added sugars: 18g); Chol 75mg; Iron 1mg; Sodium 166mg; Calc 74mg

BUTTERSCOTCH BLONDIES

CLASSIC: Calories per serving: 285, Sat Fat: 8.8g, Sodium: 149mg, Sugars: 22g
MAKEOVER: Calories per serving: 154, Sat Fat: 3.2g, Sodium: 101mg, Sugars: 14g

HANDS-ON: 12 MIN. TOTAL: 52 MIN.

Whole-wheat pastry flour is more finely ground than regular whole-wheat flour, with a delicate texture that yields lighter, more tender bar cookies.

4.5 ounces whole-wheat pastry flour
  (about 1 cup)
½ teaspoon baking powder
½ teaspoon salt
¼ cup butterscotch morsels
2 tablespoons half-and-half
¾ cup packed brown sugar

3 tablespoons canola oil
3 tablespoons butter, melted
1 teaspoon vanilla extract
2 large eggs
⅓ cup semisweet chocolate chips
Cooking spray

CRAZY TRICK
Melted butterscotch stands in for some of the butter to save 2.5g sat fat.

1. Preheat oven to 350°.

2. Weigh or lightly spoon flour into a dry measuring cup; level with a knife. Combine flour, baking powder, and salt in a medium bowl; stir with a whisk until thoroughly combined.

3. Combine butterscotch morsels and half-and-half in a medium microwave-safe bowl; microwave at HIGH 45 seconds, stirring every 15 seconds. Stir until smooth. Add brown sugar, canola oil, butter, vanilla, and eggs; beat with a mixer at high speed 2 minutes. Add flour mixture to butterscotch mixture, stirring just until combined. Stir in chocolate chips. Pour batter into an 8-inch square metal baking pan coated with cooking spray. Bake at 350° for 40 minutes or until a wooden pick inserted in center comes out with moist crumbs clinging. Cool in pan on a wire rack.

Serves 16 (serving size: 1 square): Calories 154; Fat 7.6g (sat 3.2g, mono 2.9g, poly 1g); Protein 2g; Carb 20g; Fiber 1g; Sugars 14g (est. added sugars: 13g); Chol 30mg; Iron 1mg; Sodium 101mg; Calc 30mg

BROWNED BUTTER
CHOCOLATE CHIP COOKIES

CLASSIC: Calories per serving: 187, Sat Fat: 5.8g, Sodium: 120mg, Sugars: 17g
MAKEOVER: Calories per serving: 96, Sat Fat: 2g, Sodium: 42mg, Sugars: 10g

HANDS-ON: 17 MIN. TOTAL: 42 MIN.

Butter moves quickly from nutty and brown to bitter and burned, so be sure to take the pan off the heat once the butter turns amber-brown. Blending light brown sugar with granulated sugar adds moisture to these cookies.

6 tablespoons unsalted butter
2 tablespoons canola oil
5.6 ounces all-purpose flour (about 1¼ cups)
3.3 ounces whole-wheat flour (about ¾ cup)
1 teaspoon baking powder
½ teaspoon kosher salt
¾ cup packed brown sugar
⅔ cup granulated sugar
½ teaspoon vanilla extract
2 large eggs, lightly beaten
½ cup semisweet chocolate chips
⅓ cup dark chocolate chips

1. Preheat oven to 375°.

2. Heat butter in a small saucepan over medium heat; cook 5 minutes or until browned. Remove from heat; add oil. Set aside to cool.

3. Weigh or lightly spoon flours into dry measuring cups; level with a knife. Combine flours, baking powder, and salt, stirring with a whisk. Place butter mixture and sugars in a large bowl; beat with a mixer at medium speed until combined. Add vanilla and eggs; beat until well blended. Add flour mixture, beating at low speed just until combined. Stir in chocolate chips.

4. Drop dough by level tablespoonfuls 2 inches apart onto baking sheets lined with parchment paper. Bake 12 minutes or just until bottoms of cookies begin to brown. Cool slightly.

Serves 40 (serving size: 1 cookie): Calories 96; Fat 4g (sat 2g, mono 1.2g, poly 0.4g); Protein 1g; Carb 15g; Fiber 1g; Sugars 10g (est. added sugars: 10g); Chol 14mg; Iron 1mg; Sodium 42mg; Calc 14mg

WEDDING COOKIES

CLASSIC: Calories per serving: 122, Sat Fat: 4.1g, Sodium: 35mg, Sugars: 4g
MAKEOVER: Calories per serving: 68, Sat Fat: 1.2g, Sodium: 30mg, Sugars: 3g

HANDS-ON: 28 MIN. TOTAL: 1 HR. 50 MIN.

Also known as Russian teacakes or snowball cookies, these dense, crumbly, gluten-free cookies are perfectly bite-sized. A combination of garbanzo bean flour, sorghum flour, and xantham gum creates a tender dough that holds together without the addition of a ton of butter.

2.6 ounces potato starch (about ½ cup)
2.3 ounces cornstarch (about ½ cup)
2.1 ounces garbanzo bean flour (about ½ cup)
2.1 ounces sweet white sorghum flour (about ½ cup)
1 teaspoon xanthan gum
¼ teaspoon salt
½ cup sifted powdered sugar
5 tablespoons butter, softened
2 teaspoons vanilla extract
2 tablespoons canola oil
1 tablespoon 1% low-fat milk
2 large egg yolks
½ cup pecans, finely chopped
⅓ cup powdered sugar

1. Preheat oven to 350°.

2. Weigh or lightly spoon potato starch, cornstarch, and flours into dry measuring cups; level with a knife. Combine potato starch, cornstarch, flours, xanthan gum, and salt in a medium bowl, stirring with a whisk.

3. Place ½ cup powdered sugar, butter, and vanilla in a large bowl; beat with a mixer at medium speed until well blended. Add canola oil, milk, and egg yolks, beating until blended. Gradually add flour mixture, beating until blended. Stir in pecans.

4. Shape dough into 38 (1-inch) balls, and place 2 inches apart on baking sheets lined with parchment paper. Flatten tops of cookies slightly with fingers. Bake at 350° for 10 to 12 minutes or until bottoms of cookies are lightly browned.

5. Immediately roll warm cookies in ⅓ cup powdered sugar; cool completely on a wire rack, reserving powdered sugar. Reroll cooled cookies in remaining powdered sugar.

Serves 38 (serving size: 1 cookie): Calories 68; Fat 3.7g (sat 1.2g, mono 1.6g, poly 0.6g); Protein 1g; Carb 8g; Fiber 1g; Sugars 3g (est. added sugars: 3g); Chol 14mg; Iron 0mg; Sodium 30mg; Calc 5mg

SWAG BARS

CLASSIC: Calories per serving: 203, Sat Fat: 3.7g, Sodium: 146mg, Sugars: 22g
MAKEOVER: Calories per serving: 155, Sat Fat: 1.9g, Sodium: 121mg, Sugars: 12g

HANDS-ON: 25 MIN. TOTAL: 25 MIN.

These no-bake bars come together quickly with heart-healthy pantry ingredients, such as whole-grain cereal and dark chocolate. Make sure the cereal is well crushed (try packing it in a sealed zip-top plastic bag and using a rolling pin) so it incorporates into the peanut butter mixture.

1 3/4 cups creamy peanut butter
3/4 cup sugar
3/4 cup light-colored corn syrup
1 1/2 cups (6 ounces) chopped lightly salted, dry-roasted peanuts

3 1/2 cups (4 ounces) whole-grain flaked cereal, finely crushed
Cooking spray
1/3 cup (2 ounces) chopped dark chocolate

1. Combine first 3 ingredients in a heavy saucepan over medium-high heat. Cook 4 minutes or just until mixture begins to boil, stirring constantly. Remove from heat; stir in peanuts and cereal. Spread mixture into a 13 x 9–inch metal baking pan coated with cooking spray.

2. Place dark chocolate in a small microwave-safe bowl. Microwave at HIGH 1 minute or until chocolate melts, stirring every 20 seconds. Drizzle chocolate over peanut mixture. Score into 36 bars while warm.

Serves 36 (serving size: 1 bar): Calories 155; Fat 9.2g (sat 1.9g, mono 4.2g, poly 2.5g); Protein 5g; Carb 16g; Fiber 2g; Sugars 12g (est. added sugars: 10g); Chol 0mg; Iron 2mg; Sodium 121mg; Calc 113mg

BUTTERSCOTCH BARS

CLASSIC: Calories per serving: 226, Sat Fat: 5.3g, Sodium: 191mg, Sugars: 22g
MAKEOVER: Calories per serving: 148, Sat Fat: 3g, Sodium: 87mg, Sugars: 15g

HANDS-ON: 12 MIN. TOTAL: 67 MIN.

The flour-and-oats mixture serves as both a solid base for the soft butterscotch chip layer and a crumbly, streusel-like topping.

1 cup packed brown sugar
5 tablespoons butter, melted
1 teaspoon vanilla extract
1 large egg, lightly beaten
9 ounces all-purpose flour (about 2 cups)
2 1/2 cups quick-cooking oats
1/2 teaspoon salt
1/2 teaspoon baking soda
Cooking spray
1 1/4 cups butterscotch morsels (about 8 ounces)
3/4 cup fat-free sweetened condensed milk
1/8 teaspoon salt
1/2 cup finely chopped walnuts, toasted

1. Preheat oven to 350°.

2. Combine sugar and butter in a large bowl. Stir in vanilla and egg. Weigh or lightly spoon flour into dry measuring cups; level with a knife. Combine flour, oats, 1/2 teaspoon salt, and baking soda in a bowl. Add oat mixture to sugar mixture; stir with a fork until combined (mixture will be crumbly). Place 3 cups oat mixture in the bottom of a 13 x 9–inch metal baking pan coated with cooking spray; press into bottom of pan. Set aside.

3. Place butterscotch morsels, sweetened condensed milk, and 1/8 teaspoon salt in a microwave-safe bowl; microwave at HIGH 1 minute or until butterscotch morsels melt, stirring every 20 seconds. Stir in walnuts. Scrape mixture into pan, spreading over crust. Sprinkle with remaining oat mixture, gently pressing into butterscotch mixture. Bake at 350° for 30 minutes or until topping is golden brown. Place pan on a wire rack; run a knife around outside edge. Cool completely.

Serves 36 (serving size: 1 bar): Calories 148; Fat 5.1g (sat 3g, mono 0.9g, poly 1.1g); Protein 3g; Carb 23g; Fiber 1g; Sugars 15g (est. added sugars: 15g); Chol 11mg; Iron 1mg; Sodium 87mg; Calc 31mg

BUTTER CRUNCH
LEMON BARS

CLASSIC: Calories per serving: 330, Sat Fat: 5.3g, Sodium: 155mg, Sugars: 32g
MAKEOVER: Calories per serving: 187, Sat Fat: 3.5g, Sodium: 127mg, Sugars: 22g

HANDS-ON: 45 MIN. TOTAL: 9 HR. 5 MIN.

A buttery, crunchy pastry crust forms the base for a tangy lemon filling. You can substitute fresh orange juice and grated orange rind for lemon, if you wish. These are best served chilled.

CRUST:
⅓ cup butter, softened
¼ cup packed dark brown sugar
¼ teaspoon salt
¼ teaspoon ground mace or nutmeg

4.5 ounces all-purpose flour (about 1 cup)
Cooking spray

FILLING:
1 cup 1% low-fat cottage cheese
1 cup granulated sugar
2 tablespoons all-purpose flour
1 tablespoon grated lemon rind
3 ½ tablespoons fresh lemon juice

¼ teaspoon baking powder
1 large egg
1 large egg white
Powdered sugar (optional)

CRAZY TRICK
Blending cottage cheese creates a smooth, creamy base full of protein.

1. Preheat oven to 350°.

2. To prepare crust, place first 4 ingredients in a large bowl; beat with a mixer at medium speed until smooth. Weigh or lightly spoon 4.5 ounces (about 1 cup) flour into a dry measuring cup; level with a knife. Add flour to butter mixture; beat at low speed until well blended. Press crust into bottom of an 8-inch square metal baking pan coated with cooking spray. Bake at 350° for 20 minutes.

3. To prepare filling, place cottage cheese in a food processor; process 2 minutes or until smooth, scraping sides of bowl once. Add granulated sugar and next 6 ingredients (through egg white); process until well blended. Pour filling over crust.

4. Bake at 350° for 25 minutes or until set (edges will be lightly browned). Cool. Cover and chill 8 hours. Sprinkle with powdered sugar before serving, if desired.

Serves 12 (serving size: 1 bar): Calories 187; Fat 6g (sat 3.5g, mono 1.7g, poly 0g); Protein 4g; Carb 31g; Fiber 2g; Sugars 22g (est. added sugars: 22g); Chol 29mg; Iron 1mg; Sodium 127mg; Calc 50mg

CLASSIC FUDGE BROWNIES

HANDS-ON: 8 MIN. TOTAL: 2 HR. 8 MIN.

Over the years, it has been trendy to replace the fat source in brownie recipes with applesauce, prune puree, yogurt–you name it. We find that none of these options gives you the fudgy, moist texture you really want in a brownie. So in this recipe, we've kept the saturated fat in check by replacing some of the butter with canola oil and using cocoa powder in addition to chocolate. Brewed coffee adds both moisture and richness.

3.4 ounces all-purpose flour (about ¾ cup)
1 cup granulated sugar
½ cup unsweetened cocoa
⅓ cup packed brown sugar
½ teaspoon baking powder
½ teaspoon salt
4 ounces bittersweet chocolate, chopped

2 tablespoons butter
¼ cup canola oil
¼ cup brewed coffee
1 teaspoon vanilla extract
2 large eggs, lightly beaten
Cooking spray

1. Preheat oven to 350°.

2. Weigh or lightly spoon flour into a dry measuring cup; level with a knife. Combine flour and next 5 ingredients (through salt) in a medium bowl, stirring with a whisk.

3. Place chocolate and butter in a medium microwave-safe bowl. Microwave at HIGH 1 minute or until melted, stirring every 20 seconds. Stir oil and next 3 ingredients (through eggs) into chocolate mixture. Add chocolate mixture to flour mixture; stir to combine.

4. Spoon batter into an 8-inch square metal baking pan coated with cooking spray. Bake at 350° for 30 minutes or until set and a wooden pick inserted in center comes out with moist crumbs clinging. Cool in pan on a wire rack. Cut into 16 pieces.

Serves 16 (serving size: 1 brownie): Calories 184; Fat 9g (sat 3.1g, mono 3g, poly 1.2g); Protein 3g; Carb 27g; Fiber 2g; Sugars 20g (est. added sugars: 15g); Chol 27mg; Iron 1mg; Sodium 115mg; Calc 15mg

WHOLE-WHEAT
SHORTBREAD

CLASSIC: Calories per serving: 168, Sat Fat: 6.5g, Sodium: 83mg, Sugars: 6g
MAKEOVER: Calories per serving: 93, Sat Fat: 1.9g, Sodium: 55mg, Sugars: 3g

HANDS-ON: 15 MIN. TOTAL: 1 HR. 22 MIN.

To keep saturated fat at a reasonable level, canola oil steps in for some of the butter called for in traditional recipes.

9 ounces whole-wheat pastry flour
 (about 2 cups)
1/2 cup powdered sugar
1/4 cup cornstarch
1/2 teaspoon salt

1/2 cup butter, softened
1/2 cup canola oil
1/4 cup granulated sugar
1 teaspoon vanilla extract

1. Preheat oven to 325°.

2. Weigh or lightly spoon flour into dry measuring cups; level with a knife. Combine flour, powdered sugar, cornstarch, and salt, stirring with a whisk.

3. Place butter, oil, granulated sugar, and vanilla in a large bowl; beat with a mixer at medium speed until well blended. Add flour mixture; beat just until combined.

4. Turn dough out onto a baking sheet lined with parchment paper. Pat dough out into a 10 x 8–inch rectangle. Pierce entire surface liberally with a fork. Bake at 325° for 35 minutes or until set and lightly browned around edges. Remove from oven; immediately cut hot dough into 36 pieces (a pizza wheel works nicely). Cool on pan 2 minutes on a wire rack. Remove cookies from pan; cool completely on wire rack.

Serves 36 (serving size: 1 cookie): Calories 93; Fat 5.8g (sat 1.9g, mono 2.6g, poly 1g); Protein 1g; Carb 10g; Fiber 1g; Sugars 3g (est. added sugars: 3g); Chol 7mg; Iron 0mg; Sodium 55mg; Calc 6mg

PEACH "FRIED" PIES

CLASSIC: Calories per serving: 730, Sat Fat: 19g, Sodium: 796mg, Sugars: 34g
MAKEOVER: Calories per serving: 312, Sat Fat: 5.7g, Sodium: 203mg, Sugars: 23g

HANDS-ON: 40 MIN. TOTAL: 3 HR.

Vodka in a pastry crust? Yes! It keeps the dough moist and tender.

CRUST:
12.4 ounces all-purpose flour (about 2 3/4 cups), divided
2 tablespoons sugar
1 teaspoon salt

9 tablespoons frozen unsalted butter, cut into small pieces
1/4 cup vodka, chilled
1/4 cup cold water

FILLING:
8 ounces dried peaches
1 cup water
3/4 cup sugar

1/2 cup orange juice
1 teaspoon ground cinnamon

REMAINING INGREDIENTS:
1 tablespoon fat-free milk
1 large egg, lightly beaten

Cooking spray

CRAZY TRICK
Water bonds with flour to form gluten, but too much can make a crust tough. Too little and your crust will be dry. Vodka is 60% water, so it keeps pastry dough nice and moist.

1. To prepare crust, weigh or lightly spoon flour into dry measuring cups; level with a knife. Combine 11.25 ounces (2 1/2 cups) flour, sugar, and salt in a food processor; pulse 10 times. Add frozen butter; process until mixture resembles coarse meal. Freeze flour mixture for 15 minutes. Place bowl back on processor. Combine vodka and cold water. Add vodka mixture slowly through food chute, pulsing just until combined. Divide dough into 12 equal portions. Shape each dough portion into a ball; flatten each ball into a 3-inch circle on a lightly floured surface. Roll each dough portion into a 5-inch circle, adding 1/4 cup flour as needed to prevent dough from sticking. Stack dough circles between single layers of wax paper or plastic wrap to prevent sticking. Cover stack with plastic wrap; refrigerate at least 2 hours or overnight.

2. To prepare filling, combine peaches, water, sugar, orange juice, and cinnamon in a medium saucepan. Bring to a simmer; cover and cook 1 hour, stirring occasionally. Remove from heat, and mash with a potato masher; cool.

3. Preheat oven to 425°. Place a large foil-lined baking sheet in oven. Remove dough from refrigerator. Working with 1 circle at a time, spoon 2 level tablespoonfuls peach mixture into center of each circle. Fold dough over filling; press edges together with a fork to seal. Combine milk and egg in a small bowl. Brush pies with egg mixture. Cut three diagonal slits across top of each pie. Remove hot baking sheet from oven, and coat with cooking spray. Place pies, cut sides up, on baking sheet, and place on middle oven rack. Bake at 425° for 18 minutes or until lightly browned.

Serves 12 (serving size: 1 pie): Calories 312; Fat 9.4g (sat 5.7g, mono 2.4g, poly 0.5g); Protein 5g; Carb 50g; Fiber 2g; Sugars 23g (est. added sugars: 15g); Chol 41mg; Iron 2mg; Sodium 203mg; Calc 15mg